Lecture Notes in Computer Science 12441

More information about this subseries at http://www.springer.com/series/7411

Karim Djemame · Jörn Altmann ·
José Ángel Bañares · Orna Agmon Ben-Yehuda ·
Vlado Stankovski · Bruno Tuffin (Eds.)

Economics of Grids, Clouds, Systems, and Services

17th International Conference, GECON 2020
Izola, Slovenia, September 15–17, 2020
Revised Selected Papers

 Springer

Editors
Karim Djemame (iD)
School of Computing
University of Leeds
Leeds, UK

José Ángel Bañares (iD)
University of Zaragoza
Zaragoza, Zaragoza, Spain

Vlado Stankovski (iD)
University of Ljubljana
Ljubljana, Slovenia

Jörn Altmann (iD)
Seoul National University
Gwanak-gu, Seoul, Korea (Republic of)

Orna Agmon Ben-Yehuda (iD)
Technion – Israel Institute of Technology
Haifa, Israel

Bruno Tuffin (iD)
Rennes Bretagne-Atlantique
Inria
Rennes Cedex, France

ISSN 0302-9743   ISSN 1611-3349 (electronic)
Lecture Notes in Computer Science
ISBN 978-3-030-63057-7   ISBN 978-3-030-63058-4 (eBook)
https://doi.org/10.1007/978-3-030-63058-4

LNCS Sublibrary: SL5 – Computer Communication Networks and Telecommunications

This Springer imprint is published by the registered company Springer Nature Switzerland AG
The registered company address is: Gewerbestrasse 11, 6330 Cham, Switzerland

Preface

We are glad to introduce the proceedings of the 17th International Conference on the Economics of Grids, Clouds, Systems, and Services (GECON 2020). GECON 2020 was held during September 15–17, 2020, virtually hosted by the University of Ljubljana, Slovenia, due to the 2020 COVID-19 pandemic. The conference, which is held annually, is now firmly established as a place of convergence among economics and computer science researchers, with the ultimate aim of building a strong multi-disciplinary community in this increasingly important area.

Nowadays, economics plays a pervasive role in the ICT world and is essential in strategic decisions concerning the development of new technologies. It influences its deployment, rollout plans, and is concerned in everyday operations and resource allocation optimization. However, the relationship between ICT and economics is really a two-way one, since the integration of technologies such as the Internet of Things (IoT), artificial intelligence (AI), edge, fog and cloud computing, and block-chain is going to change the way economic transactions are carried out. A conference such as GECON, therefore, plays a leading role due to its blending of skills and knowledge from both worlds.

We received 40 submissions in response to our call for papers. Each paper was peer-reviewed by at least three members of the International Program Committee (PC). Based on significance, novelty, and scientific quality, we selected 11 full papers (a 27% acceptance rate), which are included in this volume. Additionally, three shorter work-in-progress papers and six extended abstracts describing the work shown on posters during the conference are also integrated in the volume.

This volume has been structured following the six sessions that comprised the conference program:

- Smartness in Distributed Systems
- Decentralising Clouds to Deliver Intelligence at the Edge
- Digital Infrastructures for Pandemic Response and Countermeasures
- Dependability and Sustainability
- Economic Computing and Storage
- Poster session

The first session on "Smartness in Distributed Systems" had four full papers. The session started with the Best Paper Award entitled "A Consensus for Message Queue Based on Byzantine Fault Tolerance" by Jiahui Zhang et al. In this paper, the authors propose a consensus mechanism based on Byzantine fault tolerance in the context of a consortium blockchain. The objective of the work is to increase the resiliency of message queue-based consensus algorithms, since these algorithms do not tolerate malicious nodes. In the next work "Automatic QA-pair generation for incident tickets handling - An application of NLP" by Mick Lammers et al., the authors describe their experience of building a question answer system for IT support based on a large ticket dataset. The paper "ProtectDDoS: A Platform for Trustworthy Offering and Recommendation of Protections" by Muriel Franco et al., proposes a Blockchain-based solution for offering and selecting counter-DDoS services based on trustworthy service information and recommendations. Finally, the paper "Delivering Privacy-Friendly Location-Based Advertising over Smartwatches: Effect of Virtual User Interface" by Emiel Emanuel and Somayeh Koohborfardhaghighi, presents an empirical study of users' perception of a new design for enhancing privacy of location-based services.

The second session focused on "Decentralising Clouds to Deliver Intelligence at the Edge" and included two work-in-progress papers and two extended abstracts. The first work-in-progress paper "GEM-Analytics: Cloud-to-Edge AI-Powered Energy Management" by Daniele Tovazzi et al., presents a platform that exploits fog computing to enable AI-based methods for energy analysis at the edge of the network. The next work-in-progress paper, entitled "Using LSTM Neural Networks as Resource Utilization Predictors: The case of training Deep Learning models on the Edge" by John Violos et al., tackles the cost reduction issue by proposing an edge resource prediction model, which is used to optimize the resources by minimizing resource waste and preventing QoS infringements. The next work presented is an extended abstract, entitled "Towards a semantic edge processing of sensor data in a smart factory" by Paula-Georgiana Zălhan et al. This work presents an experimental work, to support the decision making on the point in the pipeline where the semantic annotation should take place. Finally, the next extended abstract "Distributed Cloud Intelligence: Implementing an ETSI MANO-Compliant Predictive Cloud Bursting Solution using Openstack and Kubernetes" by Francescomaria Faticanti et al., presents a cloud platform for cloud bursting based on deep learning.

The third session on "Digital Infrastructures for Pandemic Response and Countermeasures" was made up of two full papers. In "A MDE Approach for Modelling and Distributed Simulation of Health Systems," Unai Arronategui et al., present a model-driven engineering approach to support the modeling of healthcare systems in epidemic episodes combining different perspectives, and the translation to efficient code for scalable distributed simulations. This was followed by the paper "South Korea as the role model for Covid-19 policies? An analysis of the effect of Government policies on infection chain structures" by Alexander Haberling et al., which provides an analysis of the impact of policies to the COVID-19 pandemic based on a social network analysis, applying a combined method of network analysis and multiple regression.

The fourth session covered the "Dependability and Sustainability" topic and included four full papers. In "A Network Reliability Game," Patrick Maillé et al., present a game theory model on the interactions among participants (nodes) in an ad-hoc network, considering reliability investments and demand of all nodes for reliable access to a given point. In "NuPow: Managing Power on NUMA Multiprocessors with Domain-Level Voltage and Frequency Control," Changmin Ahn et al., introduce NuPow, a hierarchical scheduling and power management framework for architectures with multiple cores per voltage and frequency domain and non-uniform memory access (NUMA) properties. The paper demonstrates the feasibility of the hierarchical design with domain-specific control for the cores, the frequency and voltage domains by providing and evaluating a working implementation on the Intel Single-Chip Cloud Computer (SCC). In "Multi-Tier Power-Saving Method in Cloud Storage Systems for

Content Sharing Services," Horleang Choeng et al., explore the notion of power-saving for storage systems through a novel methodology, targeting cloud content sharing services, with the aim to reduce the number of accesses in disks that are in power-saving mode. In "Instant Live Migration," Changyeon Jo et al., present the design of a distributed shared memory system that is tailored to virtual environments, e.g. cloud data centers, where live migration of virtual machines is key. The proposed system uses remote direct memory access to reduce remote memory access latency and runs virtual machines without a significant performance degradation.

The "Economic Computing and Storage" topic was covered in the fifth session, which includes two full papers. In "Towards Economical Live Migration in Data Centers," Youngsu Cho et al., argue that live migration-aware service-level objectives and smart live migration open new opportunities for economical live migration in warehouse-scale computing, and present a framework based on machine learning techniques to predict key parameters of virtual machines live migration. In "Index-Selection for Minimizing Costs of a NoSQL Cloud Database," Sudarshan Chawathe proposes a cost-model for secondary indexing in provider-hosted Cloud NoSQL stores and, in particular, for Amazon Web Services (AWS) DynamoDB with the aim of helping cloud users' cost optimization.

The conference program also included a poster session for authors to present their on-going work. In "The Influence of Online Reviews on API Adoption: A Developer-centric View," Konrad Kirner et al., discuss how online customer reviews affect developers when selecting an online API and propose a framework to study such influence. In "Power of the Chunks: Bridging Education Services and Consumer Expectations through Reusable Knowledge Modules," Djamshid Sultanov et al., discuss a new way of optimizing curriculum composition (as an educational service) by considering the consumer expectations. System dynamics is used for investigating stakeholders' value creation and exchange in terms of educational service offerings and fulfilment of consumer expectations. In "Exascale Computing Deployment Challenges," Karim Djemame et al., argue that Exascale computing deployment drives a once in a generation shift of computation, and, therefore, requires fundamentals of computer science to be re-examined. Moreover, it requires a significant degree of co-design and close attention to the economics underlying the deployment challenges ahead.

Additionally to these topic sessions, this year's GECON featured two keynotes, evenly distributed, and a Wild-and-Crazy-Ideas session.

The keynote speaker on the first day was Prof. Schahram Dustdar, from TU Wien, Austria. Prof. Dustdar's keynote "The New Convergence - Research challenges in the IoT/Edge/Fog/Cloud Continuum" presented edge computing, IoT, AI, and human augmentation as major technology trends, driven by recent advancements in edge computing, IoT, and AI accelerators. As humans, things and AI continue to grow closer together, systems engineers and researchers are faced with new and unique challenges. In this talk, Dustdar analyzed the role of edge computing and AI in the cyber-human evolution and identified challenges that edge computing systems will consequently be faced with. A closer look is needed at how a cyber-physical fabric will be complemented by AI operationalization, to enable seamless end-to-end edge intelligence systems.

The keynote speaker on the second day was Iain James Marshall, CEO of Amenesik. His keynote "Building the European Cloud Service Federation for Business Needs" is concerned with the current state of cloud application development and deployment. As cloud application deployment is still very much a manual process today, it requires a substantial software development team to be engaged and maintained throughout the entire cloud application life cycle. In his talk, Marshall envisages a technological rupture from this theme in the form of fully automated cloud service federation, which does not only support both specialized and generic applications but also allows fully automated cost and revenue sharing between the collaborating federation members. He illustrated how this technology, which emerged during the European Union's Horizon 2020 BASMATI project, can be applied in several use case specific service federations, which are defined in the context of the SERENE H2020 Innovation Action project, in conjunction with an underlying generic cloud service federation offer. Moreover, he detailed the environment and processes, which are needed to make this technology successful and sustainable.

The Wild and Crazy Ideas session was organized by the conference host Assoc. Prof. Vlado Stankovski on the topic of the new Horizon 2020 Next Generation Internet project entitled "OntoChain: Trusted, Transparent, and Traceable Ontological Knowledge on Blockchain."

Acknowledgments. Any conference is the fruit of the work of many people, and GECON is no exception. In particular, we wish to thank the authors, whose papers make up the body of the conference, the members of the Program Committee and the reviewers, who devoted their time to review the papers on a tight time schedule. We wish to thank the invited speakers, for bringing new viewpoints and inputs to the GECON community. Furthermore, we would like to thank Alfred Hofmann, Anna Kramer, and the whole team at Springer, which continues an established tradition of publishing GECON proceedings in its renowned LNCS series. Finally, we wish to thank the attendees, whose interest in the conference is the main driver for its organization.

September 2020

Karim Djemame
Jörn Altmann
José Ángel Bañares
Orna Agmon Ben-Yehuda
Vlado Stankovski
Bruno Tuffin

Organization

GECON 2020 was organized by the Faculty of Computer and Information Science of the University of Ljubljana, Slovenia. (https://www.fri.uni-lj.si/).

Executive Committee

Conference Chair

Vlado Stankovski   University of Ljubljana, Slovenia

Conference Vice-chairs

Karim Djemame	University of Leeds, UK
Orna Agmon Ben-Yehuda	Technion, Israel
Jörn Altmann	Seoul National University, South Korea
José Angel Bañares	University of Zaragoza, Spain

Public Relations Chair

José Ángel Bañares   Università di Zaragoza, Spain

Local Logistics

Janez Brežnik	University of Ljubljana, Slovenia
Petar Kochovski	University of Ljubljana, Slovenia
Uroš Paščinski	University of Ljubljana, Slovenia
Sandi Gec	University of Ljubljana, Slovenia

Proceedings Chair

Karim Djemame   University of Leeds, UK

Poster Chair

Orna Agmon Ben-Yehuda   Technion, Israel

Wild and Crazy Ideas Session Chair

Orna Agmon Ben-Yehuda   Technion, Israel

Roundtable Session Chair

Jörn Altmann   Seoul National University, South Korea

Special Session Chair

Maurizio Naldi   Università di Roma, LUMSA, Italy

Special Topic Session on Decentralising Clouds to Deliver Intelligence at the Edge

Seugwoo Kum	Korean Electronics Technology Institute, South Korea
Domenico Siracusa	Fondazione Bruno Kessler, Italy

Program Chairs

Bruno Tuffin	Inria, France
Vlado Stankovski	University of Ljubljana, Slovenia

Program Committee

Alvaro Arenas	IE University, Spain
Aurilla Aurelie Arntzen	University of South-Eastern, Norway
Unai Arronategui	University of Zaragoza, Spain
Ashraf Bany Mohamed	University of Jordan, Jordan
Stefano Bistarelli	Università di Perugia, Italy
Rajkumar Buyya	The University of Melburne, Australia
María Emilia Cambronero	University of Castilla-La Mancha, Spain
Emanuele Carlini	ISTI-CNR, Italy
Jeremy Cohen	Imperial College London, UK
Massimo Coppola	ISTI-CNR, Italy
Costas Courcoubetis	SUTD, Singapore
Daniele D'Agostino	CNR-IMATI, Italy
Patrizio Dazzi	ISTI-CNR, Italy
Alex Delis	University of Athens, Greece
Patricio Domingues	Escola Superior de Tecnologia e Gestão de Leiria, Portugal
Sebastian Floerecke	University of Passau, Germany
Giancarlo Fortino	University of Calabria, Italy
Felix Freitag	Universitat Politècnica de Catalunya, Spain
Saurabh Kumar Garg	University of Tasmania, Australia
Daniel Grosu	Wayne State University, USA
Netsanet Haile	Seoul National University, South Korea
Bahman Javadi	Western Sydney University, Australia
Odej Kao	TU Berlin, Germany
Stefan Kirn	University of Hohenheim, Germany
Tobias Knoch	Erasmus University Medical Center, The Netherlands
Bastian Koller	HLRS, University of Stuttgart, Germany
Somayeh Koohborfardhaghighi	University of Amsterdam, The Netherlands
George Kousiouris	National Technical University of Athens, Greece
Dieter Kranzlmüller	Ludwig Maximilian University of Munich, Germany
Dimosthenis Kyriazis	University of Piraeus, Greece
Joerg Leukel	University of Hohenheim, Germany
Leonardo Maccari	University of Trento, Italy
Ivan Merelli	ITB-CNR, Italy
Roc Meseguer	Universitat Politècnica de Catalunya, Spain

Paolo Mori	IIT-CNR, Italy
Leandro Navarro	Universitat Politècnica de Catalunya, Spain
Marco Netto	IBM, Italy
Mara Nikolaidou	Harokopio University of Athens, Greece
Alberto Nuñez	Complutense University of Madrid, Spain
Frank Pallas	TU Berlin, Germany
Dana Petcu	West University of Timisoara, Romania
Ioan Petri	Cardiff University, UK
Congduc Pham	University of Pau and Pays de l'Adour, France
Ilia Pietri	Intracom S.A. Telecom Solutions, Greece
Omer Rana	Cardiff University, UK
Ivan Rodero	Rutgers University, USA
Rizos Sakellariou	The University of Manchester, UK
Benjamin Satzger	Microsoft, USA
Lutz Schubert	OMI, Ulm University, Germany
Jun Shen	University of Wollongong, Australia
Gheorghe Cosmin Silaghi	Babes-Bolyai University, Romania
Aleksander Slominski	IBM, USA
Stefan Tai	TU Berlin, Germany
Rafael Tolosana-Calasanz	University of Zaragoza, Spain
Bruno Tuffin	Inria, France
Iraklis Varlamis	Harokopio University of Athens, Greece
Dora Varvarigou	National Technical University of Athens, Greece
Luís Veiga	Universidade de Lisboa, Portugal
Claudiu Vinte	Bucharest University of Economic Studies, Romania
Stefan Wesner	Ulm University, Germany
Phillipp Wieder	GWDG - University of Göttingen, Germany
Dimitrios Zissis	University of the Aegean, Greece

Subreviewers

Tayebeh Bahreini	Wayne State University, USA
Hossein Badri	Wayne State University, USA
Bernhard Egger	Seoul National University, South Korea
Zacharias Georgiou	University of Cyprus, Cyprus
Ivan Mercanti	Scuola IMT Alti Studi Lucca, Italy
Francesco Santini	University of Perugia, Italy
Moysis Symeonidis	University of Cyprus, Cyprus

Steering Committee

Karim Djemame	University of Leeds, UK
Jörn Altmann	Seoul National University, South Korea
Jose Ángel Bañares	University of Zaragoza, Spain
Orna Agmon Ben-Yehuda	Technion, Israel
Steven Miller	Singapore Management University, Singapore

Omer F. Rana   Cardiff University, UK
Gheorghe Cosmin Silaghi   Babes-Bolyai University, Romania
Konstantinos Tserpes   Harokopio University of Athens, Greece
Maurizio Naldi   Università di Roma, Italy

Contents

Digital Infrastructures for Pandemic Response and Countermeasures

Dependability and Sustainability

Economic Computing and Storage

Poster Session

Smartness in Distributed Systems

A Blockchain Consensus for Message Queue Based on Byzantine Fault Tolerance

Jiahui Zhang[1]([✉]), Jingling Zhao[1], Xuyan Song[2], Yiping Liu[2], and Qian Wu[3]

[1] School of Computer Science, Beijing University of Posts and Telecommunications, Beijing, China
{zjhq,zhaojingling}@bupt.edu.cn
[2] School of Cyberspace Security, Beijing University of Posts and Telecommunications, Beijing, China
{sungxy,2019111009}@bupt.edu.cn
[3] Cyber Emergency Response Team, Beijing, China
wuqian@cert.org.cn

Abstract. Blockchain technology is developing rapidly, and many companies that develop and apply blockchain technology have gradually risen. Most companies choose to use the consortium blockchain. Because the consortium blockchain is for small-scale groups or institutions, identity authentication is required to join the consortium blockchains. Therefore, security can be guaranteed to a certain extent. Blockchain is often considered as a distributed accounting system. An important mechanism to ensure the stable operation of this accounting system is to ensure consistency among the distributed ledgers. The consensus mechanism in the blockchain is the algorithm that accomplishes this function. To improve throughput, many consortium blockchains use message queues as the consensus algorithm. However, the message queue consensus cannot tolerate malicious nodes. Aiming at this problem, this paper designs and implements a consensus for message queue based on Byzantine fault tolerance, which improves and combines message queue and PBFT. Moreover, it is verified through experiments that the consensus algorithm can reach the general level of TPS. The system can still operate normally when malicious nodes appear within the tolerable range, which has certain robustness and efficiency.

Keywords: Blockchain · Byzantine fault tolerance · Consensus · Consortium blockchain · Message queue

1 Introduction

Blockchain has recently received widespread attention around the world. It has been adopted in many applications in various fields [1]. There are currently three main categories of it: public blockchain, private blockchain and consortium blockchain. Due to the completely decentralized nature of the public blockchain, it cannot meet the needs of enterprises, so in practice, companies often choose partially decentralized consortium blockchain. In addition, the consensus mechanism is the core part of the blockchain [2].

© Springer Nature Switzerland AG 2020
K. Djemame et al. (Eds.): GECON 2020, LNCS 12441, pp. 3–14, 2020.
https://doi.org/10.1007/978-3-030-63058-4_1

The processing speed of the consortium blockchain is faster than the public. Because the identity and the number of nodes has been specified, a relatively loose consensus mechanism is used. This paper focuses on the improvement of consensus algorithms in the context of consortium blockchain.

Hyperledger Fabric is currently the most typical application for consortium blockchain[1]. The consensus algorithm used in Hyperledger Fabric v1.0 is the Kafka based ordering service[2]. The core part of the algorithm mainly uses Kafka as a message queue to ensure the consistency of the received messages between nodes. Many consortium blockchain systems are using message queue consensus algorithms. This algorithm has higher throughput than traditional consensus algorithms such as Practical Byzantine Fault Tolerance Algorithm (PBFT), Proof of Work (POW), etc. It is suitable for high-throughput application scenarios. However, this consensus algorithm has some drawbacks. It cannot tolerate malicious nodes. Once there are nodes in the system that are controlled as malicious nodes, malicious nodes may be forged block, and the information stored in the blocks between nodes will be inconsistent, leading to errors in the consensus. If the transactions in the blocks involve financial transactions in the real world, it will cause losses to the entire blockchain system.

Thus, according to the above analysis of the problems in the message queue consensus mechanism, this paper designs and implements a consensus for message queue based on Byzantine fault tolerance. This consensus is named as BFTMQ and it will be used later. The novelty of the paper is to solve the problem that the message queue consensus mechanism cannot tolerate malicious nodes, and maintains the high throughput and tolerance of downtime nodes based on the message queue consensus mechanism. In summary, this paper makes the following contributions:

1. BFTMQ is designed to solve the problem that the message queue consensus mechanism cannot tolerate malicious nodes;
2. The designed consensus algorithm is implemented and tested on a simulated blockchain system. The experimental results verify the feasibility of the consensus algorithm and ensure stable throughput and tolerance of malicious nodes;
3. Introduced the famous consensus algorithms used by the consortium blockchain, and explained the key processes and advantages and disadvantages of them.

The remainder of this paper is organized as follows: Sect. 2 introduces the related work about the consensus. BFTMQ is explained in Sect. 3. The experimental results are discussed in Sect. 4. Finally, a summary and future work are presented in Sect. 5.

2 Related Work

Practical Byzantine Fault Tolerance Algorithm (PBFT) is the famous consensus mechanism used by the existing consortium blockchain. As the application scope of the

---

[1] What is Hyperledger Fabric, [Online]. Available: https://hyperledgerfabric.readthedocs.io/en/latest/blockchain.html#what-is-hyperledgerfabric.

[2] Hyperledger Fabric Glossary, [Online]. Available: http://hyperledgerdocs.readthedocs.io/en/latest/glossary.html.

consortium blockchain continues to expand, traditional PBFT consensus algorithm is difficult to meet the needs in real life. Hyperledger Fabric 2.0 version uses the Raft consensus algorithm, which is also equivalent to a message queue. It reduces the node configuration requirements and is an optimization of the Kafka based ordering service. Many consortium blockchains have adopted consensus algorithms based on message queues. The following sections will introduce the consensus mechanism of PBFT and Raft, and their advantages and disadvantages.

2.1 Practical Byzantine Fault Tolerance Algorithm

PBFT is a consensus algorithm suitable for alliance chains. In the PBFT consensus algorithm network, there are f Byzantine nodes. When the total number of nodes N in the network is greater than $3f$, the distributed system can reach consensus. PBFT is a distributed consistency algorithm based on state machine copy replication. It consists of a consistency protocol, a view replacement protocol, and a checkpoint protocol. The consistency protocol is used to ensure data consistency across nodes across the entire network, through three-phase communication between nodes. In the implementation of the consistency protocol, if the master node fails, it will trigger the view replacement protocol to replace the master node. The checkpoint protocol is triggered periodically to clean up the communication messages stored by each node during the execution of the consistency protocol and synchronize the status of each node. The consistency protocol is the core protocol that the PBFT algorithm can complete consensus. It is mainly divided into three phases: pre-prepare, pre-pare and commit. The execution process is shown in Fig. 1.

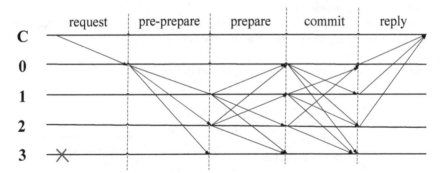

Fig. 1. PBFT algorithm consistency protocol implementation process.

1. Pre-preparation phase: The master node will generate a pre-preparation message for the request sent by the client, and broadcast the pre-preparation message to all slave nodes.
2. Preparation stage: After receiving the pre-preparation message sent by the master node, the secondary node will generate the preparatory message and broadcast the preparatory message to other nodes, while writing the pre-preparation message and

the preparatory message into the log file. At this stage, each node receives the preparation message broadcast by all other nodes. The node will verify the authenticity of the message, and compare the received preparation message with the preparation message in its own log. If more than $(f + 1)$ preparation messages are correct, it will enter the confirmation phase.

3. Confirmation phase: All nodes generate confirmation messages and broadcast them to other nodes. At this stage, the same verification work as the preparation phase will be completed. After the verification is passed, the consensus process of this request can be completed [3].

PBFT can achieve the consistency of the blockchain, eliminating excess calculations and avoiding waste of resources. However, there are problems with the efficiency of PBFT. It depends on the number of nodes participating in the protocol. This protocol is not suitable for blockchain systems with too many nodes, and it has poor scalability.

2.2 Raft

In the version of Hyperledger Faric v2.0, Raft is adopted as the consensus algorithm. The Raft protocol uses a "leader and follower" model. The primary node is dynamically elected among the orderer nodes, and the other orderer nodes are the follower nodes. Raft can tolerate faulty nodes. For this reason, Raft is called "crash fault tolerant" (CFT) [4].

The Raft protocol defines three roles, which can be said to be three states:

1. Follower: At the beginning, all nodes in the system are initially in the Follower state;
2. Candidate: Responsible for election voting;
3. Leader (leader): Responsible for synchronization of logs, processing client requests, and maintaining heartbeat contact with Follower.

The transition between roles (states) is shown in Fig. 2.

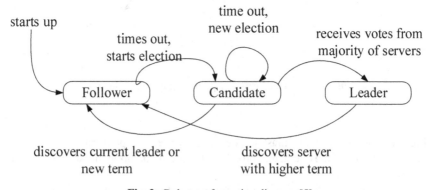

Fig. 2. Role transformation diagram [5]

When the system is initially started, all nodes are followers. If they do not receive the heartbeat signal of the leader for a period of time, the followers will be converted to Candidate. If a Candidate node receives votes from most nodes, this Candidate can be converted to a Leader, and the remaining Candidate nodes will return to the Follower state. Once a Leader finds that an anther Leader node has a higher term (Term) than it does, it will be converted to a Follower[3].

During Raft operation, Log Replication is the main activity. Log replication is to ensure data consistency between orderer nodes. The client sends the request to Leader, and Leader writes it to the local log. Then, send AppendEntries requests to other Followers. After the follower writes the data locally, it returns OK. As long as more than half of the successful returns are received (including Leader), Leader changes the status of the data to Committed. Leader then returns the consensus result to the client. Finally, Leader sends an AppendEntries request to Follower again. After receiving the request, Follower changes the Uncommitted data in the local log to Committed. This completes the log replication process, and the logs of all orderer nodes are consistent[4].

Raft is similar to the Kafka based consensus, but it is easier to install than Kafka. However, it still cannot tolerate Byzantine nodes. Fabric is still working on this.

3 Methodology

This paper designs an improved consensus mechanism suitable for the consortium blockchain, and solves the problem that the consortium blockchain cannot reach consensus in the scenario that malicious nodes exist. In order to further integrate the message queue consensus with PBFT, two consensus algorithms are improved respectively. The orderer nodes in the message queue consensus are divided between primary nodes and secondary nodes, which is convenient for block consensus. Since the transactions are already ordered at the message queue consensus phase, the confirmation phase in the PBFT consensus mechanism can be eliminated. Therefore, the three phases in the PBFT consensus mechanism are adjusted to two phases. Finally, BFTMQ is designed.

3.1 Algorithm Design

We define the node running the consensus algorithm as the orderer node. They are the nodes used for ordering and generating the blocks. First, orderer nodes are required to complete the transaction collection and ordering process, which is completed by a message queue. The message queue is quite a container for messages. When we need to use messages, we can fetch them for our own use. It is a first-in-first-out data structure, so messages are consumed in order when consuming messages. Therefore, it can guarantee the consistency of transactions by ordering. After a period of time, orderer nodes need to generate blocks for broadcasting. In order to ensure the consistency of the blocks, orderer nodes need to perform Byzantine fault tolerance consensus. The schematic diagram of the consensus process is shown in Fig. 3.

---

[3] The Ordering Service, [Online]. Available: https://hyperledger-fabric.readthedocs.io/en/latest/orderer/ordering_service.html#raft.

[4] Consensus agreement-RAFT & PBFT [Online]. Available: https://www.cnblogs.com/helloworldcode/p/11094099.html, last accessed 2020/05/05.

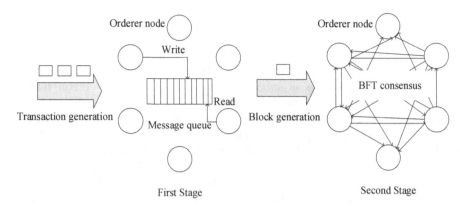

Fig. 3. Schematic of the consensus process.

First Stage. First stage mainly completes the ordering of transactions, ensuring that the order of transactions received by each orderer node is consistent. Moreover, it is responsible for packaging transactions to generate blocks for broadcast. This phase of consensus uses the message queue consensus and elects the primary node, which is responsible for generating blocks and initiating BFT Consensus. The election details of the master node will be described in detail in the second stage.

The message queue model can use existing message queue tools, such as Kafka, MSMQ, and so on. We can also design and implement a message queue model independently, which it can complete asynchronous message sequence consistency. In order to visualize the message queue implementation process, we use Kafka as the message queue, and describe the implementation process of the message queue consensus in detail.

The message queue based on Kafka requires Kafka tools[5]. Kafka needs Zookeeper to run. In order to simplify the consensus mechanism, this paper will deploy each Kafka node under the same broker of the same Zookeeper[6]. Kafka nodes and Zookeeper nodes are collectively referred to as orderer nodes. Orderer nodes are represented as a set O.

All Kafka nodes act as both producers and consumers. Since only one consumer in the same group can consume data, this is an inherent characteristic of Kafka. However, consumers need to consume the same data at the same time. Therefore, set all consumers in different groups to ensure that all Kafka nodes can consume data under the same broker. Kafka producer-consumer model is shown in Fig. 4. The producer is responsible for writing the received transactions to the offset, and consumers in different groups can read the same transaction into local memory and then perform data processing.

Kafka producer-consumer system records the order of information in the channel according to the offset, similar to the index of the data. Therefore, the transaction message pulled by the orderer nodes is accompanied by its offset in the channel, which is convenient for viewing the orderliness of the transaction and recording where the transaction is processed. The data stored in the channel is not easy to process, so the

---

[5] Kafka documentation, [Online]. Available: https://kafka.apache.org/documentation/.

[6] Zookeeper documentation, [Online]. Available: https://zookeeper.apache.org/doc/.

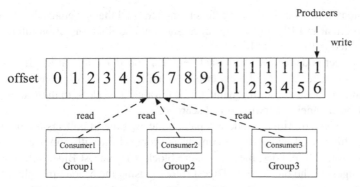

Fig. 4. Schematic diagram of Kafka producer-consumer model.

transaction needs to be stored in the local database according to the offset to facilitate subsequent packaging and processing. The database is a leveldb database, which is a k-v type database. When storing transactions, use offset as the key and transactions as the value.

After a period of time, the transactions collected during this period are packaged to generate blocks. In order to ensure the consistency of the blocks received by each node and prevent malicious nodes from publishing wrong blocks, it is necessary to perform BFT consensus among orderer nodes before the blocks are broadcast to the entire network. Therefore, the second stage of consensus will be entered.

Second Stage. The second phase of the consensus is mainly to perform consensus verification on the blocks generated by the primary node in the first phase to ensure the consistency of the broadcasted blocks. Let the maximum number of tolerable malicious nodes in O be f, then the size of the O set must satisfy the formula (1)

$$|O| \geq 3f + 1 \tag{1}$$

The algorithm defines the following:

Let v be the view number, which in turn increases with view change.

Let p be the primary node and s be the secondary node. Both the primary node and the secondary nodes are orderer nodes, represented by the numbers $\{0, 1 \ldots |O| - 1\}$.

The selection of the primary node is determined by v and block height h, which satisfies the formula (2)

$$p = (h + v) \quad mod \ |O| \tag{2}$$

PBFT is a Client/Server (C/S) response mode, which needs to be converted into a P2P mode. Therefore, the client role is removed, so the request phase is omitted. The consensus has undergone two stages of consensus proposal (Proposal) and consensus confirmation (Confirm) [6].

Algorithmic Process. Based on the above logic, the detailed algorithm flow of BFTMQ is as follows:

1. The client node (the client here refers to the terminal that generates the transaction, not the client in PBFT) generates a transaction, and the transaction information is transmitted in the form of broadcast;
2. When a peer node receives a transaction, it is flooded and forwarded. If it is orderer nodes, verify the legality of the transaction and confirm that the transaction is not in the Kafka publish-subscribe channel. If it is valid, it is added to the Kafka publish-subscribe channel, otherwise, it is discarded.
3. After the elected primary node has passed the Δ_t time, it collects the transactions during this period and issues a consensus proposal P_p with a message format of $\ll$Proposal, v, h, p, bd>, block>, where block is broadcast Block information, bd is the digest of the block, bd = Digest (block), using the Merkel tree algorithm;
4. The secondary nodes s_i, after receiving the consensus proposal, verify the validity of the proposal, and after confirmation, send a confirmation message C_C to other orderer nodes, the format is <Confirm, v, h, i, bd_i>, where bd_i is the block summary information of master node p forwarded from node s_i, which represents the node's confirmation of the block sent by the primary node;
5. After any orderer node receives 2f identical confirmation messages, it believes that consensus is reached and can broadcast the block to the entire network; if after checking the proposal, it is found to be not true, the secondary node suspects the primary node and broadcasts a view change message, which will introduce the view change process in detail later;
6. After receiving the block, other peer nodes consider the consensus to be completed and write the block into the database;
7. Orderer nodes start a new round of consensus after the consensus task is completed.

The specific process of the consensus algorithm is shown in Fig. 5.

3.2 View Change Protocol Design

When the secondary node detects that the master node does not initiate a consensus proposal after Δ_t time, it suspects that there is a problem with the primary node. The secondary node will send a view change message to notify other orderer nodes to change the view. The view change process changes as follows:

1. Let the new view be $v_{new} = v_{old} + 1$, the secondary node sending the view change is s_v, and the format of the view change is <ChangeView, v_{old}, v_{new}, s_v, h>
2. When other secondary nodes receive the message, check if the v_{old}, v_{new}, and h fields are correct. If correct, broadcast a change confirmation message in the format <ChangeConfirm, v_{new}, v_{old}, h, i>, where i is the number of the node. During the view change process, consensus proposals and consensus confirmation messages are rejected.
3. After any one of the orderer nodes receives the change confirmation of the other 2f orderer nodes, the view change is confirmed and the view number becomes v_{new}.

If the master node encounters a network delay when initiating a consensus proposal, resulting in the secondary node not receiving the consensus proposal within Δ_t time, it

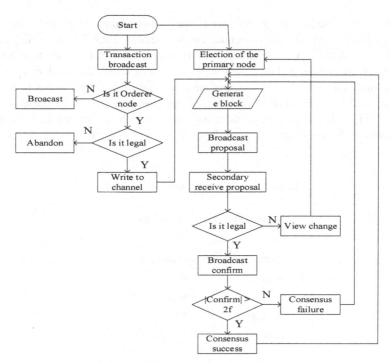

Fig. 5. Flow chart of consensus algorithm.

mistakes the master node as a malicious node and executes the view change protocol. This process will not affect the protocol execution and block synchronization. When the view change was initiated, all the secondary nodes refused to accept the consensus proposal of the old master node, and until the change is completed, they will accept the consensus proposal of the new master node. If view changes are frequently initiated due to network delays, consider extending the Δ_t time.

4 Experimental Evaluation

This chapter tests BFTMQ from two aspects: transaction throughput and system fault tolerance to verify the effectiveness and practicability of the new algorithm.

4.1 Experiment Preparation and Execution

In order to be able to conduct experiments, this paper designed and implemented simulated transaction nodes to simulate the process of user-generated transactions. There is no limit on the trading account in the node, which guarantees that the simulated transaction occurs at the fastest speed, thereby achieving the test of throughput.

The entire blockchain system is written in Go language, using a virtual machine to simulate multiple nodes in the blockchain. This experiment uses Kafka to implement the message queue. According to the Hyperledger Faric document, orderer nodes are no less than 4 nodes, and zookeeper nodes are 1, 3 or 5 [7]. In addition, if the number of nodes in the PBFT is four, at least one error node can be tolerated. Therefore, according to the characteristics of the two consensus algorithms, the experimental test sets a zookeeper node, three Kafka nodes, and these four nodes are all orderer nodes, which can perform ordering and BFT consensus. The experiment also set up two peer nodes to receive and store the block information after the orderer nodes complete the consensus. In addition, there is also a transaction simulation node, which is a process that simulates the occurrence of transactions. The specific node configuration environment is shown in Table 1.

Table 1. Node configuration environment

Software/hardware	Version/model
Operating system	Ubuntu 16
Memory	8 GB RAM
JDK	8
Go	10.4
Zookeeper	3.5.5
Kafka	2.11-2.2.1

In the experiment, each process is started in turn. The transaction simulation node cyclically generates and sends transaction data to the consensus module. The consensus module executes the BFTMQ algorithm to generate blocks, and records blocks in the distributed ledger of orderer nodes and peer nodes on the entire network to form an immutable and distributed blockchain database. A schematic of this experiment is shown in Fig. 6.

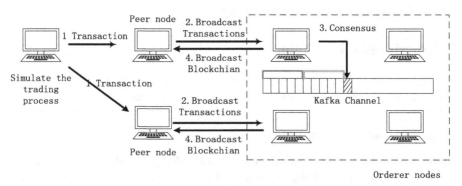

Fig. 6. Schematic diagram of BFTMQ experiment.

---

[7] Bringing up a Kafka-based Ordering Service, [Online]. Available: https://hyperledger-fabric.rea dthedocs.io/en/latest/kafka.html.

4.2 Performance Testing

The two major indicators of concern in the consensus algorithm are throughput and fault tolerance. According to the experimental design of the previous section, the experiment and statistics of the two indicators are performed separately, and demonstrate the effectiveness and advantages of the consensus algorithm.

Throughput. Throughput is a measure of a system's ability to process transactions, requests, and transactions per unit time, and is an important indicator of the system's concurrency capabilities. In this paper, TPS (Transaction per Second) is used to indicate the size of the throughput, which refers to the total number of transactions divided by time sent to the transaction confirmation and written in the blockchain, see formula (3)

$$TPS_{\Delta_t} = SumTransactions_{\Delta_t}/\Delta_t \tag{3}$$

Among them, Δ_t is the time interval between transaction issuance and block confirmation, that is, the time interval of the block generation, and $SumTransactions_{\Delta_t}$ is the number of transactions included in the block during this time interval.

Take six different time intervals of 5 s, 10 s, 20 s, 40 s, 60 s, and 100 s. Each time interval is tested 20 times, and the average of 20 times is taken as the TPS of each time interval, and get the relationship between TPS and block time as shown in Fig. 7.

Since the BFT consensus mechanism was added after the completion of message queue consensus, and the throughput of BFT consensus is much smaller than message queue consensus, it has a certain impact on the throughput of this consensus mechanism. Therefore, this consensus mechanism is suitable for the consortium blockchain system without high throughput requirements.

Fault Tolerance. According to the algorithm design in Sect. 2, BFTMQ is the most tolerated malicious node $f \leq (|O| - 1)/3$, In order to ensure the security of the system, there are four orderer nodes, let $f = 0, 1, 2$ to observe the performance of the system. The malicious node acts as the master node to generate the wrong block for consensus verification, and uses the TPS index to determine the transaction whether the block is confirmed within the normal range and compared with Kafka ordering consensus. Through experiments, we can draw Fig. 7.

It can be seen from the figure that when the malicious node is 1, Kafka ordering consensus protocol cannot be reached, there is no block in the system broadcast to the entire network, and transactions cannot be conducted within the regular time. At this time, TPS = 0, the entire network is immediately unable to work, it is easy to cause network paralysis. However, BFTMQ can tolerate malicious nodes in the normal range and maintain the operation of the system.

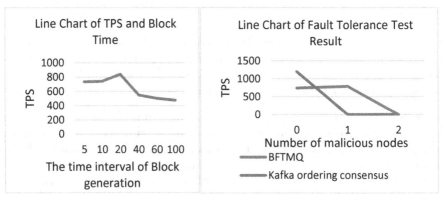

Fig. 7. Line chart of TPS and fault tolerance test results (left) TPS relationship between two consensus mechanisms with different numbers of failed nodes (right).

5   Conclusions and Future Work

According to the experimental results in Sect. 4, it is proved that BFTMQ designed in this paper can be used as the consensus mechanism of the consortium blockchain, which can correctly perform the ordering and consensus, and solves the problem that message queue consensus cannot tolerate malicious nodes. The dual function of tolerating malicious nodes is realized. However, although the algorithm has a higher throughput than traditional PBFT, it cannot reach the throughput of 10,000+ transactions. Therefore, future work needs to further optimize the BFT algorithm, improve throughput, and reduce latency.

References

1. Chen, W., Xu, Z., Shi, S., Zhao, Y., Zhao, J.: A survey of blockchain applications in different domains (2019). arXiv:1911.02013 [cs.CR]
2. Cao, Z.: A consensus mechanism suitable for alliance chains. Cyberspace Secur. **10**(01), 100–105 (2019)
3. Fang, W., Wang, Z., Song, H., et al.: A blockchain-oriented optimized PBFT consensus algorithm. J. Beijing Jiaotong Univ. **43**(05), 58–64 (2019)
4. Fatourou, P.: The distributed computing column. Inform. Econ. J. **17**(4), 109–122 (2013)
5. Ongaro, D., Ousterhout, J.: In search of an understandable consensus algorithm (2014)
6. Duan, J., Karve, A., Sreedhar, V., et al.: Service management of blockchain networks. In: 2018 IEEE 11th International Conference on Cloud Computing (CLOUD). IEEE Computer Society (2018)

Automatic Q.A-Pair Generation for Incident Tickets Handling: An Application of NLP

Mick Lammers[1], Fons Wijnhoven[1] (ID), Faiza A. Bukhsh[1(✉)] (ID),
and Patrício de Alencar Silva[2] (ID)

[1] Department of Computer Science, University of Twente, 7500AE Enschede, The Netherlands
mick-lammers@hotmail.com,
{a.b.j.m.wijnhoven,f.a.bukhsh}@utwente.nl
[2] Programa de Pós-Graduação em Ciência da Computação, Universidade Federal Rural do Semi-Árido (UFERSA), Mossoró, Rio Grande do Norte, Brazil
patricio.alencar@ufersa.edu.br

Abstract. Chatbots answer customer questions by mostly manually crafted Question Answer (Q.A.)-pairs. If organizations process vast numbers of questions, manual Q.A. pair generation and maintenance become very ex-pensive and complicated. To reduce cost and increase efficiency, in this study, we propose a low threshold QA-pair generation system that can automatically identify unique problems and their solutions from a large incident ticket dataset of an I.T. Shared Service Center. The system has four components: categorical clustering for structuring the semantic meaning of ticket information, intent identification, action recommendation, and reinforcement learning. For categorical clustering, we use a Latent Semantic Indexing (LSI) algorithm, and for the intent identification, we apply the Latent Dirichlet Allocation (LDA), both Natural Language Processing techniques. The actions are cleaned and clustered and resulting Q.A. pairs are stored in a knowledge base with reinforcement learning capabilities. The system can produce Q.A. pairs from which about 55% are useful and correct. This percentage is likely to in-crease significantly with feedback in its usage stage. By this study, we contribute to a further understanding of the development of automatic service processes.

Keywords: Service request handling · Service management · Q.A. pair generation system · ICT user support management · Natural language processing

1 Introduction

I.T. Shared Service Centers are the beating heart of large organizations. They take on everything that has to do with the facilitation of I.T., like personal computers, mobile devices, workplaces, servers, applications, and VPN's. I.T. Incident management is a large part of shared service centers' responsibility [7]. As of now, incident management is performed in almost all service centers using a ticketing system. A ticketing system registers incident calls and requests for service from clients. The tickets are then either sent to persons who can act on them or persons who know most about the context of

© Springer Nature Switzerland AG 2020
K. Djemame et al. (Eds.): GECON 2020, LNCS 12441, pp. 15–27, 2020.
https://doi.org/10.1007/978-3-030-63058-4_2

these tickets. Especially in highly complex large-scale environments, the existing ticking systems would be most useful but are less effective because of difficulties in generating Q.A. (which stands for question-answer) pairs and high costs of maintaining Q.A. pairs manually [2, 6]. In this research, a system is designed by which the ticket data is used to create this actionable knowledge in a manner that limits the amount of manual work in QA-pair creation and maintenance using Natural Language Processing and Machine Learning. The objective of this research is to "to find an optimal design for a low-cost QA-pair generation system for a large-scale I.T. incident tickets dataset."

A state-of-the-art research is performed to identify components and techniques in QA-pair generation in Sect. 2. We provide summaries of related work and draw design conclusions for our solution in Sect. 3. Based on this literature study, we define the research gap and goals, and we build our own solution of categorizing incidents, ticket intents, and solutions in Sect. 4.

We demonstrate and test the proposed solution by the case of the SSC-ICT IT Shared Service Center of 8 Dutch ministries. SSC-ICT supports about 40,000 civil servants who almost all have a laptop and phone to be supported as well as a virtual working environment for performing their jobs. Furthermore, SSC-ICT provides services for over one thousand applications and receive around 30,000 tickets a month in ticket management system TopDesk, mainly via phone (60%), e-mails (15%), and face-to-face contact (10%). Given the highly textual nature of Q.A. pairs, natural language processing seems to be particularly useful in Q.A. pair generation. After designing this system, we evaluate its effectiveness, draw generalizable conclusions, and define the needs for further research.

2 State-of-the-Art

QA pairs have a question and an answer. In incident management, the question is often referred to as "intent." The intent is the user's intent for creating the ticket. The answers are called actions, resolutions, or just answers. Previous studies that describe the development of Q.A. pair generating systems are described below. These studies were found using the literature research methodology of [15]. In total, 200 articles are found using forward and backward snowballing. After inclusion/exclusion criteria (for details see [9]), we have selected 60 most relevant articles. In the following, we will highlight only a few.

The study found in [5] designed a cognitive support system for a specific client with 450 factories operating in 190 countries. For extracting the intents, they used a combination of n-gram and Lingo techniques [11], as well as field experts to manually identify intents. Another very well-known system used by [1] describes a cognitive system developed by researchers from IBM for a service desk. The knowledge extraction processes applied is divided into three steps: problem diagnosis, root cause analysis, and resolution recommendation. A similar study found in [12] designed a system to automatically analyze natural language text in network trouble tickets. Their case is a large cloud provider of whom they analyze over 10,000 tickets. An overview of the different steps and knowledge discovery techniques mentioned in well-known studies is given in Table 1.

Table 1. Q.A.-pair identification steps and techniques from the literature.

Author	Q.A.-pair identification steps				Identification techniques			
	Category clustering	Root-cause analysis	Intent identification	Resolution finding	Reinforcement learning	Unsupervised		Supervised
						POS patterns	Topic modeling	Classifier
N. Berente et al. (2019)		●		●			●	●
Suman et al. (2018)			●				●	
P. Dhoolia et al. (2017)		●	●	●	●	●		
S. Agarwal et al. (2017)		●	●	●				●
Vlasov et al. (2017)		●	●	●				●
Mani et al. (2014)	●		●	●		●		
Jan et al. (2014)			●				●	
Potharaju & Nitarotaru (2013)			●	●		●		

3   Design Principles of Q.A.-Pair Generation

All the articles discussed use an intent identification process as well as a resolution recommendation process (except for [8] who focus on intent identification techniques only). Reinforcement learning and root cause analysis are used only in a small number of articles. Root cause analysis is used where the datasets are smaller in contrast to reinforcement learning that is more valuable with larger numbers of tickets and potential feedback mechanisms.

The largest dataset used in the described articles has 80,000 tickets, less than half of the number of tickets of this research. Consequently, the datasets from the articles have fewer categories, and they identify relatively few problems, 130 at the most, then the expected 1,000 problems from SSC-ICT.

This, along with tests that showed that clustering techniques on the complete corpus showed inconsistent clustering results. Moreover, good results on using a Latent Semantic Analysis (LSA) based method for grouping tickets based on subjects provide the foundation to add a component to the pipeline, which we call categorical clustering. In this step, we first group the tickets in large categories. After that, we apply for each category a unique iteration of the intent identification component.

Furthermore, we decided not to implement Root Cause Analysis in this iteration of the system due to a lack of resources. A methodological overview of the steps followed is provided in Fig. 1.

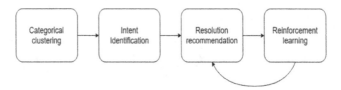

Fig. 1.   Four steps of a Q.A.-pair generation system

In **step one**, the tickets need to be ordered on categories, because detecting intents right away leads to very inconsistent and noisy clusters. For identifying categories, keyword based-clusters (supervised) and word-embedding based clustering (unsupervised) are mentioned in the literature [3]. The downside to keyword-based categorization is that unimportant words like operations or adjectives may also be identified as clusters. Therefore, Categorization using word-embeddings, Latent Semantic Analysis (LSA), is the best method for this process, as it benefits from the single keyword categories, and it excludes low-informative words automatically.

Step two involves intent identification or problem identification by which specific problems are identified from tickets. This can be done by a supervised learning methodology in which intents are identified beforehand, and new tickets are classified based on one of these intents or in an unsupervised way in which topics are created using either POS patterns in tickets or from topical word embeddings. Supervised intent identification is most effective in a rule-based environment. Unsupervised methodologies for intent identification are either word embeddings (LDA/LSA) or patterns in word or POS forms.

Step three identifies resolutions or action recommendations (i.e. the A in Q.A.) from resolution texts. In this process, action fields are cleaned from source-related or e-mail related noise. Furthermore, hot sentences are extracted, and duplicate actions are removed. The sorting and providing of these actions are improved by step four.

Step four involves the process of increasing the accuracy of the system based on client feedback. Client feedback will act as being the assessor on the accuracy of the action recommendation of the system. This assessment can then be used to classify the action as relevant or irrelevant to the intent, based on which new intents can be solved better. Relevant examples of feedback mechanisms are the number of clicks on a specific action, a like/dislike option, or search history.

4   Design of Q.A.-Pair Generation System

4.1   Ticket Data Description

For our case, the ticket data includes a dataset from the start of February 2018 till the 31st of December 2018. This is a dataset of 340,000 tickets with 40+ attributes. We focused on all first-line tickets, and with this step, we exclude 40,000 tickets. Then, we chose to include only incidents, requests for service, and requests for information. Other ticket types were mainly computer-generated tickets and, therefore, not of interest to this research. This results in a final dataset of 210,000 tickets. The selected tickets have the attributes listed in Table 2.

The 'short description' (containing intent information) and the 'action' fields are the main sources for Q.A. pair generation. The request field appeared too inconsistent for use. We keep the request field, the category, and subcategory fields out of this research scope because these categories are not problem-focused.

4.2   Categorical Clustering

The column with the "short description" along with their ticket id's, is exported from the excel dataset and converted to the XML-format. This is a file of 450,000 lines. For the categorical clustering, three techniques are attempted based on outcomes of the state-of-the-art research: LDA, POS Patterns, and Lingo3G clustering. LDA did not show good results. The resulting clusters are overlapping. POS patterns were also not effective. The POS patterns were too specific and did not capture the global category. Lingo3G, however, worked very well on the dataset. After having tweaked with the attribute settings, amongst other things promoting short (one-word) labels and increasing the expected number of clusters, a process-based ticket cluster overview appeared (vide Fig. 2). For Lingo3G, we used the custom parameters on top of the standard parameters as shown in Table 3.

Lingo3G applies a custom version of LSA (Latent Semantic Analysis) using Term Frequency – Inverse Document Frequency (TF-IDF) word embeddings on a text corpus and then applying Singular Value Decomposition (SVD) for dimensionality reduction. Its algorithm consists of preprocessing, frequent phrase extraction, cluster label induction, and cluster content discovery steps.

Table 2. Attributes used for Q.A.-pair generation

Data field	Description
Ticket id	A unique id for each ticket, automatically generated
Short description	A summary of the ticket problem, written by the service desk operator
Request	The full description of the ticket, in case of an e-mail, the full e-mail is displayed here. In other cases, it is like a short description
Action	A summary of the suggested action steps by the operator
Type of ticket	Type of customer request, such as a request for service, internal management notification, request for information, security incident, SCOM (a monitoring system), complaint
Category	The highest level of Categorization: User-bound services, Applications, Premise-bound services, Housing & hosting, Security
Subcategory	Each of the main categories has at least five subcategories. In total there are 42 subcategories. 50% of the tickets are covered by three subcategories: location specific services, housing and hosting services, and security services
Practitioners group	This is the division that solved the ticket, 85% of the ticket has the service desk as practitioner group, the other tickets are solved by about 300 different small groups
Entry type	The means by which the customer contacted the service desk: telephone, e-mail, physical service desk, portal, website, manually

Table 3. Custom parameters for Lingo3G application

Parameter	Description
Minimum cluster size: 0.0010%	Lowers the threshold for minimal cluster size
Cluster count base: 20	Increases the number of resulting clusters
gMaximum hierarchy depth: 1	Limits optional clustering depth to 1 layer
Phrase-DF cut-off scaling: 0.20	Decreases the length of labels
Word-DF cut-off scaling: 0.00	Further limits the length of labels to 1 word
Maximum top-level clustering passes: 8	Increases the computational effort
Default clustering language: Dutch	Change NLP language to Dutch

The preprocessing step removes stop words from an external list that is created by a field expert. This also identifies synonyms and label name. Because the input consists of only one sentence, we skip the frequent phrase extraction process. Lingo3G generates 138 clusters from the ticket data. With the largest being 10% of the whole ticket corpus and the smallest 0.05%. The ten largest clusters accumulate to 65% of the ticket corpus, 15% is part of the other 107 clusters, 20% is not categorizable.

Evaluation

We evaluated the categories manually on hierarchical independence, synonymity, and informativity. Synonymity is about whether there is another synonymous cluster or not, for instance, in the case of SSC-ICT, the clusters "mail" and "e-mail." Hierarchical independence is about whether a cluster should be subjective to another cluster. For instance, the tickets in the cluster "paper" are 95% of the time regarding "printer" and should, therefore, be part of the "printer" cluster. Further Categorization would then happen in the next component, intent identification. Relevance is about whether a category describes an actual single subject. For instance, "defect" is not a category because it does not provide any information about the subject apart from that it is probably defective. In the evaluation process, 21 clusters were removed, and the tickets were reallocated. This resulted in 117 final categories. A visualization of the weighted clusters is provided in Fig. 2.

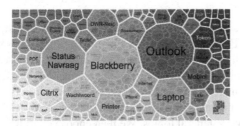

Fig. 2. High-level cluster results from Lingo3G

4.3 Intent-Level Clustering

For the intent-level clustering process, we tried two techniques: POS patterns and LDA. The POS patterns technique is used in most reviewed articles. Due to the high expectations of LDA in text clustering (in research but also in online communities and data science companies that we had contact with) and also the high scores of the technique in the article of [8], we decided to attempt this technique.

External Evaluation

We evaluated the techniques on the coverage, the number of total intents, and the clustering quality. For the clustering quality, we chose for the external evaluation of samples using a golden test set. We chose this method because we believe the internal evaluation is not practical due to the subjectiveness of the clusters.

We create this golden test set by manually clustering a sample of 1,000 tickets for 3 categories by 3 independent people, of which the best classification was chosen each time. We give a quantitative score to the degree to which the technique's results comply with the golden test set. The score given is the proportion of tickets in a cluster that is both in the golden test set as well as in the technique's resulting cluster. A score of 0.50 for a technique thus means that on average, each ticket's parent cluster contains 50% the same tickets as the parent cluster of the golden test set.

Option 1: POS patterns
For the identification of unique problems, we applied POS Patterns to the "Korte omschrijving" (Dutch phrase for 'short description') text. From the related works, it was clear that this was the go-to method to extract intents for short text and high variety corpus. We use the combination of operation-entity POS patterns, as suggested by [5]. The operations are verbs. The entities are nouns and adjectives.

For preprocessing, the first stopwords are removed using an online freely available stopword-list. Labels of the categories in which the tickets are classified are removed as well, to avoid redundant intent labels. Next, we tag the remaining words on 'Part of Speech.' If a verb is detected, the system combines the nearest nouns or adjectives with them to form a two-word phrase. If no verb is identified, the system uses the remaining words as an intent. We found that in most cases, there existed no verb in sentences. We show the results in Table 4. The total amount of tickets that the system converts to intents is about 110,000; this is slightly more than 50% of the categorized tickets.

Option 2: LDA
For this experiment, we used the complete dataset of the outlook cluster, which comprises about 15,000 tickets. For preprocessing, we lemmatized the dataset, and we used the same dutch stopword list that we used for the POS patterns. We use these files as input for training the LDA model. For determining the number of topics, we have used well known methodology, namely the perplexity score, of the clustering results. However, this methodology recommends using a maximum of 30 topics, which we find small, and the results also show very general topics. We then choose to go for 100 topics.

As summarized in Table 4, the main difference between the techniques lies in the number of tickets covered by the algorithms. LDA covered 100% of the dataset tickets and POS only 36%. The reason for the low score of the POS pattern technique is the high exclusion of words that are not part of the set POS patterns. Many short descriptions do not have a verb, which is the main ingredient of POS patterns. For this reason, we use LDA for the intent identification process.

4.4   Resolution Recommendation

For the resolution recommendation process, we combine the tickets in the clusters with their respective actions. Using the ratio of verbs as well as numbers in a sentence, we successfully removed all e-mail related noise like signature and salutation as well as TopDesk similar noise consisting of the name of the operator and timestamp. Next, we remove empty action fields and combine double actions; this increases the weight rate that we match to these actions. A domain expert manually labeled 2,000 actions as solutions to intents. 30% of the tickets appear to contain useful actions. The smallest intents of the system contain at least 20 tickets. So even the smallest intents have, on average 6 useful actions. It then depends on the reinforcement learning component to recommend these useful actions first.

4.5   Reinforcement Learning

We developed an interface for a user to type in a short description of any incident upon which the system will identify the corresponding cluster and provide previously

Table 4. Number of tickets automatically converted to intents

Method	POS patterns	LDA
Total tickets	210.000	210.000
Threshold	10	10
Coverage	36%	100%
# of intents External evaluation	1490	1500
Large (Outlook)	0.4063	0.4106
Medium (Excel)	0.4200	0.4844
Small (P-direkt)	0.3062	0.2403
Average	0.3775	0.3784

applied actions for the incident. The user can then leave feedback for the action that was most suitable to his incident using a like-button. This feedback is used automatically to improve the sorting of actions using reinforcement learning. Further potential improvements are identifying intent variations, identifying flaws in the intent disambiguation process, learning new intents, and learning new mappings between words and intents.

4.6   The Architecture of the Q.A. Pair Generator

Figure 3 depicts the complete process of training a Q.A. pair system and recommending actions to customer input. For training the system, the categorical clustering and intent identification are used. First, the categories are determined using LSA indexing. Then, the tickets are appointed to one of around 100 categories (for the SSC-ICT dataset). After that, the intents are identified.

The QA pair generator preprocesses the short descriptions of the tickets and the complete corpus of brief descriptions for a category transformed into a TF-IDF corpus, in which the preprocessed short descriptions are the documents Once we trained the model, the tickets are given a dominant topic, which is the intent. The system than grabs the action fields for each of the tickets of each intent excludes doubles and actions that are remarkably similar using the Levenshtein distance, and thus produces a list of actions for each intent. When the customer has chosen an intent that he or she thinks fits best, the Q.A. pair can produce a resolution from a matching action list. The list is sorted based on the feedback of customers as well as on a score that is provided by a deep learning classifier that can distinguish useless and useful actions.

5   Discussion

As summarized in Table 5, the success rate of the intent identification process is, on average, around 55%. The success rate is calculated by subtracting the number of tickets in "non-informative clusters" from both the "total number of tickets" and the "number of tickets clustered correctly" and then dividing the "tickets clustered correctly" by the

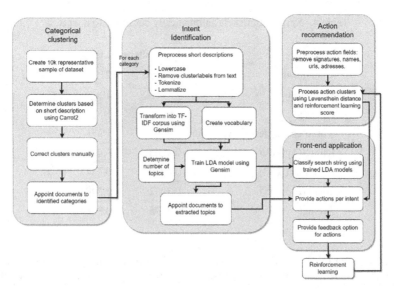

Fig. 3. Q.A. pair generator: process view

"total number of tickets." This score means that, on average, the system can identify a correct intent for a ticket 55% of the time. Furthermore, we conclude that between 10 and 20% of the tickets that are part of a category are described too vaguely to extract any meaning out of them. On top of the 12% of the category clustering component (88% success rate), we say that between 20 and 30% of all tickets are described too vaguely by the operators.

For all tickets clustered well, about 30% contains a useful action. Looking at the intents, which are almost always larger than 10 tickets and often larger than 100 tickets, the chance that intent has at least one user action is large. Furthermore, if this does not appear to be the case, the action could always be added manually by an operator. So once enough feedback is received from users, the right actions are filtered from the less informative actions, and the system will be able to recommend a useful action to an intent most of the time.

Table 5. Intent classification success for three identified categories

Category	"Outlook"	"Excel"	"P-direkt"
Total number of tickets	13341	721	286
Tickets clustered correctly	8034	436	220
Number of tickets in non-informative clusters	1323	167	89
Success rate	55.8%	48.6%	66.5%

6 Conclusion and Further Research

From research on comparable State of the Art systems, we identified the following components for a Q.A. pair generation system: Intent Identification, action recommendation, and Reinforcement Learning. We added to this the element of Categorization due to the large dataset and wide variety of tickets of SSC-ICT. We also identified specific relevant techniques for Q.A. pair generation. For Categorization, we identified LSI, LDA, and POS patterns. To avoid the risk of overfitting, we created three golden cluster sets of three different sizes and different types of categories for our evaluation method. Furthermore, we determined that the number of tickets covered, along with a threshold for intent-size, was relevant for evaluation. For the action recommendation component, we decided that the percentage of unique and useful actions proposed is a good measure. However, this is meant for future use of the system, thus not evaluated in this research, in contrary to the other two components. The reinforcement learning component also requires feedback to be able to be evaluated. Furthermore, its results can be seen in increased results for the other three components rather than having its own measure.

The main subjects that this research puts forward which are not extensively researched are that of categorization clustering, the use of Topic Modelling (LDA), our clustering quality evaluation method, and the reinforcement learning for improving the intent identification component. We believe that decreasing the number of expected topics by one hundredfold by first applying categorization clustering is the reason why LDA could be utilized as successful as we did for a dataset that is as big as ours. However, as of 2017, GuidedLDA has been discovered, a method to seed keywords in LDA topics, steering the algorithm in a preferred direction to identify topics around. GuidedLDA and its potential have, however, barely been researched yet. We are curious to see how far this steering can go, especially in combination with applying reinforcement learning. Its potential seems unlimited, reaching towards topic databases in which topics instead of lexical keywords are stored, with hundreds of weighted terms per topic.

The deep Categorization that this research suggests using categorization clustering as well as intent identification makes advanced business intelligence possible. The complete system, including the result recommendation and reinforcement learning component, has multiple use cases as well. Frequently Asked Questions (FAQ) could be easily identified and updated; the system could be used as a knowledge base for operators or be made available for all customers. Furthermore, this Q.A. pair system is the first necessary step towards building a chatbot.

This paper provides a low-cost and quick set-up method for being able to categorize the largest ticket datasets on problem-level. Topic modeling shows to be able to handle inconsistent and short ticket summaries well, in contrast to Part of Speech modeling, which depends on the accuracy of POS taggers and the presence of known verbs and nouns. The methodology in this paper is an excellent way to kickstart your use of Artificial Intelligence and see quick results. Furthermore, it provides and is designed with great opportunities for further enhancement of the system using reinforcement learning based on user feedback.

In this paper, we have presented the workflow of the solution (vide Fig. 3), POS, and LSA are traditional for natural language processing. As a future work direction, a one-state solution could be implemented using a deep neural network extracting the intent automatically and matching it intelligently to the desired action when training data is available, although we need to find if the proposed solution is not expensive.

Another possible future research direction could be to incorporate modern word-embedding techniques like *cbow* or *skip-gram* and could be character-based for dealing with spelling mistakes. This would boost the accuracy of the Q.A pair solution. Moreover, incorporating reinforcement learning for the neural network seems more natural as for the existing solution, but will it be cost-effective or not is still an open question.

References

1. Agarwal, S., Aggarwal, V., Akula, A.R., Dasgupta, G.B., Sridhara, G.: Automatic problem extraction and analysis from unstructured text in I.T. tickets. IBM J. Res. Dev. **61**(1), 4:41–4:52 (2017). https://doi.org/10.1147/JRD.2016.2629318
2. Bensoussan, A., Mookerjee, R., Mookerjee, V., Yue, W.T.: Maintaining diagnostic knowledge-based systems: a control-theoretic approach. Manag. Sci. (2008). https://doi.org/10.1287/mnsc.1080.0908
3. Berry, M.W., Kogan, J.: Text Mining: Applications and Theory. Wiley (2010). https://doi.org/10.1002/9780470689646
4. Berente, N., Seidel, S., Safadi, H.: Research commentary—data-driven computationally intensive theory development. Inf. Syst. Res. **30**(1), 50–64 (2019)
5. Dhoolia, P., et al.: A cognitive system for business and technical support: a case study (2017). https://doi.org/10.1147/JRD.2016.2631398
6. Grosan, C., Abraham, A.: Rule-based expert systems. In: Grosan, C., Abraham, A. (eds.) Intelligent Systems. ISRL, vol. 17, pp. 149–185. Springer, Heidelberg (2011). https://doi.org/10.1007/978-3-642-21004-4_7
7. Iden, J., Eikebrokk, T.R.: Using the ITIL process reference model for realizing I.T. governance: an empirical investigation. Inf. Syst. Manag. **31**(1), 37–58 (2014). https://doi.org/10.1080/10580530.2014.854089
8. Jan, E., Chen, K., Ide, T.: A probabilistic concept annotation for I.T. service desk tickets. In: Proceedings of the 7th International Workshop on Exploiting Semantic Annotations in Information Retrieval - ESAIR 2014, pp. 21–23 (2014). https://doi.org/10.1145/2663712.2666193
9. Lammers, M.: A QA-pair generation system for the incident tickets of a public ICT Shared Service Center. Mater thesis, University of Twete (2019). http://essay.utwente.nl/77562/
10. Mani, S., Sankaranarayanan, K., Sinha, V.S., Devanbu, P.: Panning requirement nuggets in stream of software maintenance tickets. In: Proceedings of the 22nd ACM SIGSOFT International Symposium on Foundations of Software Engineering - FSE 2014, pp. 678–688 (2014). https://doi.org/10.1145/2635868.2635897
11. Osiński, S., Stefanowski, J., Weiss, D.: Lingo: search results clustering algorithm based on singular value decomposition. In: Kłopotek, M.A., Wierzchoń, S.T., Trojanowski, K. (eds.) Intelligent Information Processing and Web Mining. AINSC, vol. 25, pp. 359–368. Springer, Heidelberg (2004). https://doi.org/10.1007/978-3-540-39985-8_37
12. Potharaju, R., Nita-Rotaru, C.: Juggling the jigsaw : towards automated problem inference from network trouble tickets. In: NSDI, pp. 127–141 (2013)
13. Roy, S., Malladi, V.V., Gangwar, A., Dharmaraj, R.: A NMF-based learning of topics and clusters for IT maintenance tickets aided by heuristic. In: Mendling, J., Mouratidis, H. (eds.) CAiSE 2018. LNBIP, vol. 317, pp. 209–217. Springer, Cham (2018). https://doi.org/10.1007/978-3-319-92901-9_18

14. Vlasov, V., Chebotareva, V., Rakhimov, M., Kruglikov, S.: AI user support system for SAP ERP (2017)
15. Wolfswinkel, J.F., Furtmueller, E., Wilderom, C.P.M.: Using grounded theory as a method for rigorously reviewing literature. Eur. J. Inf. Syst. **22**(1), 45–55 (2013). https://doi.org/10.1057/ejis.2011.51

ProtectDDoS: A Platform
for Trustworthy Offering
and Recommendation of Protections

Muriel Franco$^{(\boxtimes)}$, Erion Sula$^{(\boxtimes)}$, Bruno Rodrigues$^{(\boxtimes)}$, Eder Scheid$^{(\boxtimes)}$,
and Burkhard Stiller$^{(\boxtimes)}$

Communication Systems Group CSG, Department of Informatics IfI,
University of Zürich UZH, Binzmühlestrasse 14, 8050 Zürich, Switzerland
{franco,rodrigues,scheid,stiller}@ifi.uzh.ch, erion.sula@uzh.ch

Abstract. As the dependency of businesses on digital services increases, their vulnerability to cyberattacks increases, too. Besides providing innovative services, business owners must focus on investing in robust cybersecurity mechanisms to countermeasure cyberattacks. Distributed Denial-of-Service (DDoS) attacks remain one of the most dangerous cyberattacks, *e.g.*, leading to service disruption, financial loss, and reputation harm. Although protection measures exist, a catalog of solutions is missing, which could help network operators to access and filter information in order to select suitable protections for specific demands.

This work presents *ProtectDDoS*, a platform offering recommendations of DDoS protections. *ProtectDDoS* provides a blockchain-based catalog, where DDoS protection providers can announce details regarding their services, while users can obtain recommendations of DDoS protections according to their specific demands (*e.g.*, price, attacks supported, or geolocation constraints). *ProtectDDoS*'s Smart Contract (SC) maintains the integrity of data about protections available and provides tamper-proof reputation. To evaluate the feasibility and effectiveness of *ProtectDDoS*, a prototype was implemented and a case study conducted to discuss costs, including interactions with the SC.

Keywords: Cybersecurity · DDoS protection · Recommender system · Smart Contract (SC) · Marketplace

1 Introduction

Denial-of-Service (DoS) attacks represent a significant threat to any commercial organization and individuals, which rely on Internet-based services. In the last years, such attacks have become more complex and sophisticated, and, in turn, difficult to predict and mitigate [6]. Even more dangerous are the so-called Distributed Denial-of-Service (DDoS) attacks, as the attack itself derives from multiple hosts distributed over the network, such as those using botnets. Consequently, the targets affected (*e.g.*, companies and governments) are usually

© Springer Nature Switzerland AG 2020
K. Djemame et al. (Eds.): GECON 2020, LNCS 12441, pp. 28–40, 2020.
https://doi.org/10.1007/978-3-030-63058-4_3

confronted with economic impacts. Not only do these attacks cause financial damages due to the unavailability of services and loss of online traffic, but in critical cases, they inflict long-term damage to the corporate reputation, causing drastic drops of stock prices [1].

Furthermore, the number of DDoS attacks has almost tripled in the last three years, with an averaged financial loss of dozens of thousands of USD (US$) per hour of such an attack. *E.g.*, it was estimated that in 2009 only in the United Kingdom (UK) DDoS did cost more than USD 1 billion [4], which includes revenue losses and cyber insurance premiums. These numbers continue to grow due to the increasing amount of exposed Internet-of-Things (IoT) devices and Artificial Intelligence (AI) techniques. Cybersecurity predictions point out that the number of DDoS attacks globally will reach 17 million by 2020, causing several economic and societal impacts.

Based on this threat landscape, large companies and governments are spending about USD 124 billion on information security products and protection services. However, many of the problems plaguing cybersecurity are economic in nature [7]. Often systems fail, because organizations do not bear to assess full costs of a failure neither the risks involved. It is still more prevalent when, for example, considering organizations and users with restrictions of budget or technical expertise to invest in cybersecurity, such as Small- Medium-sized Enterprises (SME). Therefore, it is clear that an efficient risks analysis and investments in proper cybersecurity solutions are critical for the next years for both organizations and governments with services or systems exposed on the Internet. These investments must not focus solely on reactive protection against DDoS attacks, but also target the planning and decision process of cybersecurity to predict attacks and possible losses arising from a cyberattack. Therefore, multiple layers of precaution to protect the critical services against DDoS attacks are required.

As of today, the variety of DDoS protection services has increased as well. While competition in this sector may show benefits for consumers, such as higher quality for the same price or diversified products, organizations often struggle with choosing a protection service that suits their needs. Solutions that help with the selection of a DDoS protection can support the organization in the decision-making process. More specifically, by providing the user with essential information related to the many DDoS protection services available, taking into account filters and characteristics of the cyberattack (*e.g.*, fingerprints and log files), the user may simplify decisions. However, there are no intuitive solutions (*e.g.*, dashboards) that ease the access to a broad set of DDoS protections, while ensuring the integrity of the information from protections available, *i.e.*, tamper-proof information. Besides that, there is still a lack of integration of catalogs and mechanisms that help to decide which is the most suitable protection, taking into account specific DDoS scenarios and user demands.

This paper presents *ProtectDDoS*, a blockchain-based platform for the offering and support of an recommendation for protection services against DDoS attacks. *ProtectDDoS* provides a blockchain-based catalog, where protection providers can announce protections and interested users can filter its protections by applying different parameters, such as price, the type of DDoS attack supported, and deployment time. In addition, DDoS attacks fingerprints [10] can be used as an input to find the most suitable protection for a determined type of attack. This paper's **contributions** are summarized as follows:

- A Smart Contract (SC) is implemented to store *(i)* the hash of protection services and the private address of protection providers to verify the origin and integrity of protections available and *(ii)* protections' reputations based on users' feedback, which can be used to avoid protections with misbehavior or insufficient performance for a certain scenario determined.
- A dashboard is offered, fully integrated with a recommender system for protection services, called *MENTOR*, allowing the user to use a Web-based interface to obtain a recommendation of the most suitable solution according to his/her demands and predefined filters.

The remainder of this paper is organized as follows. Background and related work are reviewed in Sect. 2. Section 3 introduces the platform for offering and recommending DDoS protections, including implementation details. Section 4 discusses the feasibility of the solution proposed, and a case study is presented. Section 5 provides a functional evaluation in order to measure the costs of the *ProtectDDoS*. Finally, Sect. 6 summarizes the paper and comments on future work are added.

2   Background and Related Work

As businesses strengthen their digital dependency, they also become more vulnerable to cyberthreats. Therefore, besides the need for speed in innovation, decision-makers in cybersecurity (*e.g.*, network operator, company owner, or an expert team) have to be able to implement robust security mechanisms, while managing costs and risks associated with the business [9]. Such activities involve:

1. **Identify** security risks and associated costs and *(ii)* determine impacts of cybersecurity in the business or service. In turn, it is possible to estimate overall impacts (*e.g.*, financial loss occasioned by a business disruption) in order to decide whether to invest in cybersecurity.
2. **React** against an imminent cyberattack or **assume** risks, paying for the damage or delegating that to third-parties (*e.g.*, cyberinsurers).

For (1) such overall estimations can be done using different approaches. For instance, the Return On Security Investments (ROSI) [12] offers a benchmark to determine, when a specific investment in cybersecurity is recommended based on the potential financial loss given an assessed risk. Based on that, decision-makers have to decide how to handle a possible or imminent threat. Between the different choices, the decision-maker can determine a plan to prevent cyberattacks and its impacts proactively. In the context of (2) and once an attack happens, prevention is cheaper than reactions, when an attack already surpassed the infrastructure.

If companies do not invest correctly in cybersecurity, the security of their operations depends on luck and impacts of attacks can be devastating, which is not acceptable by companies that have to maintain reputation.

The market for protection services has grown together with investments in cybersecurity. Several providers are offering protections for different kinds of attacks (*e.g.*, data leaks, DDoS, and malwares) and demands. For example, [2] provides a repository listing providers offering many protection services to address different cybersecurity threats, such as advanced threat protection, anti-virus, secure communications, and anti-phishing. The number of protections available is large and is growing in parallel with investments in cybersecurity. In only one such a repository 1,200 providers are listed, and one can, for example, obtain information to contract more than 80 protection services against DDoS attacks. However, even though there are few catalogs centralizing information from different cybersecurity solutions [2], there is still a lack of platforms that use such information to simplify the decision-process and cybersecurity planning of companies. Table 1 provides a comparison of different cybersecurity-oriented solutions that implement approaches to offer or recommend services.

Table 1. Comparison of related work in terms of the functionality designed

Solution	Functionalities				
	User-friendly catalog	Supports recommendation	Filters	Allows integrity verification	Reputation mechanisms
[3]	No	Yes	Yes	No	No
[2]	Yes	No	Yes	No	No
[8]	No	Yes	Yes	No	No
[5]	No	Yes	Yes	No	No
[11]	Yes	No	No	Yes	Yes
ProtectDDoS	Yes	Yes	Yes	Yes	Yes

In previous work, the recommender system for protection services called *MENTOR* was introduced to help during the decision of which is the most suitable protection for demands determined [3] in which a recommendation engine that can suggest recommendations based on a list of parameters and user demands. However, *MENTOR* is still in early stages and does not yet provide user interfaces or a catalog for protection providers to submit their solutions. Furthermore, the reputation of protections based on user feedback is not being considered during the recommendation process. The work of [8] provides a recommender system to predict cyberattacks by identifying attack paths, demonstrating how a recommendation method can be used to classify future cyberattacks. [5] introduced an interactive user interface for security analysts that recommends what data to protect, visualizes simulated protection impact, and builds protection plans. However, none of them supports neither characteristic of DDoS attacks nor intuitive interfaces for users to add their demands nor log files to receive recommendations.

By using the concepts of Blockchains (BC) and Smart Contracts (SC), different solutions have been proposed to enable the validation of integrity and origin of solutions for different purposes. BCs were initially conceived as a distributed ledger to be the backbone of the Bitcoin cryptocurrency. However, BCs capacity to provide an immutable, trustworthy, and decentralized collection of records has attracted the attention of both industry and academia [14]. The concept of SCs is implemented by the second generation of BCs, such as Ethereum and NEO. Fees involved in SCs are lower than for traditional systems requiring a trusted intermediary. [11] introduces *BUNKER*, a BC-based marketplace for Virtual Network Functions (VNFs), to provide immutable and trusted information concerning VNF packages acquired by end-users. This solution stores the hash of VNF packages in a BC to guarantee the integrity of the VNF being acquired by end-users. This feature is useful for both providers and users interested in protections, since the integrity of the protection, the provider's identity, and its reputation can be verified for any offered solution, before users decide on one specific cybersecurity solution.

3   The *ProtectDDoS* Platform

The *ProtectDDoS* platform allows users to describe their demands for protections in order to obtain a proper level of protection against different types of DDoS attacks from an extensive list of options available, which facilitates the decision process to select the most suitable protection. These protection services can be acquired proactively before an attack happens or acquired to react during an imminent attack. Thus, *ProtectDDoS* offers mechanisms to support decisions required during cybersecurity planning and management. Besides that, protection providers can announce their solutions to build a heterogeneous catalog of protections against DDoS, thus, achieving a broad audience of companies and users interested in contract/acquire protections. Also, *ProtectDDoS* allows, through a Web-based interface, users to *(i)* upload fingerprints of DDoS attacks to find specific protections, *(ii)* verify, supported by the BC, the integrity and origin of information of different protections, *(iii)* receive the recommendation of the best solution according to its demands, and *(iv)* provide feedback of contracted protections, thus, supporting a reputation system for protections available. The *ProtectDDoS*'s code is publicly available at [13].

3.1   Architecture

Figure 1 introduces the architecture of the *ProtectDDoS* platform and its main components. The architecture is divided into three different layers: the *(i)* User Layer provides components required for actors to interact with *ProtectDDoS* and protections available through an intuitive and modern interface, the *(ii)* Data

Layer, which is in charge of steps involved in process handling of information related to protections, and it serves as a link to the upper and lower layers, and the *(iii)* BC Layer, which consists of an SC running inside the Ethereum BC containing information (*e.g.*, hash and reputations of protections) to be used by the other layers, such as to verify integrity services' information or its developer. Also, the integration with the *MENTOR* recommender system is available by using the *MENTOR* API (Application Programming Interface) , which is fully integrated with the *ProtectDDoS* architecture, thus, allowing for calls to receive a recommendation of the best protection service according to previously defined filters and configurations of the user.

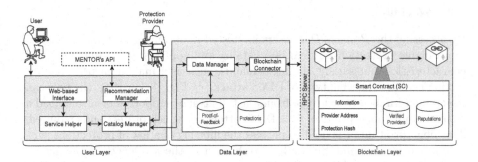

Fig. 1. *ProtectDDoS*'s conceptual architecture

The *User Layer* provides a *Web-based interface* (*i.e.*, dashboard) access to the catalog as well as details protections and the recommendation process. The *Service Helper* plays a crucial role in the integration of the catalog and the recommendation process by applying the filters predefined on the entire dataset of protections available, thus, removing protections that are not suitable for user's requirements. The *Catalog Manager* requests information from the Data Layer to build the catalog of protections available, applies these filters, and sends the list of protections to start the recommendation process. Finally, the *Recommendation Manager* is in charge of constructing the calls for the recommendation API (*i.e.*, MENTOR's API). For that, this component transforms user requirements and information from selected protections into a defined JSON data structure [13] containing all relevant information for the recommendation.

The *Data Layer* contains the *Protections database* to store all information of protections available, such as developer, name, price, and types of attacks supported. Also, a database is provided to store all log files (*e.g.*, pcap) containing information regarding the contracted protection performance, which helps during the audition and validation of bad or good feedback provided by users. This database is managed by the *Data Manager*, which is the interface to the *Data Layer* and is in charge of the process to answer requests for information. Furthermore, the *BC Connector* is an adaptor, implemented to enable communications with the SC running inside the BC. The *BC Connector* performs calls to interact with the SC (*e.g.*, verify the protection hash or validate the provider address) by sending BC transactions though a *Remote Procedure Call (RPC) server* provided by the BC.

Finally, the *BC Layer* deploys the SC to store a list of verified providers based on their address on the BC, reputations of each protection according to the users' feedback, the hash of the proof-of-feedback files, and the hash of the protection associated with the address of the provider that submitted the service. It is worth reinforcing that all this information is immutable, which allows any interested party to audit the information following the full history of the information stored.

3.2 Workflow

By accessing the *ProtectDDoS*, users interested in obtaining protection can verify available protection services in a catalog and apply filters to select a set of characteristics that satisfy his/her demands, such as a maximum price or protection against a specific type of DDoS attack (*cf.* Fig. 2). For that, the user can select a determined attack type from a list of attacks supported or also upload a file containing fingerprints of that DDoS attack for which protection is required. This fingerprint input is used to process the filtering of a list of protections suitable for such a demand. Such a list can be sent to the *MENTOR* recommender system through the API provided in order to receive, as a response, the best protection selected by the recommendation process implemented in *MENTOR*.

Also providers of protection services can access the Web-based interface and store new protections to become available in the catalog. The process of uploading a new protection service comprises of two essential steps:

1. The service information is hashed, using the SHA-256 algorithm and subsequently submitted to the BC.
2. Upon successful storage, the service provider's address and the transaction hash are retrieved by the RPC server and stored off-chain.

The first operation is handled using an SC and will cost a fee to be completed (*cf.* Sect. 5). As the costs to store all information required would be high, only the hash of this service information is stored. When interacting with an SC, an Ethereum account is required. Ethereum was used, since it offers a clear path program SCs in Solidity. The second operation retrieves the hash of any protection from the BC, thus, offering to any user checks, whether this service information has been compromised or the provider cannot be verified. Hence, the service hash is required and a specific function in the SC is invoked.

Also, a DDoS fingerprint is supported by *ProtectDDoS* as defined in the DDoSDB platform [10]. Parameters that be configured for the catalog filter or recommendation of protections and include: *(i)* Service Type, which can be reactive or proactive, *(ii)* Attack Type (*e.g.*, SYN Flood or DNS Amplification) defined directly from a list or identified by a using a fingerprint filed optionally and uploaded by the user, *(iii)* Coverage Region to indicate the location

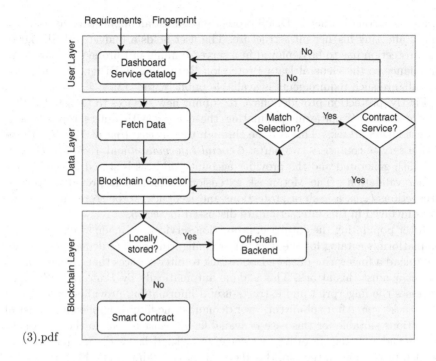

Fig. 2. *ProtectDDoS*'s workflow

(*e.g.*, continents, countries, or even cities), where a cloud-based protection has to be deployed, *(iv)* Deployment Time, which determined how long (*e.g.*, in seconds, minutes, or hours) it may take until the protection is deployed and active, and *(v)* the Budget available by the user to fund this protection.

4   Proof-of-Concept and Case Study

A Proof-of-Concept (PoC) was implemented in a public domain approach to showcase the *ProtectDDoS* [13]. The *User Layer* was implemented using *ReactJS 16.8*, a JavaScript library for building user interfaces. This library facilitates the overall process of developing user interface components using the *JSX* syntax extension. It also boosts productivity and facilitates further maintenance. The *Service Helper*, the *Catalog*, and the *Recommendation Manager* were implemented using *Python 3.6.5*, while *MENTOR*'s API was implemented using *Flask 1.0.2*. SQLite 3.30.1 was defined as the database to store information at the *Data Layer*. Its connection is implemented by using *SQLAlchemy 1.3*, an open-source SQL toolkit and object-relation mapper. For the *BC layer* Ethereum was defined as the BC to be used, including *Solidity* for the SC development.

A case study was conducted to provide evidence of the feasibility and usability of *ProtectDDoS*. This case considers a scenario where *(i)* a protection provider wants to submit a new protection to be listed in the platform and *(ii)* a user wants to contract a reactive DDoS protection against an application layer attack that is affecting his/her infrastructure. The user holds a budget of USD 5,000. The protection has to be deployed in a server running in Europe to ensure legal compliance to the General Data Protection Regulation (GDPR). The interface to configure such requirements is available publicly, too [13].

Firstly, protection providers have to submit new services to be listed within the *ProtectDDoS* platform, populating the catalog with different protections against DDoS attacks. This is done through the *Service Upload Tab*. Each protection service comprises two parts: *General Information* and *Technical Details*. The hash generated and the provider account's address is stored in the BC for further validations. The Metamask extension enables users/providers to send transactions (*e.g.*, a hash of protections and feedback) to be stored on the BC. Costs involved in this interaction are discussed in Sect. 5.

After populating the database, protection services are made available within the platform's catalog for the user. After configuring his/her demands, the user can upload a fingerprint of the DDoS attack to filter services that are suitable to protect against this attack. This is done automatically by *ProtectDDoS*, which processes the fingerprint and extracts useful information, providing evidence of the attack type. After submitting user demands, the filter is applied and a list of protections suitable for this case is available. This list is sent to the *MENTOR* recommender system in order to receive an ordered list with the most recommended protection on the top. Based on this list containing suitable services, for example, the recommendation engine can decide that the best option is a service with a deployment time in seconds, which includes features to mitigate this type of attack with the cost of USD 2,400. Although other solutions may be cheaper, they are providing features that are not considered ideal, taking into account all user demands and the fingerprint of the attack being addressed.

The user can verify, whether the protection service offered has been manipulated or not, *i.e.*, by validating the integrity and origin of the protection information being provided. Thus, the *Service Hash* and *Transaction Hash* are required. This information can be obtained by clicking on the *See More* button of a specific service. At this point, the user can either copy the service hash or have a closer look at the transaction itself by selecting the transaction hash. If the user decides to go for the transaction hash, an *Etherscan* page will be opened, which will provide further details regarding the transaction itself. Otherwise, if the user decides select the service hash, an Ethereum account and the browser extension Metamask will be required to execute the validation. Thus, through the *Verify Page*, the user can quickly validate a particular service by its hash. Within this verification interface the protection is verified, meaning that this particular service is stored inside the BC and the integrity of this service is ensured (*i.e.*, the information regarding the protection was not modified after its submission). However, in this case here, the provider linked to this service hash is highlighted as untrusted, meaning that the real identity of this provider cannot be ensured.

Furthermore, the user can access the Web-based interface and provide feedback regarding a previously contracted protection, which includes a rating from *zero* to *three*, comments, and a log file (*e.g.*, pcap format) containing the proof-of-feedback. This proof-of-feedback is stored in the platform's database and its hash is stored in the BC in order to ensure that changes in the log can be identified during further audits or analysis. By using such a reputation approach, the platform can be configured to remove from the recommendation process or even from the catalog protections that are representing misbehavior, such as not delivering the functionality promised or with a worse performance while mitigating the DDoS attack specified.

5 Functional Evaluation

Despite these benefits introduced by the *ProtectDDoS* platform, costs and security have to be considered upon using a public BC.

5.1 Costs

Costs are concerned with additional fees and the time to store information. These fees are not high, but should be considered to store, for instance, a large number of protections and their reputations. Thus, an analysis of the current state of the Ethereum BC was conducted to investigate costs. Fees exist for every transaction that requires to store data in an SC. This fee is described in "Gas", which is the price being paid for BC miners to successfully conduct the execution of a transaction or a contract. This fee is paid using Ether (ETH), which is Ethereum's cryptocurrency. Besides ETH, fees can also be represented in sub-units "Gwei": 1 ETH is ≈1 billion Gwei. For the costs analysis, the price of 1 ETH was equaling USD 144 as of the quotation in December 2019.

To execute the functionality provided by the SC, the contract needs to be compiled and successively deployed to the desired BC network. At this moment the owner of the SC will be confronted with costs that occur only once, *i.e.*, during the deployment. The deployment of the latest, fully working SC here at the time of writing generated a total cost of 0.01041256 ETH, which amounts up to USD 1.50. This cost can be broken into two main components: 520,628 units of Gas used to deploy the actual contract and a 20 Gwei gas price paid per unit. Important to note is that whenever the SC is updated, the owner will have to deploy it again, and if a new feature is added to the SC, the cost will increase. In addition, the cost of 0.0076 ETH (≈USD 1.10) resembles to add a new provider as *Verified*. Such costs can be paid by the owner of the catalog or by providers that want to announce themselves on the platform.

Upon the design of the functionality to store a protection service to the BC, two possible approaches were investigated: *(i)* store the full protection service information or *(ii)* store only a hash of the protection. Although the approach *(i)* enables users to, eventually, verify every characteristic of the protection, the costs of writing large amounts of data on the BC increase exponentially. Therefore, the approach *(ii)* is a more suitable alternative in terms of costs, since the amount to be paid to store a new protection service is lower. Upon submission, the provider paid *0.002154 ETH* (≈*USD 0.31*) to store the hash generated and its address. In case a new account address for the hash generated has been stored, the system allows for a storage and submission of this service again with a cost of *0.001082 ETH* (≈*USD 0.16*). Also, there are costs concerning the storage of ratings provided by the user and the reputation of each protection service. This cost has to be paid by the SC owner (*i.e.*, the platform) ensuring that the user is not burdened with this fee. It is important to mention that there are no fees to retrieve information from any SC. Hence, the functions *verifyService()* and *getReputation()* do not show any cost involved.

5.2   Security

One of the main characteristics of a BC is its ability to unearth, causing applications to remove trusted third parties, while trust levels can be relatively increased by the transparency and immutability of the process. In the context of security applications, such as the *ProtectDDoS*, two additional concerns exists with the exposure of confidential data and the handling of protection service requirements. Therefore, it is important to consider the solution's deployment approaches in order to ensure that the information stored is not exposed or tampered with. In this sense, a possible deployment absorbing requests from multiple clients (*i.e.*, on external premises) implies a centralization process, which is just the opposite of the decentralization proposed by BCs (*cf.* Fig. 3).

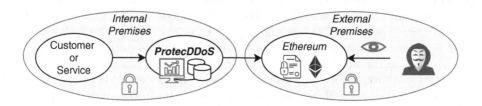

Fig. 3. *ProtectDDoS*'s deployment

In this sense, Fig. 3 presents an ideal implementation approach of the service as a decentralized application and is maintained within internal premises. Thus, the *ProtectDDoS* platform operates as a decentralized application, where public data on protection services are announced and the instance in internal premises can act as a reverse proxy selecting, among services advertised, which ones have all characteristics desired. Similarly, protection service advertisers also operate instances of the *ProtectDDoS* platform on internal premises. Henceforth, aspects of confidentiality and integrity related to the security needs of customers are maintained on internal premises and characteristics of the service advertised cannot be tampered with either.

6   Summary and Future Work

This paper developed and evaluated *ProtectDDoS* a Web-based platform that introduces a trustworthy catalog and recommendation of protections against DDoS attacks. *ProtectDDoS* builds on BC-based SCs to allow for the validation of integrity and the origin (*i.e.*, provider) of protections available. Also, by using SCs the reputation of protections can be stored in an immutable manner. Moreover, the *ProtectDDoS* platform explores the recommendation of protections by integrating them with the cybersecurity recommender system *MENTOR*, thus, allowing users to receive recommendations of the best protection according to specific demands. *ProtectDDoS* also allows through the user-friendly Web interface the upload of DDoS attack fingerprints and the configuration of different parameters to specify specific user demands and characteristics of attacks in order to find the most suitable protection against a DDoS attack. The feasibility of the solution was evaluated in a prototypical implementation based on the dedicated case study. The evaluation provided measures the benefits and additional costs in the context of BCs in use.

Future work includes *(i)* the support of leasing protections directly from the platform by using SCs, thus, storing and enforcing automatically respective agreements between providers and users, *(ii)* the development of mechanisms to process and extract meaningful information from different configurations and log files provided by users, thus, extending the information supported by *ProtectDDoS*, and *(iii)* the proposal of DDoS visualizations to help users to understand attack behaviors and the performance of protections contracted. Furthermore, an in-depth analysis of the recommendation process and the performance of protections recommended for each DDoS attack will be conducted. Finally, an integration of *ProtectDDoS* with cybersecurity economics-aware solutions [9] might be performed in order to provide for an accurate and cost-effective offering and recommendation of protections.

Acknowledgements. This paper was supported partially by *(a)* the University of Zürich UZH, Switzerland and *(b)* the European Union's Horizon 2020 Research and Innovation Program under Grant Agreement No. 830927, the CONCORDIA Project.

References

1. Abhishta, A., Joosten, R., Nieuwenhuis, L.J.: Comparing alternatives to measure the impact of DDoS attack announcements on target stock prices. J. Wirel. Mob. Netw. Ubiquit. Comput. Dependable Appl. (JoWUA) **8**(4), 1–18 (2017)
2. Cybertango: The cybersecurity directory - DDoS protection companies (2019). https://www.cybertango.io/cybersecurity-vendors/DDoS. Accessed 1 May 2020
3. Franco, M.F., Rodrigues, B., Stiller, B.: MENTOR: the design and evaluation of a protection services recommender system. In: 15th International Conference on Network and Service Management (CNSM 2019), Halifax, Canada, October 2019, pp. 1–7 (2019)
4. Hellard, B.: DDoS attacks could cost the UK £1bn (2019). https://www.itpro.co.uk/security/33279/ddos-attacks-could-cost-the-uk-1bn. Accessed 1 May 2020

5. Li, T., Convertino, G., Tayi, R.K., Kazerooni, S.: What data should i protect? Recommender and planning support for data security analysts. In: 24th International Conference on Intelligent User Interfaces (IUI 2019), Los Angeles, USA, March 2019, pp. 286–297. ACM (2019)
6. Mansfield-Devine, S.: The growth and evolution of DDoS. Netw. Secur. **2015**(10), 13–20 (2015)
7. Moore, T.: Introducing the economics of cybersecurity: principles and policy options. In: Workshop on Deterring CyberAttacks, Washington, DC, USA, April 2010, pp. 1–21 (2010)
8. Polatidis, N., Pimenidis, E., Pavlidis, M., Mouratidis, H.: Recommender systems meeting security: from product recommendation to cyber-attack prediction. In: Boracchi, G., Iliadis, L., Jayne, C., Likas, A. (eds.) EANN 2017. CCIS, vol. 744, pp. 508–519. Springer, Cham (2017). https://doi.org/10.1007/978-3-319-65172-9_43
9. Rodrigues, B., Franco, M., Parangi, G., Stiller, B.: SEConomy: a framework for the economic assessment of cybersecurity. In: Djemame, K., Altmann, J., Bañares, J.Á., Agmon Ben-Yehuda, O., Naldi, M. (eds.) GECON 2019. LNCS, vol. 11819, pp. 154–166. Springer, Cham (2019). https://doi.org/10.1007/978-3-030-36027-6_13
10. Santanna, J., van Hove, K.: DDoSDB: collecting and sharing information of DDoS attacks (2019). https://ddosdb.org/. Accessed 1 May 2020
11. Scheid, E.J., Keller, M., Franco, M.F., Stiller, B.: BUNKER: a blockchain-based trUsted VNF pacKagE repository. In: Djemame, K., Altmann, J., Bañares, J.Á., Agmon Ben-Yehuda, O., Naldi, M. (eds.) GECON 2019. LNCS, vol. 11819, pp. 188–196. Springer, Cham (2019). https://doi.org/10.1007/978-3-030-36027-6_16
12. Sonnenreich, W., Albanese, J., Stout, B., et al.: Return on security investment (ROSI)-a practical quantitative model. J. Res. Pract. Inf. Technol. **38**, 45–52 (2006)
13. Sula, E., Franco, M.: Web-based interface for the recommendation of DDoS attack protections (2019). https://gitlab.ifi.uzh.ch/franco/ddosrecommendation. Accessed 1 May 2020
14. Bocek, T., Stiller, B.: Smart contracts – blockchains in the wings. In: Linnhoff-Popien, C., Schneider, R., Zaddach, M. (eds.) Digital Marketplaces Unleashed, pp. 169–184. Springer, Heidelberg (2018). https://doi.org/10.1007/978-3-662-49275-8_19

Delivering Privacy-Friendly Location-Based Advertising Over Smartwatches: Effect of Virtual User Interface

Emiel Emanuel and Somayeh Koohborfardhaghighi(✉)

Amsterdam Business School, University of Amsterdam, Amsterdam, The Netherlands
emiel.emanuel@student.uva.nl, s.koohborfardhaghighi@uva.nl

Abstract. The expansion of smartwatches and positioning technologies have offered marketers the opportunity to provide consumers with contextually relevant advertising messages. However, perceived privacy risk and a lack of privacy control are preventing consumers from using location-based advertising (LBA). This study explores how variation in the design of the user interfaces of smartwatches (regular user interface vs. virtual user interface) affects the perceived ease of privacy control, perceived privacy risk, and ultimately the intention of consumers to use LBA. A simple mediation analysis is conducted on the data collected from a between-subjects experiment (N = 335). The obtained results extend the growing literature on the topic of LBA and privacy concerns related to it. The results indicate that a smart-watch augmented with a virtual user interface increases perceived ease of privacy control. Also, this has a direct positive effect on perceived privacy risk and the intention to use LBA. However, perceived privacy risk does not mediate the relationship between perceived ease of privacy control and the intention to use LBA. The findings of this study have important implications for various commercial players.

Keywords: Location-based advertising · Perceived privacy risk · Perceived ease of privacy control · Virtual user interface · Smartwatches · Social contract theory

1 Introduction

The expansion of mobile devices and positioning technologies has offered novel possibilities and challenges to revolutionize e-commerce mobile applications. The producers of mobile devices in cooperation with marketers provide consumers with the flexibility to make use of services considering their mobility patterns and needs. With the positioning technologies, marketers can provide mobile users contextually relevant advertising messages via mobile instruments on a geographic reference point, when they are at the edge of making a purchase. Wearable devices and smartwatches in particular are perfect devices to execute these new marketing opportunities. The location tracking feature of smartwatches can be beneficial for both companies and consumers. Using real-time intent data, a smartwatch user might receive an ad with an attractive offer from the nearby

© Springer Nature Switzerland AG 2020
K. Djemame et al. (Eds.): GECON 2020, LNCS 12441, pp. 41–53, 2020.
https://doi.org/10.1007/978-3-030-63058-4_4

store which might be in line with his or her needs. For marketers, the personalization of advertisements offers cost efficiencies in comparison to traditional mass marketing [1].

Location-based advertising can be executed more effectively using a smartwatch than other mobile devices such as smartphones. However, privacy concerns are preventing the consumers from accepting location-based advertisements due to the following reasons. First, according to the authors of [2] high privacy concerns exist on location tracking because consumers do not have the technical skills to protect and control their privacy. The authors argued in the paper that the use of smartwatches for marketing purposes and growth of data transactions have only intensified privacy concerns as consumers feel uncomfortable with the amount of data acquired by companies. Apple and Google have initiated some practices to resolve this problem by giving the consumer more control over mobile location privacy. Facebook also is launching variety of new tools to provide consumers with more control over their privacy. The smartwatch market also is expected to respond to the privacy concerns of its consumers. Therefore, in this study we argue that it is essential to reduce perceived privacy risk by shifting the privacy control from third parties to the consumer. That is to say, designers by augmenting smartwatches with a virtual touchscreen (i.e., which can be projected on objects) can provide a larger display and stimulate personal privacy control. Therefore, based on the line of argument presented so far the main research question in this research is: How does a privacy control facilitated through a virtual user interface in smartwatches affect a consumer's perceived privacy risk and intention to use location-based advertising?

As the main contribution of this research, first we investigate the relationship between perceived ease of privacy control (facilitated through a virtual user interface) and the intention to use location-based advertising. Second, we investigate the mediation role of the perceived privacy risk with the intention to use location-based advertising.

Previous literature in this area are focused solely on the smartphones, however, we test our model within the context of smartwatches. To the best of our knowledge, no empirical research exists in addressing how the design of a virtual user interface in smartwatches affects the perceived ease of privacy control, perceived privacy risk, and ultimately the intention of consumers to use LBA.

The rest of this paper is organized as follows: In Sect. 2, the relevant literature on wearable technology and personal privacy control is presented. In Sect. 3, we formulate our theoretical model and we present our hypotheses. This is followed by an extensive explanation of the research design in Sect. 4. The results of our analysis are presented in Sect. 5. In Sect. 6, we provide the conclusion and discussion over our findings.

2   Literature Review

2.1   Wearable Technology

Technology is advancing every day and the use of mobile devices like smartphones is still increasing. According to [3] there seems to be a shift from carrying these mobile devices to wearing them. Wearable technologies consist of microchips, sensors and wireless communication components to operate. This technology differentiates itself from smartphones by being designed to be worn casually in everyday life and their presence may be disregarded [4]. There are two main groups of wearable tech devices, namely; smart textiles and wearable computers. Smart textiles are better for long-term monitoring as they are not skin attached, however, wearable computers have a broader range of functions and capabilities due to the presence of an interactive screen [7]. Wearable tech devices which are attached to the skin make consumers' streaming data available to providers and multiple real-time analytics applications [5]. Besides, the potential applications of wearable technology in observing health and medical conditions can lead to interesting practical implications (e.g., continuous monitoring of patients). On top of that, wearable technology can be utilized to improve personal comfort in domestic environments like automatically altering lighting, temperature or entertainment preferences as users change their locations [6]. According to the author of [6] the costs to create such technologies are decreasing which stimulates the use of wearable tech devices.

2.2 Location-Based Advertising (LBA)

In 2001, location tracking functions were presented in Japan. Telecommunication operators and merchants use global positioning systems for commercial purposes. Location tracking functions and utilization of its potentials are essential in the marketing field as marketers can turn this feature into business profits [8, 9]. Marketers are able to target (potential) customers with customized services and offerings, both inside and even before entering a store. Firms are able to create a strong connection with their customers and deliver a personalized experience [6]. In other words, location-based information is essential for companies due to marketing reasons and providing location-based services to their customers. The purpose of location-based services (LBS) is to deliver contextual and personalized information to consumers through wireless technologies.

Due to the development of information and communication technology, the LBS market is expanding rapidly. According to [10], in the US, over 70% of the smartphone consumers utilized LBS in 2013. Also, the LBS industry was forecasted to have a global revenue of 43.3 billion US dollar by 2019. LBA is a sub-part which falls under the broad definition of location-based marketing (LBM). Xu and Teo in [11] proposed that LBA causes a five to ten times higher click-through rate when comparing to the common internet advertising messages. Looking at this billion dollar industry and the rising annual expenses of companies on LBS and LBA, it is therefore essential that users be stimulated to use LBA. In conclusion, the willingness to provide location information is valuable to location-based service providers. However, the collection of location data is held back by the privacy concerns of the consumers. As smartwatches are commonly regarded as highly personal devices, LBA over such devices might be experienced as intrusive and increases their perceived privacy risks. Consequently, this may slow down the effectiveness and expansion of LBA [12].

2.3 Perceived Privacy Risk in Sharing Personal Data

Xu et al. [13] defined perceived privacy risk as: "a user's concern about possible loss of privacy, including collection, improper access and unauthorized secondary use." The concept of perceived privacy risk handles the rights of consumers whose data are shared [14]. There are several concerns related to information privacy such as accessing the information which is shared with other devices, accessing personal data through the cloud or an alternative remote storage system or even selling information or its utilization by a third party for other purposes than what initially agreed on. All these factors increase the perceived privacy risk of consumers of smartwatches. Liu et al. in [15] showed that perceived privacy risk is a major predictor of the willingness to disclose personal information. Besides it was reported that the disclosed personal data has a negative effect on the user's payoff. Also, the result of that study showed that the intention of consumers to share location information is explained by obtaining personalized services in return.

2.4 Perceived Privacy Risk and the Intention to Use LBA

The relationship between smartphone users and LBA providers can be seen as an implicit social contract. The social contract theory implies that the consumers of LBA evaluate the possible benefits compared to the privacy costs. On one hand, through LBA consumers benefit from personalization and customization of advertisements with respect to their needs and locations. On the other hand, consumers share their personal data which is beneficial for marketers.

Xu and Teo in [11] described the social contract as the consumer's tradeoff between making personal information available and receiving economic or social benefits in exchange. In the context of this research, the perceived privacy risk is related to when, how and to what extent personal information of consumers is shared with others. Consequently the benefit is related to the obtained value from LBA providers in exchange of location data. According to Okazaki and Hirose [14], consumers of mobile advertising are most concerned about the significant amount of data collected from their devices which then can be stored indefinitely for potential use in the future. The results of another study [16] show that consumers have had the feeling that they were always being watched by an unknown company because they were not aware of the mechanism through which their personal location information were collected.

To conclude, the collection and usage of location-based information may evoke privacy concerns. As the result, this may inhibit consumers from using LBA. Consumers are concerned about whether their data is collected and appropriately utilized. Zhou in his research [17] showed that ultimately 35% of LBA users completely switched off the location tracking capability due to privacy concerns which puts LBA providers at a disadvantage. Therefore, LBA providers need to understand the perceived privacy risk and take effective measures to reduce the negative effect of perceived privacy risk on the intention to use LBA. As we mentioned before, a good relationship with consumers can be acquired when they can have a certain level of control over their personal information and its distribution. That is to say, the amount of control over personal information has a positive effect on the user's payoff [15].

2.5 Privacy Control, Virtual User Interface and Perceived Ease of Privacy Control

Privacy control reflects an individual user's perceived ability to manage his or her information disclosure [13]. Conceptualization of perceived control differs from the commonly used term control. Perceived control is a cognitive construct and, as such, may be subjective. Particularly, perceived control has been defined as a psychological construct reflecting an individual's beliefs at a given point in time, in one's ability to effect a change in the desired direction on the environment [18, 19]. In the context of LBA, Xu and Teo [16] showed that perceived privacy risk is lower when consumers can exert personal control over location in-formation. Tucker in [20] investigated the consequences of handling privacy issues by giving privacy control to Facebook users. The result of that study showed that by shifting control to consumers Facebook users were almost twice as likely to show positive reactions regarding personalized advertisements. Thus, shifting control from companies to consumers, can also benefit the LBA providers. Mobile users are able to turn on and off the location-based services just by push buttons on their touchscreens. Furthermore, users can control the accuracy and the extent to which location information is given to LBS providers. Smart-watches on the other hand are dependent upon other devices due to their small displays, which reduces the mobility, availability and ease of use. Ultimately, the intention to use LBA is diminished. As opposed to the current situation where a connection with another device has to be made first, the result of one study [21] shows that increased privacy control makes it possible to adjust privacy preference settings at runtime.

Regarding the impact of screen size on the perceived privacy control, Kim [23] showed that smartwatches which possess larger screens have a positive effect on the personal privacy control. Lim, Shin, Kim and Park in [22] argued that controllability of a smartwatch can be enhanced by using a technology which makes use of unified infrared line array sensors fixated along the side of the smartwatch. This way the location, swipe and click movements of the finger can be observed on the back of the hand. This is an example of an around device interface (ADI) which has been increasingly researched. ADIs are stimulating the pragmatic and controlling qualities of devices with small user interfaces. However, this innovation solves only a part of the problem. Still, the user interface of the smartwatches remains relatively small in comparison to smartphones. As mentioned, perceived ease of privacy control can be stimulated by making the smartwatch less dependent on other devices. A new Samsung patent file shows a projector integrated into the smartwatch so that the user can use objects as a touchscreen. The smartwatch would be able to project interfaces, a keyboard and menu options on the consumer's hand or arm. This new feature deals with the limited screen size of the smartwatch, making it independent of other devices. The virtual user interface of the smartwatch allows it to resolve the limitation of the screen size and stimulate the perceived ease of privacy control.

3   Conceptual Model and Hypotheses

Based on the literature review presented so far on the relationship between perceived ease of privacy control, perceived privacy risk and the intention to use LBA, we present our proposed conceptual framework and hypothesis in this section. The proposed conceptual model is presented in Fig. 1. We aim to address how the design of a virtual user interface in smartwatches affects the perceived ease of privacy control, perceived privacy risk, and ultimately the intention of consumers to use LBA. Therefore, we formulate our hypothesis as follow:

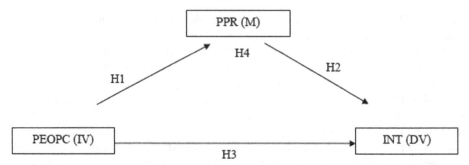

Fig. 1. Proposed Conceptual Model. PEOPC = Perceived Ease of Privacy Control, PPR = Perceived Privacy Risk, INT = Intention to Use LBA, IV = Independent Variable, M = Mediator, DV = Dependent Variable.

H1:   Perceived Ease of Privacy Control (enhanced through a virtual user interface) reduces Perceived Privacy Risk in smartwatches.
H2:   Perceived Privacy Risk reduces the Intention to use LBA in smartwatches.
H3:   Perceived Ease of Privacy Control stimulates the Intention to Use LBA in smartwatches.
H4:   Perceived Privacy Risk mediates the relationship between Perceived Ease of Privacy Control and the Intention to use LBA in smartwatches.

4   Methodology and Data

To answer the proposed research question and to test our hypotheses, a one-way between-subjects experiment with two conditions representing two levels of user interfaces (regular smartwatch user interface vs. virtual user interface) is conducted. After signing an informed consent form, participants were randomly assigned to either the regular smartwatch user interface group or the virtual user interface group. The actual goal of the experiment was not explicitly disclosed. Participants were provided with a short movie about a smartwatch, after which they were asked to provide their overall opinion on the type of interface under study.

The experimental group was provided with a movie informing them about a smartwatch augmented with the virtual user interface. The control group was provided with a movie informing them about a smartwatch with a regular user inter-face. It is expected that the virtual smartwatch user interface group will have a lower perceived privacy risk, a higher sense of perceived ease of privacy control and a higher intention to use LBA than the regular smartwatch user interface group.

The various constructs will be measured using a seven-point Likert-type scale, ranging from 1 (strongly disagree) to 7 (strongly agree). List of constructs and their items are presented in Table 1.

The independent variable 'perceived ease of privacy control' is measured with three validated items using a seven-point Likert scale. This variable is operationalized, for example, by the following item: "I can exactly see what data is disclosed to LBA providers and I am able to set a specified and limited amount of options regarding the disclosure". Since this is a new construct, we introduced our own items to measure it.

Table 1. Measurement model

Constructs	Items	Measures of Constructs (measured on a seven-point Likert scale)	Cronbach's Alpha (CA)
Perceived Privacy Risk (PPR) [28]	PPR_1 PPR_2 PPR_3	Please indicate to what extent you agree with the following statements: • I think service providers may keep private location information in a non-secure way • I think service providers may use my location information for other purposes, like tracking my daily activities to obtain information about me • I think service providers may share my location information with other firms without my permission	.878
Intention to Use LBA (INT) [27]	INT_1 INT_2 INT_3	Please indicate to what extent you agree with the following statements: • I would provide the LBA service provider with my location information it needs to better serve my needs • I intend to use LBA in the next 12 months • The benefits of LBA outweigh the cost of my privacy concerns	.840
Perceived Ease of Personal Privacy Control (PEOPC)	PEC_1 PEC_2 PEC_3	Please indicate to what extent you agree with the following statements: • I can exactly see what data is disclosed to LBA providers and I am able to set a specified and limited amount of options regarding the disclosure • I can alter the privacy preferences where and whenever I want • I can exercise personal control of my privacy	.899

The mediator 'perceived privacy risk' is measured with three validated items using a seven-point Likert scale (1 = strongly disagree, 7 = strongly agree). Perceived privacy risk is operationalized, for example, by the following item: "When I share location information with an LBA provider I believe I cannot be personally identified" [28].

The dependent variable 'intention to use LBA' is measured with three validated items using a seven point Likert scale. The intention to use LBA is operationalized, for example, by the following item: "I am very likely to provide the LBA service provider with my personal information it needs to better serve my needs" [27].

Previous studies on the topics of perceived privacy risk and personal privacy control proposed a number of supplementary factors which could be of potential influence on the intention to use LBA. Such factors include consumer's general attitude towards LBA (i.e., ATT), previous privacy experience (i.e., PPRV) and Consumers' degree of innovativeness (i.e., INNV) [24–26]. That is why, we consider such factors as our control variables (i.e., in addition to general control variables such as age gender and education).

For the statistical analyses, scores will be collected and transferred into SPSS. Dummy variables will be composed for the two conditions regarding the independent variable. Descriptive statistics, skewness, kurtosis and normality tests are conducted for all variables. The outliers are evaluated to guarantee that no data entry or instrument errors are generated. A simple mediation also is executed to investigate the mediating role of perceived privacy risk between the relationship of perceived ease of privacy control and the intention to use LBA.

The target group of this research are potential and actual users of smartwatches. The research is conducted using a non-probability convenience sampling technique which includes self-selection and snowball sampling. Participants are gathered via social media, e-mail and face-to-face meetings. Data were collected online through Qualtrics using a cross-sectional design. Out of the 446 participants who started the experimental survey, 335 completely finished it. This equals a completion rate of 75%. 52% of the participants were male and 48% were females. Approximately 51% of the participants were between 22 and 25 years old with a minimum age of 17 and a maximum of 67. Around 81.5% of the participants had an education of at least HBO (higher vocational education) or university. Furthermore, 90.4% of the respondents were European. Correlation analysis is conducted and the results are presented in Table 2.

Table 2. Result of the correlation analysis.

Variables	M	SD	Age	Gender	Education	PEOPC	INT	PPR	ATT	INNV
Age	28.5	10.7								
Gender	1.48	.50	−.12*							
Education	8.71	1.39	.03	.17**						
PEOPC	3.45	1.67	−.12*	.15**	.05					
INT	3.92	1.58	.08	.12*	−.03	.51**				
PPR	3.87	1.81	.20**	−.05	−.06	−.34**	−.18**			
ATT	3.39	1.28	.11*	.09	.02	.27**	.62**	.00		
INNV	3.27	1.18	.13*	.16**	.10	.05	.18**	.10	.3**	
PPRV	4.31	1.72	−.10	.02	.02	−.20**	−.28**	.27**	−.14**	.08

*. Correlation is significant at the 0.05 level (2-tailed).
**. Correlation is significant at the 0.01 level (2-tailed).

5   Empirical Analysis

5.1   Hypotheses Testing (Experimental Group)

A simple mediation analysis was done with model four in PROCESS (i.e., PROCESS is a macro for mediation analysis in SPSS). The independent variable (PEOPC) in the analysis was the perceived ease of privacy control.

The results of our analysis have been shown in Table 3. According to our obtained results, the relationship between the perceived ease of privacy control and the intention to use LBA was not mediated by perceived privacy risk. As a condition for mediation analysis, the mediating variable must be significantly related to the dependent variable when both the independent variable and mediating variable are predictors of the dependent variable. In our experiment, the regression of perceived privacy risk and the intention to use LBA was not significant. Therefore, we could not meet the right condition to run a mediation analysis.

The regression of the perceived ease of privacy control and the intention to use LBA was significant. The regression of the perceived ease of privacy control and perceived

Table 3. Effects on Experimental Group

Antecedent		Consequent						
		PPR (M)				INT (Y)		
		Coeff.	SE	p		Coeff.	SE	P
PEOPC (X)	a1	−.46**	.607	<.001	c1'	.46**	.059	<.001
PPR (M)		–	–	–	b1	−.067	.055	.224
ATT (C)		.027	.102	.791		.56**	.071	<.001
INNV (C)		.041	.097	.671		−.045	.067	.505
PPRV (C)		.230**	.072	.002		−.17**	.052	.001
		R2 = .321				R2 = .312		

Note: N = 169
*. Coefficient is significant at the 0.05 level (2-tailed)
**. Coefficient is significant at the 0.01 level (2-tailed)

privacy risk was also significant. The evidence will support the idea that perceived ease of privacy control affects the intention to use LBA independent of its effect on perceived privacy risk.

Regarding the influence of our control variables, the results show that consumers who previously experienced privacy issues expressed higher perceived privacy risk comparing to those who have not had such experiences in the past. This issue consequently lowers the intension of such users to use LBA. Such results confirm the idea that individuals who have been exposed to or have been the victim of personal information abuses should have stronger concerns regarding information privacy [25]. We could not find any evidence for the potential influence of consumers' degree of innovativeness on their perceived privacy risk or their intension to use LBA.

5.2   Hypotheses Testing (Control Group)

The results of our analysis have been shown in Table 4. Similar to our previous findings, the relationship between the perceived ease of privacy control and the intention to use LBA was not mediated by perceived privacy risk. In our experiment, the regression of perceived privacy risk and the intention to use LBA was not significant. Therefore, we could not meet the right condition to run a mediation analysis. Also, the regression of the perceived ease of privacy control and the intention to use LBA was not significant. The regression of the perceived ease of privacy control and perceived privacy risk was significant. Regarding the influence of our control variables, we could not find any evidence for the potential influence of consumers' degree of innovativeness or their previous privacy issues on their perceived privacy risk or their intension to use LBA. However, we observed the significant influence of the consumers' general attitude towards LBA on their perceived privacy risk or their intension to use LBA. The more individuals become in favor of LBA, they care less about their information privacy [29].

Table 4. Effects on Control Group

Antecedent		Consequent						
		PPR (M)				INT (Y)		
		Coeff.	SE	p		Coeff.	SE	P
PEOPC (X)	a1	−.25**	.609	.004	c1'	.092	.054	.087
PPR (M)		–	–	–	b1	.039	.046	.400
ATT (C)		.272*	.111	.015		.638**	.067	<.001
INNV (C)		.211	.131	.107		.111	.078	.157
PPRV (C)		.131	.086	.128		.021	.051	.687
		R2 = .106					R2 = .456	

Note: N = 169
*. Coefficient is significant at the 0.05 level (2-tailed)
**. Coefficient is significant at the 0.01 level (2-tailed)

5.3 Summary of Findings

In this study we explored how variation in the design of the user interfaces of smart-watches (regular user interface vs. virtual user interface) affects the perceived ease of privacy control, perceived privacy risk, and ultimately the intention of consumers to use LBA. Figure 2 and Fig. 3 deliver a summary of the obtained results. Hypothesis 1 is accepted for both the experimental group and control group. However, the effect is stronger in the experimental group. Hypothesis 3 is accepted for the experimental group and rejected for the control group. Hypothesis 2 is rejected for both the experimental group as well as the control group. Hypothesis 4 is rejected for both the experimental group as well as the control group.

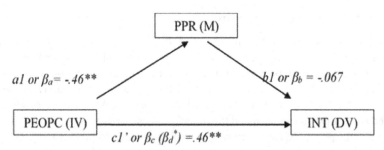

Fig. 2. Model with path coefficients of the experimental group. PEOPC = Perceived Ease of Privacy Control. PPR = Perceived Privacy Risk. INT = Intention to Use LBA. IV = Independent Variable. M = Mediator. DV = Dependent Variable. *p < .05. **p < .01. ***p < .001

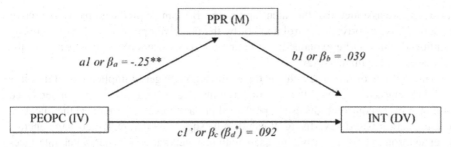

Fig. 3. Model with path coefficients of the control group. PEOPC = Perceived Ease of Privacy Control. PPR = Perceived Privacy Risk. INT = Intention to Use LBA. IV = Independent Variable. M = Mediator. DV = Dependent Variable. *p < .10. **p < .05. ***p < .01

6 Conclusion and Discussion

The main purpose of this research was to investigate the effect of augmenting a smartwatch with a virtual user interface on the user's perception of privacy risk and their intention to use location-based advertising. Furthermore, it was analyzed whether perceived privacy risk mediates relationship between perceived ease of privacy control and intention to use LBA.

First, our findings indicated that smartwatch users feel a stronger sense of perceived ease of privacy control and consequently perceive less privacy risk in the presence of a smartwatch which is augmented with the virtual user interface. The obtained results also indicated that a smartwatch augmented with a virtual user interface increases perceived ease of privacy control. Perceived ease of privacy control also in its own turn has a direct positive effect on the intention to use LBA.

To the best of our knowledge, no systematic empirical research exists addressing how the design of the user interfaces of smartwatches affects the perceived ease of privacy control and ultimately the intention of consumers to use LBA. Therefore, our obtained results indicate that augmenting smartwatches with a more sophisticated user interface helps the consumers in having a better sense of control over their data which consequently leads to a greater intention to use LBA.

Our findings are in line with the obtained results of Kim [23] who found that larger screens of smartwatches are more successful in promoting pragmatic qualities like perceived control than small screens.

We could not find any evidence that the perceived privacy risk has a negative effect on the intention to use LBA, neither for the users of a regular smartwatch nor for those with the virtual user interface. This contradicts the previous findings in [12, 17] which stated that perceived privacy concerns inhibit using LBA. A possible explanation can be derived from the social contract theory. Xu and Teo in [16] stated that it might be the case that smartwatch users place a higher value on the benefits provided by the LBA provider (i.e., like personalization) than the privacy costs (i.e., like making personal information available).

According to our obtained results perceived privacy risk did not mediate the relationship between perceived ease of privacy control and the intention to use LBA, which holds for neither the regular smartwatches nor for those with the virtual user interface.

It is therefore assumed that the intention to use LBA can be predicted by the degree of perceived ease of privacy control and not by the perceived privacy risk. As previously mentioned, this can be explained by the fact that LBA users place more value on the obtained benefits than privacy issues.

The findings of this research has the following managerial implications. First, it is useful for marketers to know that a virtual user interface increases the sense of perceived ease of privacy control, reduces the perceived privacy risk and stimulates the intention to use location-based advertising. It can thus be suggested that marketers can generate revenue through LBA by providing users with new generation of smartwatch interfaces which give users stronger sense of perceived ease of privacy control. Second, smartwatch manufacturer by further investments in the development of emerging interfaces could take bigger steps in achieving cost reduction in their production line. Removal of the actual screen and substituting it with virtual user interfaces for example could lead to cost reduction as well as creating a higher sense of control over privacy issues in smartwatch consumers. This in its own turn has the potential to reduce the perceived privacy risk and stimulate consumers' intention to use LBA.

References

1. Eastin, M.S., Brinson, N.H., Doorey, A., Wilcox, G.: Living in a big data world: predicting mobile commerce activity through privacy concerns. Comput. Human Behav. **58**, 214–220 (2016)
2. Park, Y.J., Skoric, M.: Personalized ad in your Google glass? Wearable technology, hands-off data collection, and new policy imperative. J. Bus. Ethics **142**(1), 71–82 (2017)
3. Kim, K.J., Shin, D.H.: An acceptance model for smart watches: implications for the adoption of future wearable technology. Internet Res. **25**(4), 527–541 (2015)
4. Casson, A.J., Logesparan, L., Rodriguez-Villegas, E.: An introduction to future truly wearable medical devices—from application to ASIC. In: Engineering in Medicine and Biology Society (EMBC), Annual International Conference of the IEEE. pp. 3430–3431. IEEE (2010)
5. Pipada, A.D.K.L.R., Xu, S.: The Effect of Data Security Perception on Wearable Device Acceptance: A Technology Acceptance Model (2016)
6. Thierer, A.D.: The internet of things and wearable technology: Addressing privacy and security concerns without derailing innovation (2015)
7. Van Langenhove, L., Hertleer, C., Schwarz, A.: Smart textiles: an overview. In: Intelligent textiles and clothing for ballistic and NBC protection. pp. 119–136. Springer, Dordrecht. (2012)
8. Giwa, S., Broderick, A., Omar, S.: Personalisation vs. Privacy: Consumer Perceptions of Location-based Advertising. Academy of Marketing (AM) (2015)
9. Bhaduri, A.: User controlled privacy protection in location-based services (2003)
10. Heo, J.-Y., Kim, K.-J.: Development of a scale to measure the quality of mobile location-based services. Service Bus. **11**(1), 141–159 (2016). https://doi.org/10.1007/s11628-016-0305-6
11. Xu, H., Teo, H.H.: Privacy considerations in location-based advertising. In: Designing Ubiquitous Information Environments: Socio-technical Issues and Challenges. pp. 71–90. Springer, Boston, MA (2005)
12. Limpf, N., Voorveld, H.A.: Mobile location-based advertising: how information privacy concerns influence consumers' attitude and acceptance. J. Int. Adv. **15**(2), 111–123 (2015)
13. Xu, H., Dinev, T., Smith, J., Hart, P.: Information privacy concerns: linking individual perceptions with institutional privacy assurances. J. Assoc. Inf. Syst. **12**(12), 798 (2011)

14. Okazaki, S., Li, H., Hirose, M.: Consumer privacy concerns and preference for degree of regulatory control. J. Adv. **38**(4), 63–77 (2009)
15. Liu, Z., Bonazzi, R., Fritscher, B., Pigneur, Y.: Privacy-friendly business models for location-based mobile services. J. Theor. Appl. Electronic Commerce Res. **6**(2), 90–107 (2011)
16. Xu, H., Teo, H.H.: Alleviating consumers' privacy concerns in location-based services: a psychological control perspective. In: ICIS 2004 proceedings, p. 64 (2004)
17. Zhou, T.: Understanding location-based services users' privacy concern: an elaboration likelihood model perspective. Internet Res. **27**(3), 506–519 (2017)
18. Greenberger, D.B., Strasser, S.: Development and application of a model of personal control in organizations. Acad. Manag. Rev. **11**(1), 164–177 (1986)
19. Skinner, E.A., Chapman, M., Baltes, P.B.: Control, means-ends, and agency beliefs: a new conceptualization and its measurement during childhood. J. Person. Social Psychol. **54**(1), 117 (1988)
20. Tucker, C.E.: Social networks, personalized advertising, and privacy controls. J. Market. Res. **51**(5), 546–562 (2014)
21. Ghosh, D., Joshi, A., Finin, T., Jagtap, P.: Privacy control in smart phones using semantically rich reasoning and context modeling. In: 2012 IEEE Symposium on Security and Privacy Workshops. pp. 82–85. IEEE (2012)
22. Lim, S.C., Shin, J., Kim, S.C., Park, J.: Expansion of smartwatch touch interface from touchscreen to around device interface using infrared line image sensors. Sensors **15**(7), 16642–16653 (2015)
23. Kim, K.J.: Shape and size matter for smartwatches: effects of screen shape, screen size, and presentation mode in wearable communication. J. Comput-Mediated Commun. **22**(3), 124–140 (2017)
24. Joseph, B., Vyas, S.J.: Concurrent validity of a measure of innovative cognitive style. J. Acad. Market. Sci. **12**(1–2), 159–175 (1984)
25. Smith, H.J., Milberg, S.J., Burke, S.J.: Information privacy: measuring individuals' concerns about organizational practices. MIS quarterly, p. 167–196. (1996)
26. Okechuku, C., Wang, G.: The effectiveness of Chinese print advertisements in North America. J. Adv. Res. **28**, 25–34 (1988)
27. Gefen, D., Karahanna, E., Straub, D.W.: Trust and TAM in online shopping: an integrated model. MIS Quart. **27**(1), 51–90 (2003)
28. Dinev, T., Hart, P.: Privacy concerns and internet use-a model of trade-off factors. In: Academy of Management Proceedings. vol. 2003, no. 1, pp. D1-D6. Briarcliff Manor, NY 10510: Academy of Management (2003)
29. Phelps, J.E., D'Souza, G., Nowak, G.J.: Antecedents and consequences of consumer privacy concerns: an empirical investigation. J. Int. Market. **15**(4), 2–17 (2001)

Decentralising Clouds to Deliver
Intelligence at the Edge

GEM-Analytics: Cloud-to-Edge AI-Powered Energy Management

Daniele Tovazzi[2], Francescomaria Faticanti[1,3](✉), Domenico Siracusa[1], Claudio Peroni[2], Silvio Cretti[1], and Tommaso Gazzini[2]

[1] Fondazione Bruno Kessler, TN 38123 Povo, Italy
ffaticanti@fbk.eu
[2] Energenius Srl, TN 38068 Rovereto, Italy
[3] University of Trento, Trento, Italy

Abstract. Energy analysis, forecasting and optimization methods play a fundamental role in managing Combine Heat and Power (CHP) systems for energy production, in order to find the most suitable operational point. Indeed, several industries owning such cogeneration systems can significantly reduce overall costs by applying diverse techniques to predict, in real-time, the optimal load of the system. However, this is a complex task that requires processing a large amount of information from multiple data sources (IoT sensors, smart meters and much more), and, in most of the cases, is manually carried out by the energy manager of the company owning the CHP. For this reason, resorting to machine learning methods and new advanced technologies such as fog computing can significantly ease and automate real-time analyses and predictions for energy management systems that deal with huge amounts of data. In this paper we present GEM-Analytics, a new platform that exploits fog computing to enable AI-based methods for energy analysis at the edge of the network. In particular, we present two use cases involving CHP plants that need for optimal strategies to reduce the overall energy supply costs. In all the case studies we show that our platform can improve the energy load predictions compared to baselines thus reducing the costs incurred by industrial customers.

Keywords: CHP · Fog computing · Energy analysis · AI prediction

1 Introduction

With the wide spreading of smart grids and power grids, energy management systems play a fundamental role in the control of energy consumption [11]. This kind of systems required several desired features in order to accomplish the control, forecasting and analysis of energy consumptions. These features comprehend scalability, adaptability and real-time operability of the system [2]. In

---

Supported by Energenius Srl.

K. Djemame et al. (Eds.): GECON 2020, LNCS 12441, pp. 57–66, 2020.
https://doi.org/10.1007/978-3-030-63058-4_5

particular, for industrial cogeneration plants the energy forecasting is a challenging task. The forecast involves the estimation of the energy produced by the cogenerator and the energy consumed by the factory. This estimation depends on a wide variety of operational (e.g., need for electricity and steam), economical (market prices of energy buying and selling) and environmental (weather conditions) inputs. Furthermore, part of the energy produced by cogenerators can be offered to the national grid to be redistributed to other customers. Errors on a CHP setup can have significant economic impacts.

Nowadays, several companies still manually perform energetic analyses for their facilities and costumers. This approach is obviously limited in terms of scalability and real-time operability. The deployment of cloud resources for the analysis of a huge amount of data can easily speed up this process but with a significant cost: a relevant amount of raw data should be sent to the cloud from IoT devices and smart meters causing bandwidth bottlenecks and latency issues. For this reason, several solutions have been proposed in order to bring automation and intelligence at the edge of the network. In this manner part of the computation can be performed directly where data are generated without reaching the cloud, thus reducing bandwidth consumption and improving the system reaction's times.

One of the most adopted solutions is represented by a new technological paradigm called fog computing [4]. Fog-enabled solutions extend the cloud in order to tackle the problem of data explosion in the IoT domain. Usually, the paradigm of fog computing consists of a layered architecture, including a central cloud, a series of edge units (fog nodes), gateways to connect server units and, finally, objects (things) that generate data and carry out specific operations. In this context, processing tasks can be displaced from the central cloud to the edge, going through a continuum of device with heterogeneous capabilities in terms of processing, storage and networking, which are transparently made available by modern virtualization techniques [3].

The main contribution of this work is the design and the implementation of a fog computing-based platform, GEM-Analytics, enabling Artificial Intelligence for the energy analysis and forecasting in industrial domains. We show the effectiveness of our approach deploying the proposed platform in two different use cases, tackling the optimization of Combine Heat and Power (CHP) plants of a pharmaceutical and a food factory, respectively. The application of our methods shows a significant reduction of operational costs in both cases leading to considerable monthly and annually savings for the industries.

The paper is structured as follows. Section 2 describes the architecture of the platform, the components and the AI modules used for the energy analysis. In Sect. 3 we describe the use cases and their results. Finally, a conclusion section ends the paper.

2   Architecture

A fog computing infrastructure consists in a set of heterogeneous resources geographically distributed and interconnected using different network technologies.

Such complex scenario is working at different levels: starting from physical infrastructure up to virtualization of resources, micro-services and software platforms. The specific energy vertical includes smart IoT meters to gather several parameters (e.g.. electrical, thermal, air, steam, environmental and technical). These attributes can be collected through standard protocols or from proprietary Building Management System (BMS) or Energy Management System (EMS), by edge nodes with computational resources, hosted in the same physical locations and interconnected with smart meters thorough wired or wireless local networks. The management of such physical distributed infrastructure is entrusted to the fog computing platform, that is in charge of creating, updating, deleting and monitoring services spawned in specific locations depending of their requirements.

Fog Computing Platform. The Fog Computing Platform offers resource allocation and orchestration of applications on a distributed infrastructure throughout the whole Cloud-to-Thing continuum. Such a north south (or, more informally, vertical) scenario assumes that all the components (i.e., micro-services) of an application are deployed only on a given administrative domain (i.e., a single infrastructure). This implies that the requirements imposed by an application can be satisfied without resources external to that domain.

FogAtlas [8] is a software platform, developed by Fondazione Bruno Kessler, for the management of fog/edge infrastructures. Its main features are:

Application Modelling and Positioning: to allow the owner of the application/service to define the different components (usually, micro-services) that should be distributed and their specific requirements. Based on these requirements, FogAtlas decides the positioning of the components on the infrastructure.

Zero-Touch Distribution and Orchestration of Containerised Applications: based on positioning decisions, FogAtlas orchestrates and implements each component (container) with minimal or no intervention required from the operator.

Setup, Operations and Automatic Management of a Distributed IT Infrastructure: FogAtlas provides automation in the management of each of the nodes within the infrastructure, connecting it securely to the computing cluster and monitoring its resources.

Two main components portray FogAtlas: the Application Composer and the Orchestrator. Through an Application Composer, the application blueprint and the associated requirements (traditional cloud computing requirements related to the flavours of the computational and storage resources but also network requirements like bandwidth and latency, typical of a distributed infrastructure) are expressed in a formal specification (e.g., TOSCA [5] or Kubernetes deployment manifest [9]) and forwarded to the Orchestrator. The Orchestrator, considering the current status of the distributed infrastructure (determined through the real time collection of metrics), finds the "best" region/node where to place the workload and finally invokes the Infrastructure Provisioning service in order to deploy it.

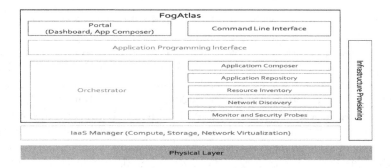

Fig. 1. FogAtlas high-level architecture.

Energy Analysis Platform. On top of FogAtlas, and leveraging on its services, sits an energy analysis platform, called GEM-Analytics, made up of two different macro-components (see Fig. 2):

Cloud Modules: represent the core component of the energy analysis. They deal with multiple functions, from data storage, to variables collection, data analysis and representation;

Edge Modules: these components reside on the fog nodes, distributed geographically and hosted by customers in local datacenter at their buildings/factories. They take care of collecting data from various sources, providing a local database to ensure redundancy of the data, sending processed and anonymized data to cloud modules and applying actuations.

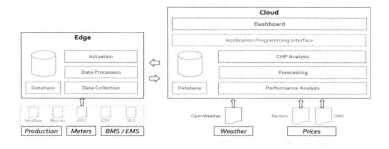

Fig. 2. GEM-Analytics platform high-level architecture.

The main objective of the platform is to run real-time energy analysis on specific energy intensive equipments with the aim of optimizing their energy consumption, and identifying inefficiencies and wrong setups. Several industrial companies deploy cogeneration plants by their premises to produce electricity and steam from natural gas. Such equipments are particularly efficient because the produce electricity from gas combustion and steam as residual output of exhausted fumes, thus allowing a significant improvement of overall efficiency compared to electricity purchase and steam production by standard boilers. However, such CHP plant is not only composed by a single cogeneration unit but can be made up of several combined units and multiple supporting boilers to ensure fault tolerance and scalability. So, the process of optimizing a CHP has to take into account numerous equipments and various sources of data, only partially related to each others, such as:

- Real-time data from energy drivers (consumed and produced electricity, consumed gas, produced steam);
- Real-time and forecasted environmental parameters (temperature and humidity) that highly impact the efficiency of the combustion processes;
- Real-time and forecasted prices of energy vectors (electricity and steam) that impact the buying and selling of energy hour-by-hour;
- Forecasted industrial production plan, that affects the amount of electricity and steam needed for the industrial process.

As soon as the datasets are collected and pre-processed, GEM-Analytics performs these operations:

i). Calculates the exact future hourly price of selling and buying energy (both electricity and natural gas) considering the future market prices and the specific energy contracts signed by the customer;
ii). Identify the efficiency curve of every equipment involved in the CHP optimization, adapting the theoretical one to real-time data and environmental parameters;
iii). Computes the forecasted amount of energy (electricity and steam) required by industry for its production cycle, based on the production plan and the environmental parameters;
iv). Evaluates the economic balance of all possible equipments setups, and selects the best configuration that meets the requirements and minimizes the overall costs. Such computation considers both the previous points and it's performed taking into account how a change in a specific equipment setup could possibly affect the system. Moreover, it considers also impact of white certificates and amount of CO_2 produced by the CHP.

The edge components are in charge of i) collecting real-time data from smart IoT meters and proprietary BMS/EMS through different drivers, ii) store these data in local database for resiliency, iii) pre-process the raw data and identify a relevant subset to be sent to the could for analytics training, and iv) run locally the algorithm model that best fit the training and validation phases and apply the setup suggested by the algorithm.

On the other side, the cloud modules collect environmental parameters from OpenWeather [14] and energy market prices from proprietary services. Then, all data coming from edge nodes and these sources are stored in a time-series database together with outcomes from analytic modules. These are in charge of i) computing the real-time performance curves of all the equipments, ii) performing general forecasting leveraging on a stack of analytic libraries (Prophet [13], scikit-learn [12], Tensorflow [1], Keras [7], Light-GBM [10], Xgboost [6]), iii) train, validate and select the model that best fit the CHP optimization and that will be used by the edge node for real-time computation and, iv) automatically retrain the models that are no longer fitting the required thresholds.

3   Case Studies

Use case 1: GEM-Analytics for pharmaceutical factory. We applied GEM-Analytics to optimize the cogeneration plant of a pharmaceutical factory in Italy with a nominal power of 7.96 MW. A peculiarity of the plant is the presence of a dual fuel boiler (in addition to a standard one) which is capable of consuming biogas, a byproduct of the fermentation processes of the factory: it is clearly convenient its usage compared to standard boilers since biogas comes for free (see Fig. 3). Moreover, the plant is subject to environmental controls which make out customer pay for the tons of CO_2 produced. We started our analysis by training predictive models to forecast the amount of electricity and steam demanded by the factoring, using as predictive variables the hourly planned production (e.g., number of fermentation equipments active per hour, phases of fermentation, ..). We used the same inputs to predict the amount of biogas produced hourly, in order to take into account the quantity of steam which comes free of charge from biogas combustion in our simulations. Finally, we also considered the variable of CO_2 emissions costs which is not present in the standard case.

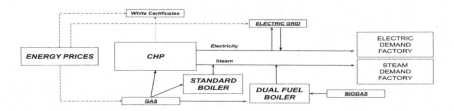

Fig. 3. CHP plant of the pharmaceutical factory in use case 1. Notice the presence of a dual fuel boiler which can consume biogas, byproduct of the factory processes.

The current usage of the CHP plant is automatically chosen in order to produce 1 MWh in addiction to the factory needs. Such overproduction is sold to the national grid. However, the cogenerator is never operated at full power to reduce costs of CO_2 emissions. The results of GEM-Analytics shows that the plant could run at a higher power (yet not at full load), reducing the total costs: see Table 1, reporting the economical results of GEM-Analytics in February 2020. The higher load of the cogenerator yields higher gas and CO_2 emissions costs (+6.41% and +10.43% respectively), but the additional amounts of electricity exported and white certificates produced lead to an overall better performance.

Total operational costs in the whole month could be reduced by 6.09% following the suggestions of GEM-Analytics, with a monthly saving of around €9K, that is €108K annually.

Table 1. GEM-Analytics economical results for use case 1 in February 2020, comparing costs of current operations with suggested ones. Negative values in electricity costs mean gains from export of excess energy cogenerated. White Certificates produced constitutes a gain, so they are reported as a negative cost. In this use case, costs from CO_2 emissions are also considered.

	Gas	Electricity	White Cert.	CO2	Total
Current (€)	335.26K	−75.31K	−166.23K	56.11K	149.84K
Suggested (€)	356.75K	−103.22K	−174.79K	61.97K	140.71K
Saving (%)	−6.41%	37.05%	5.15%	−10.43%	6.09%

From a network perspective, the FogAtlas platform allows training and validation in cloud of the analytic model that are then sent to edge node at the CHP plant for daily operations. This behaviour translates in a throughput and delay reduction up to 90% compared to a fully fledged cloud solution (see Table 2).

Table 2. Network results for use case 1 in February 2020, comparing throughput and delay of a standard cloud solution with the FogAtlas platform.

	Edge to cloud avg throughput (Mbps)	Analytic avg response delay (ms)
Cloud solution	0.538	53.92
Fogatlas	0.044	3.61
Reduction (%)	91.82%	93.30%

Use case 2: GEM-Analytics for food factory. We applied GEM-Analytics to optimize the hourly load of a food factory CHP plant in Italy.

In this case, the plant is composed by two separate cogeneration units, with nominal power of 2 MW and 1.56 MW respectively (see schema in Fig. 4). For this use case, CO_2 emission costs do not apply and the contract stipulated between the customer and the energy service provider determines the prices of exported electricity entirely from the energy market hourly index.

To predict the energy consumption of electricity and steam from the food factory we employed the Prophet [13] library, since these time series present very strong daily and weekly seasonalities, hence can be effectively forecasted with this method.

Again, the current usage level of cogenerators is determined automatically based on the amount of energy required by the production processes, with

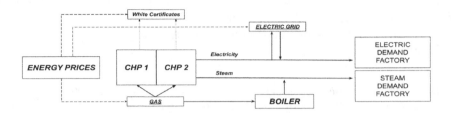

Fig. 4. Cogeneration schema of the food factory in use case 2. Notice the presence of two separated CHP plants which can be operated independently from each other.

the aim to follow a zero net exchange with the national grid. However, GEM-Analytics shows that this is not the best solution: both cogeneration units should run at a higher power, in particular in those hours in which the market index is particularly advantageous. Economical results in November 2019 are reported in Table 3: following suggestions based on electricity prices yields an obvious advantage on the electricity costs. With current strategy, €3K have been spent to import electricity while GEM-Analytics suggestions could have got €21K of revenues from electricity export. Increasing the usage of the CHP plant yields a substantial advantage also in terms of white certificates (+37.23%). Total operational costs in the whole month could be reduced by 11.15%:with a monthly saving of €10K, that is €120K annually.

Table 3. GEM-Analytics economical results for use case 2 in November 2019, comparing costs of current operations with suggested ones. Negative values in electricity costs mean gains from export of excess energy cogenerated. White Certificates produced constitutes a gain, so they are reported as a negative cost.

	Gas	Electricity	White Cert.	Total
Current (€)	132.02K	3.08K	−41.50K	93.57K
Suggested (€)	161.73K	−21.64K	−56.95K	83.14K
Saving (%)	−22.50%	810.10%	37.23%	11.15%

Similar to Use Case 1, FogAtlas platform reduces significantly (around 90%) the amount of traffic shared between edge and cloud, decreasing the latency of the analytic actuation and the overall throughput. (see Table 4).

Table 4. Network results for use case 2 in November 2019, comparing throughput and delay of a standard cloud solution with the FogAtlas platform.

	Edge to cloud avg throughput (Mbps)	Analytic avg response delay (ms)
Cloud solution	0.818	58.25
Fogatlas	0.051	4.88
Reduction (%)	93.76%	91.62%

4   Conclusions

We have proved that the combination of fog computing and AI-based energy analytics can reduce operational costs and improve real-time operability of industrial factories. Furthermore, GEM-Analytics can be adapted to a very specific vertical scenarios such as the Combine Heat and Power plant optimization and energy forecasting. Our platform computes the optimal operating strategy of energy-consuming equipment based not only on the present situation, but also on the forecasted production plan, the energy market prices and the environmental conditions. In addition, the fog computing architecture allows you to run predictive models directly in the edge nodes, drastically reducing bandwidth usage and response latency compared to a cloud solution. Our energy analysis platform currently focuses on industrial buildings and equipment with very high operating costs, given that the savings achievable are very high both in energy and economic terms. Future works will focus on extending the platform to deal with other specific scenarios such as retail shops, branch offices, banks and smart grids.

Acknowledgments. The work in this paper has been partially funded by "Programma operativo FESR 2014–2020" of Provincia autonoma di Trento, with co-financing of European ERDP funds, through project "EnergIA!" and by the European Union's Horizon 2020 Research and Innovation Programme under grant agreement no. 815141 (DECENTER: Decentralised technologies for orchestrated Cloud-to-Edge intelligence).

References

1. Abadi, M., et al.: TensorFlow: large-scale machine learning on heterogeneous systems. arXiv preprint arXiv:1603.04467 (2015)
2. Al Faruque, M.A., Vatanparvar, K.: Energy management-as-a-service over fog computing platform. IEEE Internet Things J. **3**(2), 161–169 (2015)
3. Bittencourt, L.F., Lopes, M.M., Petri, I., Rana, O.F.: Towards virtual machine migration in fog computing. In: P2P, Parallel, Grid, Cloud and Internet Computing (3PGCIC), 10th International Conference on, pp. 1–8. IEEE (2015)
4. Bonomi, F., Milito, R., Zhu, J., Addepalli, S.: Fog computing and its role in the internet of things. In: Proceedings of the First edition of the MCC Workshop on Mobile Cloud Computing, pp. 13–16. ACM (2012)
5. Brogi, A., Soldani, J., Wang, P.: Tosca in a nutshell: promises and perspectives. In: Villari, M., Zimmermann, W., Lau, K.K. (eds.) Service-Oriented and Cloud Computing. Lecture Notes in Computer Science, pp. 171–186. Springer, Berlin Heidelberg, Berlin, Heidelberg (2014). https://doi.org/10.1007/978-3-662-44879-3_13
6. Chen, T., Guestrin, C.: XGBoost: a scalable tree boosting system. In: Proceedings of the 22nd ACM SIGKDD International Conference on Knowledge Discovery and Data Mining, KDD '16, ACM, New York, NY, USA, pp. 785–794 (2016) https://doi.org/10.1145/2939672.2939785
7. Chollet, F., et al.: Keras. https://keras.io (2015)

8. Fogatlas website, https://fogatlas.fbk.eu/
9. Kdm, https://kubernetes.io/docs/concepts/workloads/controllers/deployment/
10. Ke, G., Meng, Q.E.A.: Lightgbm: a highly efficient gradient boosting decision tree. In: Advances in Neural Information Processing Systems, Curran Associates, Inc., pp. 3146–3154 (2017) http://papers.nips.cc/paper/6907-lightgbm-a-highly-efficient-gradient-boosting-decision-tree.pdf
11. Palensky, P., Dietrich, D.: Demand side management: demand response, intelligent energy systems, and smart loads. IEEE Trans. Ind. Inform. **7**(3), 381–388 (2011)
12. Pedregosa, F., Varoquaux, G.E.A.: Scikit-learn: machine learning in python. J. Mach. Learn. Res. **12**, 2825–2830 (2011)
13. Taylor, S.J., Letham, B.: Forecasting at scale. Am. Stat. **72**(1), 37–45 (2018)
14. Yanes, A.: Openweather: a peer-to-peer weather data transmission protocol. arXiv preprint arXiv:1111.0337 (2011)

Using LSTM Neural Networks as Resource Utilization Predictors: The Case of Training Deep Learning Models on the Edge

John Violos[1(✉)], Evangelos Psomakelis[2], Dimitrios Danopoulos[1], Stylianos Tsanakas[1], and Theodora Varvarigou[1]

[1] School of Electrical and Computer Engineering, National Technical University of Athens, Zografou, Greece 15771
{violos,el09727}@mail.ntua.gr, dimdano@microlab.ntua.gr, dora@telecom.ntua.gr
[2] Dept. of Informatics and Telematcs, Harokopio University of Athens, Tavros, Greece
vpsomak@hua.gr

Abstract. Cloud and Fog technologies are steadily gaining momentum and popularity in the research and industry circles. Both communities are wondering about the resource usage. The present work aims to predict the resource usage of a machine learning application in an edge environment, utilizing Raspberry Pies. It investigates various experimental setups and machine learning methods that are acting as benchmarks, allowing us to compare the accuracy of each setup. We propose a prediction model that leverages the time series characteristics of resource utilization employing an LSTM Recurrent Neural Network (LSTM-RNN). To conclude to a close to optimal LSTM-RNN architecture we use a genetic algorithm. For the experimental evaluation we used a real dataset constructed by training a well known model in Raspberry Pies3. The results encourage us for the applicability of our method.

Keywords: Resource utilization · Edge computing · Long short-term memory · Deep learning · Genetic algorithm

1 Introduction

Resource and cost optimizations are undoubtedly the hottest issues in the domain of cloud, fog and edge applications and for good reason. The variety of configuration options, cloud providers and deployment architectures, both software and hardware, are giving headaches to the system administrators, causing great losses in money and resources. These resources are especially valuable when we are talking about edge deployments as most edge devices have limited and costly resources. Even if they are interconnected in a cloudlet or IoT clusters their pooled resources are still pretty valuable and should not be wasted. Most users are overestimating their needs, ending up paying for idle resources or limiting the overall

© Springer Nature Switzerland AG 2020
K. Djemame et al. (Eds.): GECON 2020, LNCS 12441, pp. 67–74, 2020.
https://doi.org/10.1007/978-3-030-63058-4_6

system capacity as they are locking unused resources over large periods of time. There is an active interest in the relevant industry in order to tackle this issue. Amazon, for example, launched a resource optimization service which profiles our usage and makes recommendations to limit the resource waste [1].

The present work is tackling the cost reduction issue by creating a resource prediction model, which is used to optimize the resources and minimize the resource waste while preventing QoS infringements. It is obvious that in cloud and edge deployments there is a direct relation between resources and costs, the higher the allocated resources the higher the cost, even if the resources are not actually used. For that reason we focused on minimizing the waste of resources as a means of reducing the costs. The proposed LSTM-RNN based predictor is using a set of auto-optimized neural networks in order to profile the deployed applications and predict the resource utilization in the near future (8 min time step). This enables us to choose the optimal configuration for our cloud or fog deployment.

The testing and evaluation process took place using an experimental dataset created by Raspberry Pi machines. The Raspberry Pi is a common edge device chosen for its low price, its versatile, multi-purpose nature, its portability and its efficiency in power consumption as well as its low heat generation. The sample application tested was the training of a movie review classifier using Keras over Tensorflow on an IMDB database of movie reviews. This process created a realistic workload in the Raspberry Pi that was monitored using a Python script created specifically for the present work. The monitoring tool gathered information about the CPU, RAM, HDD and Network utilization at regular intervals, creating a training dataset for our algorithms.

The key contributions of this paper are:

- The proposal of a Time-Series Multi-Output Regression model for resource utilization forecasting of multiple resources in a unified model.
- An applicability study of genetic algorithms in the hypothesis space of LSTM-RNN topologies in the domain of resource utilization forecasting.
- The demonstration of an edge deployed AI application profiling approach using readily available monitoring libraries while focusing on key metrics.

The rest of the paper is structured as follows: Sect. 2 briefly reviews the literature about resource utilization forecasting techniques and AI applications deployed on the edge. Section 3 provides a description of the proposed AI application, its deployment environment, and how the profiling was conducted. Section 4 presents the design process of an LSTM-RNN model using the genetic algorithm. Section 5 describes the experimental evaluation and provides an interpretation of the results. Finally, in Sect. 6 the derived conclusion and future work are described.

2   Related Work

Resource utilization and cost are two tightly interconnected terms in edge computing. There are plenty of ways that resources affect the system costs but the most referenced one is the energy consumption. For example, Li et al. [2] are describing a system that tries to minimize the energy consumption of machine learning inference on Unmanned Aerial Vehicle (UAV) systems using a pipeline of a successive convex approximation based algorithm and the Dinkelbach algorithm. In a more close scenario as the one examined in the present, Guo et al. [3] are measuring the performance, and effectively the cost, of a mobile edge computing (MEC) network based on three factors: a) its energy consumption, b) its latency and c) its system total charge introduced by nearby computational access points. Their approach is purely mathematical, using formulas to describe and predict the three basic values for each network and application.

The main approaches of modeling the resource utilization include analytical models and machine learning models. Analytical models often use queuing theory [4] to model computing infrastructures that operate under steady request arrival rate, average service time and resource utilization with probabilistic behaviour. In addition, new models have been proposed which enhance the queuing models focusing on parallelizable tasks [5].

Machine learning models predict the resource utilization using a data-driven approach. They employ a large number of methods and techniques to discover patterns of resource usage in various circumstances from historical data. An ensemble approach [6] has been proposed integrating a multi-regression model feature selection mechanism. Sequencing resource observations is commonly exploited by time series approaches like Autoregressive Integrated Moving Average models [7]. Furthermore, a research close to our proposed model predicts CPU utilization using evolutionary neural networks [8].

The present work differentiates from the above mentioned models by combining the time series approach with deep learning models. Then it makes a smart search using genetic algorithms to identify an optimal LSTM-RNN that can forecast the resource utilization of CPUs, Ram, Disk I/O, and Network as a Multi-Output Regression Model. The genetic algorithm excels the evolutionary approach in the exploration of hypothesis space as the later use only mutation as reproduction strategy while the former use both crossover and mutation.

3   Application and Deployment Environment

3.1   Description of Applications and Data

The application we selected is a popular machine learning problem, specifically a classification of movie reviews based on the famous IMDB dataset. We trained and deployed our model using Keras, which is a high-level API to build and train models in Tensorflow, achieving almost 90% accuracy in the test dataset. It's worth mentioning that this application was selected as an indicative example which belongs to a larger category of machine learning applications specifically text classification which is a type of algorithm that can be found on the edge .i.e. document translation, language detection, spam detection, etc.

3.2   Description of Deployment Environments

We chose the Raspberry Pies3 as the deployment platform for our application. As for the specifications, this model packs a 64-bit quad-core ARM Cortex-A53 at 1.4GHz running on Raspbian operating system which is basically Debian Linux.

Having a platform that supports Linux based operating systems means we were able to have package support for most of the machine learning libraries and image packages. However, a careful setup was needed in order to install the whole Tensorflow framework on the small Raspberry (installing 3d party libraries, having small RAM, etc.) and run our application. Last, we connected to our device using the SSH protocol in order to control the application remotely (for example pause or resume the training algorithm.

3.3   Parameters of Interest

As a monitoring tool we chose to develop a python script that combines the psutil [9] and GPUtil [10] libraries, providing a plethora of monitoring tools that enable us to register metrics about the CPU, RAM, network, HDD and GPU in real time, while the target processes are running. It is a very lightweight tool, compatible with edge limitations.

The script allows us to define a set of parameters during each runtime, fine-tuning the monitoring process. These parameters include the snapshot frequency of the metrics watched, the file size limit of the logs in order to more easily process the files, and three lists of excluded devices if we have any, one for each category of devices (HDD, GPU and Network). All the data extracted by the monitoring tool are separated by category and converted in JSON format for uniformity and easier usage during the next steps of the modeling process. A JSON schema example is available at the author's GitHub Repository [11]

4   Resource Utilization Predictors Model with LSTM Neural Networks

The resource utilization predictor involves two pipelines as depicted in Fig. 1. The first pipeline is the training process which builds a multi-output regression model based on historic data. Specifically, the Raspberry Pies profile the resource usage during execution of the deployed service. The profiling output contains cpu, ram disk and network parameters. The profiling dataset is pre-processed using the min-max normalization method and piped to the hyper-parameter optimization process which trains multiple neural networks in order to identify an optimal topology.

The second pipeline Fig. 1b starts when the first pipeline has finished. It takes the current status of resource usage, it makes the pre-processing like in the training. Afterwards, the DL model provides a resource utilization prediction for the next 8 min time-step. The resource predictions are of manifold usages. In Fig. 1b, we see how we can leverage these predictions in order to employ elastic scaling.

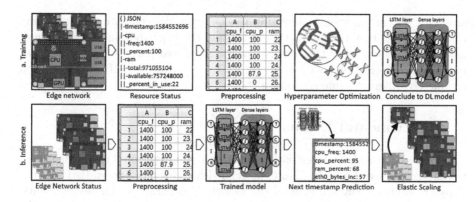

Fig. 1. LSTM-RNN with Genetic Algorithm Training and Inference

4.1   LSTM Neurons Architectural Usage

The training of DL models exhibits predictability in the sequence of resource utilization. We make the assumption that the next CPU and RAM usage may often dependent on the previous values and follows common patterns. LSTM, by having a chain-like structure, are able to connect information from long monitoring periods and map patterns of usage to predictions.

LSTM is a non-linear time series model that allows information to persist, using a memory state, and is capable to learn the order dependence between observations in a sequence. LSTM originates from RNN but outperforms it by resolving two weaknesses: the vanishing gradient problem and the short-term memory. The former makes RNN earlier layers incapable of being trained sufficiently. The latter makes RNN incapable of carrying information from earlier time observations to later ones and as a result RNN forgets faster.

The parameters of an LSTM-RNN can be optimized by minimizing an objective function. Widely used optimization techniques for LSTM-RNN are the Root Mean Square Propagation (RMPSrop) and the Adaptive Moment Estimation (Adam).

4.2   Architecture Design

Hyper-parameters decisions mainly involve the number of layers in an ANN and the number of units in each layer. In addition, it may also include the activation function type and dropout percentage. An automatic, systematic search through architecture space can be performed by a genetic algorithm.

The main steps of Genetic Algorithms are summarized as follows. Firstly, we pick a population size (N) and generate said population of ANN with random hyperparameters. Secondly, we pick a number of generations for the algorithm. We iterate over the generations performing the following steps: i) We train and test the entire population and then sort it by some metric; ii) The (B) best ANN advance to the next generation along with some randomly chosen (R), while we are being careful to avoid converging too fast; iii) We generate the remaining (N-R-B) members of the population by picking the hyper-parameters of the new networks choosing from the hyper-parameters of two parent ANN, chosen at random* from (B U R) with the probability of a random HP changing to a completely different value (mutation).

5   Experimental Evaluation

The proposed model is implemented and evaluated in Python 3 using the frameworks TensorFlow 2, pandas, NumPy, Scikit-learn, logging and statistics in the Jupyter notebook environment of the Google Colaboratory. The experiments' source code is available for any kind of reproduction and re-examination at the author's GitHub Repository [11].

5.1   Comparison with State of the Art Models

The proposed model is compared against Application and User Context Resource Predictor (AUCROP) model [12], a state of the art predictor for Resource utilization which employs traditional machine learning algorithms, and with two state of the art machine learning meta models named Auto-sklearn and XGBoost.

Auto-sklearn [13] is an automated machine learning pipeline of preprocessing, regression, and hyper-parameter tuning using a Bayesian optimization process. It contains a repository of previous optimization runs enabling training from previous saved settings. XGBoost [14] is a software library that implements the model of Gradient boosted decision trees. It is available in many programming languages including Python and compatible with Scikit-learn. XGBoost has gained much popularity because it has been used by many Kaggle and KDD Cup winning solutions.

5.2   Experimental Results and Discussion

For the evaluation we used the out-of-sample method that preserves the temporal order of records. The dataset was split into two sequences, the training sequence (66% observations) and the testing sequence (34% observations). In the context of time series applications we cannot use any shuffling mechanism as is the common practice for traditional machine learning evaluation, because we must preserve the sequence of observations. For evaluation metrics we used Root Mean Squared Error (RMSE) and Mean Absolute Error (MAE). We also log the training time and the Inference Times for a single prediction and for a batch of 100 predictions.

The Genetic Algorithm performed a smart search in hypothesis space in order to converge on an optimal LSTM-RNN Multi-Output Regression model. AUCROP, XGBoost and Auto-sklearn also used a hyper-parameter optimization approach. The list and the candidate values of the hyper-parameters are

Table 1. Single-Output & Multi-Output Evaluation

Method	RMSE	MAE	CPU-1 (%)		RAM-1 (%)		Train. Time	Infer. Time	
			RMSE	MAE	RMSE	MAE		Single	Batch
AUCROP	0.0814	0.0414	17.235	14.009	2.480	1.482	522	0,004	0,011
XGBoost	0.1139	0.0599	16.457	13.569	1.515	0.4720	181	0.060	0.010
Auto-sklearn	0.1055	0.0243	52.659	17.856	1.546	0.5260	1338	0.263	0.572
LSTM-RNN	0.0674	0.0338	16.099	12.838	1.746	0.9170	574	0.020	0.024

described in a file in the author's GitHub Repository [11]. The experimental results are summarized in Table 1.

Looking at the results, the LSTM-RNN model trained using the Genetic Algorithm achieved the best RMSE value over the dataset, while maintaining low training and inference times. In resource utilization prediction the large errors are undesirable, so RMSE is the most important evaluation metric as it assigns relatively high weight to large errors compared to MAE. Table 1 provides aggregations of all regression outputs in the first and second column and specific outputs such as CPU-1 and RAM-1 in the columns three to six.

LSTM-RNN also outperformed all other models in predicting the percentage value of CPU-1 core, measured by both RMSE and MAE. The accuracy of RAM utilization predictions appears to be slightly below XGBoost and Auto-sklearn, possibly due to a randomization factor introduced by RAM's caching policies.

6 Conclusions

The present research demonstrates how a DL approach with LSTM layers can be applied in order to tackle the problem of forecasting the resource utilization in edge devices in the use case of AI model training. LSTM-RNN can be a powerful regression model with high accuracy results if its architecture is of optimal design. A heuristic approach was used to converge on close to optimal architecture using a genetic algorithm.

There are still topics that are out of this paper's scope. Firstly, we should examine different applications deployed on the edge. Applications with erratic workloads should be more interesting. Applications that have fluctuating number of requests should need additional parameters of observations. In this case, we should find different feature engineering techniques and leverage open data related to the deployed service.

The interaction between the edge devices is also a very interesting topic. Edge devices do not work isolated. They belong in a heterogeneous infrastructure involving different types of software and hardware. Resource usage also depends on this ecosystem so predictors should take into consideration the full environment.

Acknowledgements. This work is part of the ACCORDION project that has received funding from the European Union's Horizon 2020 research and innovation programme under grant agreement "No 871793".

References

1. "Launch: Resource Optimization Recommendations," Amazon Web Services, 23 Jul 2019 https://aws.amazon.com/blogs/aws-cost-management/launch-resource-optimization-recommendations/
2. Li, M., Cheng, N., Gao, J., Wang, Y., Zhao, L., Shen, X.: Energy-efficient UAV-assisted mobile edge computing: resource allocation and trajectory optimization. IEEE Trans. Veh. Technol. **69**(3), 3424–3438 (2020)
3. Guo, Y., et al.: Intelligent offloading strategy design for relaying mobile edge computing networks. IEEE Access **8**, 35127–35135 (2020)
4. Truong, T.M., Harwood, A., Sinnott, R.O., Chen, S.: Performance analysis of large-scale distributed stream processing systems on the cloud. In: IEEE 11th International Conference on Cloud Computing (CLOUD), pp. 754–761 (2018) https://doi.org/10.1109/CLOUD.2018.00103
5. Li, X., Liu, S., Pan, L., Shi, Y., Meng, X.: Performance analysis of service clouds serving composite service application jobs .In: 2018 IEEE International Conference on Web Services (ICWS), pp. 227–234 (2018) https://doi.org/10.1109/ICWS.2018.00036
6. Kaur, G., Bala, A., Chana, I.: An intelligent regressive ensemble approach for predicting resource usage in cloud computing. J. Parallel Distrib. Comput. **123**, 1–12 (2019). https://doi.org/10.1016/j.jpdc.2018.08.008
7. Zia Ullah, Q., Hassan, S., Khan, G.M.: Adaptive resource utilization prediction system for infrastructure as a service cloud. Comput. Intell. Neurosci. (2017) https://www.hindawi.com/journals/cin/2017/4873459/
8. Mason, K., Duggan, M., Barrett, E., Duggan, J., Howley, E.: Predicting host CPU utilization in the cloud using evolutionary neural networks. Future Gener. Comput. Syst. **86**, 162–173 (2018). https://doi.org/10.1016/j.future.2018.03.040
9. GitHub, G. Rodola', giampaolo/psutil, https://github.com/giampaolo/psutil
10. GitHub, A.K.: Mortensen, anderskm/gputil https://github.com/anderskm/gputil
11. GitHub, S. Tsanakas, STsanakas/Resource_Utilization_Prediction, https://github.com/STsanakas/Resource_Utilization_Prediction
12. Violos, J., Psomakelis, E., Tserpes, K., Aisopos, F., Varvarigou, T.: Leveraging user mobility and mobile app services behavior for optimal edge resource utilization. In: Proceedings of the International Conference on Omni-Layer Intelligent Systems, Crete, Greece, pp. 7–12 (2019) https://doi.org/10.1145/3312614.3312620
13. Feurer, M., Klein, A., Eggensperger, K., Springenberg, J., Blum, M., Hutter, F.: Efficient and robust automated machine learning. In: Advances in Neural Information Processing Systems 28, C. Cortes, N. D. Lawrence, D. D. Lee, M. Sugiyama, and R. Garnett, Eds. Curran Associates Inc, pp. 2962–2970 (2015)
14. Chen, T., Guestrin, C.: XGBoost: a scalable tree boosting system. In: Proceedings of the 22nd ACM SIGKDD International Conference on Knowledge Discovery and Data Mining, pp. 785–794 (2016) https://doi.org/10.1145/2939672.2939785

Towards a Semantic Edge Processing of Sensor Data. An Incipient Experiment

Paula-Georgiana Zălhan$^{(\boxtimes)}$ ⓘ, Gheorghe Cosmin Silaghi ⓘ,
and Robert Andrei Buchmann ⓘ

Business Informatics Research Centre, Babeş-Bolyai University,
Cluj-Napoca, Romania
{paula.zalhan,gheorghe.silaghi,robert.buchmann}@econ.ubbcluj.ro

Abstract. This paper addresses a semantic stream processing pipeline, including data collection, semantic annotation, RDF data storage and query processing. We investigate whether the semantic annotation step could be moved on the edge, by designing and evaluating two alternative processing architectures. Experiments show that the edge processing fulfills the low-latency requirement, facilitating the parallel processing of the semantic enrichment for the sensor data.

Keywords: Semantic stream processing · Edge computing · Sensor data

1 Introduction

Industrial Wireless Networks (IWNs) have the potential to connect and integrate smart entities with traditional industries to provide greater flexibility, intelligence and adaptation [11]. These entities collect and transmit massive amounts of data regarding the working environment, which requires low latency processing capabilities to enable real-time monitoring of the industrial site. The stream data characteristics impose significant challenges to existing industrial systems. Thus, innovative solutions are demanded to overcome these issues by combining quantity-oriented methods with semantics-oriented techniques towards building processing pipelines that fulfill the needs of Industry 4.0 environments.

The main goal of this paper is to deliver faster insights of underlying large-scale sensor data generated in an industrial environment. Given a Semantic Stream Processing (SSP) [10] pipeline which includes [16] data collection, semantic annotation, RDF data storage and query processing, we investigate whether edge processing of semantic annotation could deliver a higher throughput of messages processed by the system. The pipeline's architecture is built with the help of various tools that include: the Apache Kafka [1] distributed streaming platform, the GraphDB [3] semantic database server and the Semantic Sensor Network (SSN) ontology [8].

To fulfill the low latency requirement of a smart factory use case, we evaluate two alternative pipeline architectures: (i) semantic annotation after the sensor

© Springer Nature Switzerland AG 2020
K. Djemame et al. (Eds.): GECON 2020, LNCS 12441, pp. 75–79, 2020.
https://doi.org/10.1007/978-3-030-63058-4_7

data is ingested into the real-time system, and (ii) semantic annotation on the "edge" – i.e., at the producer point. The experiment reported in this paper supports the decision on which approach should be considered in order to advance the proposed pipeline beyond the current, proof-of-concept status.

This paper is organized as follows. Section 2 reviews the existing SSP systems. Section 3 presents the adopted methodology and the architecture of our SSP pipeline. Section 4 describes the implemented alternatives, reports and discusses the results. Section 5 concludes the work.

2   Related Work

The RDF Stream Processing (RSP) deals with fast changing data that can be semantically modeled by means of the RDF model [6]. Initially, centralized RSP engines such as CQELS [9] were proposed. However, these systems are unable to handle large-scale data originating from heterogeneous sources. Distributed RSP engines such as Strider [14] were designed to address the above-mentioned limitations. They perform parallel processing over the incoming data using a cluster computing infrastructure. Other solutions such as SEASOR [13] are based on a middleware component to deal with the real-time property of heterogeneous incoming data streams, delivered to various destination systems. In addition to SSP, Stream Reasoning [7] extends the traditional RSP engines with rule-based, logical, reasoning capabilities. Furthermore, stream reasoning could be combined with machine learning techniques [5].

3   Solution Overview: A SSP Pipeline

In order to build our SSP pipeline [16], we adopted the Design Science Methodology (DMS) [15]. We followed an iterative development cycle with the explicit intention of improving the pipeline's performance, which is empirically investigated considering a smart factory scenario. We are specifically interested in deciding the location in the pipeline where the semantic annotation should take place, for improving the system latency. Figure 1 presents the architecture of our SSP pipeline, which is based on Apache Kafka [1] to collect and process the streaming data, GraphDB [3] to store the annotated data streams and the SPARQL query language to analyze the resulting RDF graph.

The data streams are generated by various sensors deployed in a smart factory ecosystem. The continuous data gathered from sensor sources is collected and processed by a distributed data ingestion system. Apache Kafka is employed for ingesting the sensor streams because it could handle large-scale data in a fault-tolerant manner [12]. Kafka works as a cluster connecting multiple producers and consumers to one or more servers known as brokers. Apache Zookeeper [2] is used to store metadata about the Kafka cluster.

In the Smart Factory scenario, the incoming data is categorized into topics and analyzed on the fly using the Kafka core API. To provide machine-readable

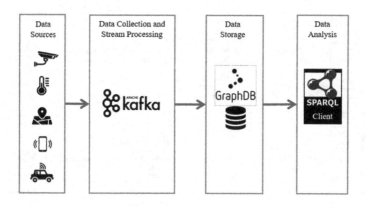

Fig. 1. The SSP pipeline [16]

descriptions of the ingested data, the streaming data previously collected is continuously annotated using the SSN ontology [8]. The annotated sensor streams are then persisted in a triplestore for later analysis. We chose GraphDB to store the RDF streams because it is one of the popular RDF stores, delivering good performance for triplestore initialization, loading and indexing [4]. The RDF streams are then retrieved and manipulated using SPARQL query language.

4   Introductory Results

The performance of the deployed SSP pipeline depends heavily on the software and hardware settings. All the tests were carried out on Ubuntu 16.04.4 LTS x64-based PC with Intel(R) Core(TM) i7-7500U, 2.70 GHz CPU, 8 GB RAM and Java 1.8. We deployed the Confluent streaming platform 4.0.0 with Apache Kafka 1.0.0 and Apache Zookeeper 3.4.10, which were the latest versions available at the time of building the SSP. For RDF parsing of the JSON streams we used RDFLlib 4.2.2 package with SPARQL 1.1 implementation. To store the annotated streams we used GraphDB SE 8.7.

To identify the proper place for semantic annotation of the raw sensor data, we implemented and evaluated two different architectures - as indicated in Fig. 2:

- *Semantic annotation on consumer side* (S1). The semantic annotation task is performed after sensor streams are written into topics.
- *Semantic annotation on producer side* (S2). The semantic enrichment task is performed directly on edge sensors.

In both scenarios, the Kafka cluster was configured on a single machine, with multiple brokers and one Zookeeper instance. The producers run in their own thread during 10 min and simultaneously publish the data streams to multi-partition topics. The timing of the produced data streams follows a Poisson process with a data rate that varies depending on the experiment.

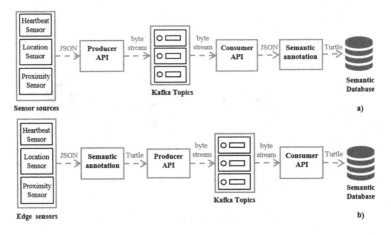

Fig. 2. a) Semantic annotation on consumer side (S1) vs. b) semantic annotation on the producer side (S2)

Table 1 summarizes the number of annotated messages and their corresponding RDF triples, in the alternative architectures. We notice that when the semantic processing is moved at the edge of the network (S2), even ten times more annotated messages are generated and implicitly, the number of corresponding RDF triples it is about ten times larger. In the semantic edge architecture (S2), the data does not waste time to travel through the pipeline. Thus, the edge computing architecture for semantic modeling of sensor streams provides advantages in terms of data processing power and network bandwidth reduction.

Table 1. Annotated messages and corresponding RDF triples in both architectures

Producers	S1		S2		Throughput multiplication[1]
	Messages	RDF triples	Messages	RDF triples	
10	529	8993	5703	96951	10.78
20	558	9486	6253	106301	11.21
30	696	11832	6207	105519	8.92
40	579	9843	6023	102391	10.40
50	357	6069	6043	102731	16.93
60	652	11084	5714	97138	8.76
70	707	12019	5902	100334	8.35
80	851	14467	5904	100368	6.94
90	751	12767	5911	100487	7.87
100	705	11985	6091	103547	8.64

Throughput multiplication of the number of annotated messages in S2 vs. S1

5   Conclusions

When building the low-latency pipeline for streaming analysis of sensor data, we adopted the Design Science for investigating the proper place to execute the semantic modeling of sensor data using the SSN ontology. We implemented two alternative architectures of the semantic stream processing system in the context of a smart factory. Experiments focus on assessing the performance of the alternative architectures and results show that the semantic edge architecture is capable of producing an increased number of annotated sensor streams. Performing the semantic enrichment of sensor data locally, not only reduces the physical distance the data travel through the semantic pipeline, but has the potential to improve the IWN's performance by reducing the latency.

References

1. Apache Kafka. https://kafka.apache.org. Accessed 22 May 2020
2. Apache Zookeeper. https://zookeeper.apache.org/. Accessed 22 May 2020
3. GraphDB. https://graphdb.ontotext.com/. Accessed 22 May 2020
4. Bellini, P., Nesi, P.: Performance assessment of RDF graph databases for smart city services. J. Vis. Lang. Comput. **45**, 24–38 (2018)
5. Chen, J., Lécué, F., Pan, J.Z., Chen, H.: Learning from ontology streams with semantic concept drift. In: Proceedings of the 26th International Joint Conference on Artificial Intelligence, pp. 957–963. IJCAI'17, AAAI Press (2017)
6. Cyganiak, R., Wood, D., Lanthaler, M.: RDF 1.1 Concepts and Abstract Syntax. W3C Recommendation, 25 February 2014. https://www.w3.org/TR/rdf11-concepts/. Accessed 22 May 2020
7. Dell'Aglio, D., Della Valle, E., van Harmelen, F., Bernstein, A.: Stream reasoning: a survey and outlook. Data Sci. **1**(1–2), 59–83 (2017)
8. Haller, A., Janowicz, K., Cox, S., Le-Phuoc, D., Taylor, K., Lefrançois, M.: Semantic Sensor Network Ontology. W3C Recommendation, 19 October 2017. https://www.w3.org/TR//vocab-ssn/. Accessed 22 May 2020
9. Le-Phuoc, D., Dao-Tran, M., Xavier Parreira, J., Hauswirth, M.: A native and adaptive approach for unified processing of linked streams and linked data. In: Aroyo, L., et al. (eds.) ISWC 2011. LNCS, vol. 7031, pp. 370–388. Springer, Heidelberg (2011). https://doi.org/10.1007/978-3-642-25073-6_24
10. Le-Phuoc, D., Manfred, H.: Semantic stream processing. In: Sakr, S., Zomaya, A. (eds.) Encyclopedia of Big Data Technologies. Springer, Berlin (2019)
11. Li, X., Li, D., Wan, J., Vasilakos, A.V., Lai, C.F., Wang, S.: A review of industrial wireless networks in the context of industry 4.0. Wireless Netw. **23**(1), 23–41 (2017)
12. Narkhede, N., Shapira, G., Palino, T.: Kafka: The Definitive Guide: Real-time Data and Stream Processing at Scale. O'Reilly Media, Inc., California (2017)
13. Pacha, S., Murugan, S.R., Sethukarasi, R.: Semantic annotation of summarized sensor data stream for effective query processing. J. Supercomput. **76**, 4017–4039 (2020). https://doi.org/10.1007/s11227-017-2183-7
14. Ren, X., Curé, O.: Strider: a hybrid adaptive distributed RDF stream processing engine. In: d'Amato, C. et al. (eds.) ISWC 2017. LNCS, vol. 10587, pp. 559–576. Springer, Cham (2017). https://doi.org/10.1007/978-3-319-68288-4_33
15. Wieringa, R.J.: Design Science Methodology for Information Systems and Software engineering. Springer, Berlin (2014)
16. Zalhan, P.G., Silaghi, G.C., Buchmann, R.A.: Marrying big data with smart data in sensor stream processing. In: Siarheyeva, A. et al. (ed.) 28th International Conference on Information Systems Development (ISD2019). AIS eLibrary (2019)

Distributed Cloud Intelligence: Implementing an ETSI MANO-Compliant Predictive Cloud Bursting Solution Using Openstack and Kubernetes

Francescomaria Faticanti[1,2]([✉]), Jason Zormpas[3], Sergey Drozdov[3],
Kewin Rausch[1], Orlando Avila García[4], Fragkiskos Sardis[3], Silvio Cretti[1],
Mohsen Amiribesheli[3], and Domenico Siracusa[1]

[1] Fondazione Bruno Kessler, Trento, Italy
ffaticanti@fbk.eu
[2] University of Trento, Trento, Italy
[3] Konica Minolta Global R&D, London, UK
[4] Atos, Madrid, Spain

Abstract. While solutions for cloud bursting already exist and are commercially available, they often rely on a limited set of metrics that are monitored and acted upon when user-defined thresholds are exceeded. In this paper, we present an ETSI MANO compliant approach that performs proactive bursting of applications based on infrastructure and application metrics. The proposed solution implements Machine Learning (ML) techniques to realise a proactive offloading of tasks in anticipation of peak utilisation that is based on pattern recognition from historical data. Experimental results comparing several forecasting algorithms show that the proposed approach can improve upon reactive cloud bursting solutions by responding quicker to system load changes. This approach is applicable to both traditional datacentres and applications as well as 5G telco infrastructures that run Virtual Network Functions (VNF) at the edge.

Keywords: Cloud bursting · Proactive control · Application metrics · Workload orchestration

1 Introduction

Today's diverse utility-based computing ecosystem cannot function without relying on the cloud paradigm. The paradigm has disturbed all the existing computing tasks. At its core, it decouples applications from hardware and allows for increased and elastic scaling of compute and storage. It achieves this, through the implementation of virtualised infrastructures and platforms on top of commodity hardware. It is worthy to note that, although legacy monolith applications can be migrated to the cloud, only cloud-native ones can fully benefit from cloud computing features such as automatic scaling, failover and self-healing.

© Springer Nature Switzerland AG 2020
K. Djemame et al. (Eds.): GECON 2020, LNCS 12441, pp. 80–85, 2020.
https://doi.org/10.1007/978-3-030-63058-4_8

To enable the users to take full advantage of the cloud computing paradigm, Konica Minolta is working on an advanced all-in-one data-driven cloud platform called Distributed Cloud Intelligence (DCI). DCI is an optimised Platform as a Service (PaaS) for the particular needs of the next chapter of applications in areas such as smart cities, data analytics, computer vision, IoT and robotics. In the following study, in close collaboration with Fondazione Bruno Kessler and Atos, DCI portrays a PaaS capable of edge-centric cloud bursting. The following work will showcase how DCI can enable businesses to efficiently handle peak IT demands. As an instance, if all of the on-premise resource capacity of an organisation is utilised, the overflow traffic is directed to a centralised cloud (e.g., public) so there's no interruption of services. Additionally, given the agreed Service Level Agreements (SLAs), DCI removes the costs of raw data transfer to the centralised cloud by performing the heavy processes and pre-processes at the edge locations. The work illustrates that leveraging deep learning techniques, DCI will tremendously lower the data transfer costs and delays. Deep learning methods perform a proactive control of system workload in order to prevent overflow situations in the resource utilisation and requirements' violations in the applications' performances.

The remainder of the paper is structured as follows. The System Architecture is shown in Sect. 2. The predictive cloud bursting method and experimental results are presented in Sect. 3. A concluding section ends the paper.

2   System Architecture

The system is comprised of three components: i) the edge datacentre where end-user applications are hosted by an organisation that wishes to employ cloud-bursting, ii) the remote cloud which can be a public cloud or a remote hosting facility that can offer its resources for task offloading, iii) and the Jump server which is a hardened host that performs light-weight orchestration functions in the form of collecting and processing performance metrics from the application and the infrastructure. The implementation presented in this paper uses Openstack as the cloud platform on the edge and remote clouds and Kubernetes as the container orchestration engine for hosting applications. Specifically, we use Openstack VMs to deploy a Kubernetes cluster that will host the end-user applications subject to cloud-bursting. The resource utilisation metrics from Openstack's VMs are monitored at the Jump server. Once the resource utilisation conditions are met on the edge, the Jump server is able to initiate a cloud burst of microservices from the edge to the remote cloud. When certain conditions are met, the Jump server will communicate directly with Openstack on the remote cloud to deploy additional Kubernetes slave instances for task offloading or delete instances that are no longer required.

3   Predictive Cloud Bursting

In this section, we analyse the integration of machine learning components to the Cloud environment in order to achieve a predictive Cloud bursting system and

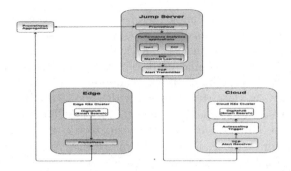

Fig. 1. System architecture based on Konica Minolta DCI

we present some experimental results. In what follows we describe how the data were collected and pre-processed for the application of the Machine Learning models. Finally, we describe the model selected to perform the forecast of peak demands and the obtained results.

Data Collection. After the metrics were identified and their effects on the behaviour of the application (Konica Minolta Semantic Search) and the system (Cloud environment) was analysed, the InfluxDB and the Prometheus API's were utilised to collect the timeseries data from these metrics. Historic data for the system's CPU Usage and Load Average were collected utilising the InfluxDB for the purpose of training the machine learning algorithm, while real-time data were collected utilising the Prometheus API's for the purpose of predicting a possible overloading of the system.

Data Pre-processing. The following three data transforms are performed on the dataset prior to fitting a model and making a forecast:

1) **Transform the time series data so that it is stationary.** Specifically, we aim to remove the increasing trends in the data. This can be skipped since our data looks stable.

2) **Transform the time series into a supervised learning problem.** Specifically, the organisation of data into input and output patterns where the observation at the previous time step is used as an input to forecast the observation at the current time time-step.

3) **Feature scaling** (also known as data normalization [1]) is the method used to standardize the range of features of data. Since, the range of values of data may vary widely, it becomes a necessary step in data pre-processing while using machine learning algorithms. This method is used to automatically scale up or down the number of resources based on demand at any time. Essentially, the process entails transforming the values of the data from the original range to a value that is within the range of 0 to 1. The formula for feature scaling is $X_{scaled} = \frac{X - \min X}{\max X - \min X}$, where X is the original feature value, and X_{scaled} is the normalized one [1].

LSTM Model Description. A recurrent neural network (RNN) is a class of artificial neural networks where connections between nodes form a directed graph along a temporal sequence [2]. This allows it to exhibit temporal dynamic behaviour. Derived from feedforward neural networks, RNNs can use their internal state (memory) to process variable length sequences of inputs. Long short-term memory is an artificial recurrent neural network architecture used in the field of deep learning. Unlike standard feedforward neural networks, LSTM has feedback connections. It can not only process single data points, but also entire sequences of data.

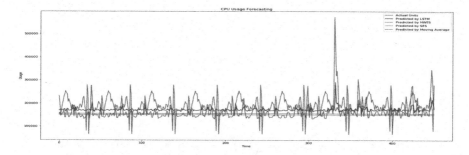

Fig. 2. An illustration of the Time Series forecasting models predicting values in actual data (CPU Usage vs Time).

Experimental Results. The purpose of our experiment was to prove that a Machine Learning algorithm could predict, in real-time, whether a system (DCI Private Cloud) would overload, thus alerting it in advance to trigger the Cloud Bursting functionality (to the DCI Public Cloud). In order to achieve this, the recurrent neural network called "Long Short Term Memory" was selected amongst multiple Statistical (e.g. Moving Average, Holt-Winter Exponential Smoothing) and Machine Learning networks (Sarima and Sarimax), as its accuracy of predicting Time-Series data outperformed all the other models as seen in Figure 2.

The methodology used to conduct the experiment was the following:
- Multiple files (pdf, txt) were uploaded to the file server.
- The LSTM model was executed to collect "new" historical Time-Series data (Systems Load Averages) from InfluxDB and was tasked to train on them.
- Using API calls to Prometheus the real-time Time-Series data (System Load Averages) were received to the program.
- The LSTM model trained on the historical data from InfluxDB and made predictions/forecasts on the real-time Time-Series data that were collected from the API calls to Prometheus.

Table 1. LSTM Model for real-time load average prediction

Upload Freq	Job	Metric Prediction Time	ML Training Time
Slow (3–10 files/m)	System Load Average	0.85 sec	3 min 56 s
Medium (1–3 files/s)	System Load Average	1.02 sec	4 min

Test Results. The model was trained [Table 1] and tested [Fig. 3] using real Time-Series data from the system's load averages. As we can see in Fig. 2 and Fig. 3, LSTM accurately predicts most of the trends in our data.

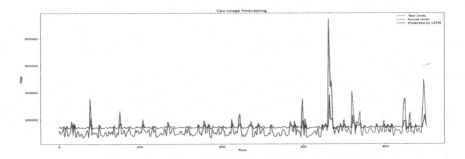

Fig. 3. CPU Usage Forecasting (CPU Usage vs Time).

4   Conclusions and Future Work

In recent years, cloud computing paradigm has attracted a growing amount of attention from industry and academic players. This has occurred because of cloud computing's ability to dynamically provision resources on-demand. In this context cloud bursting techniques are crucial to avoid overflows in resource utilisation and to monitor applications' performances. In this work we described a new cloud platform (DCI) able to perform cloud bursting using predictive control methods based on deep learning approaches. DCI demonstrates a real-time prediction-based solution that controls the auto-scaling process of cloud infrastructures by modifying the configuration of service mesh underlying the computing resources. This deep learning-based solution is independent of distributed frameworks (i.e., Kubernetes and OpenStack) and therefore applies to any other cloud infrastructures. Future works involve the support for new emerging technologies such as 5G and Edge-centring Machine Learning such (e.g., Federated Learning).

Acknowledgments. This work has received funding from the European Union's Horizon 2020 Research and Innovation Programme under grant agreement no. 815141 (DECENTER: Decentralised technologies for orchestrated Cloud-to-Edge intelligence) and internal funding from Konica Minolta by providing support for the LightEdge project in collaboration with FBK.

References

1. Data Science on Prometheus Metrics. https://github.com/AICoE/prometheus-data-science
2. Understanding   LSTM   Networks.   https://colah.github.io/posts/2015-08-Understanding-LSTMs/

Digital Infrastructures for Pandemic Response and Countermeasures

A MDE Approach for Modelling and Distributed Simulation of Health Systems

Unai Arronategui⑩, José Ángel Bañares(✉)⑩, and José Manuel Colom⑩

Aragón Institute of Engineering Research (I3A), University of Zaragoza,
Zaragoza, Spain
{unai,banares,jm}@unizar.es

Abstract. Epidemic episodes such as the COVID-19 has shown the need
for simulation tools to support decision making, predict the results of
control actions, and mitigating the effects of the virus. Simulation methods have been widely used by healthcare researchers and practitioners
to improve the planning and management of hospitals and predict the
spread of disease. Simulating all involved aspects of an epidemic episode
requires the modelling and simulation of large and complex Discrete
Event Systems (DESs), supported by modular and hierarchical models
easy to use for experts, and that can be translated to efficient code for
distributed simulation. This paper presents a model driven engineering
(MDE) approach to support the modelling of healthcare systems (HS) in
epidemic episodes combining different perspectives, and the translation
to efficient code for scalable distributed simulations.

Keywords: Healthcare modelling and simulation · Holistic analysis ·
Distributed simulation · Model elaboration

1 Introduction

According to the World Health Organization the COVID-19 outbreak can col-
lapse even the most robust health systems, resulting in the need to entirely reconfigure health sectors in response. In Spain, the diseased has shown its capacity
to spread in a matter of days, forcing the Government to adjust its response
and introduce strict lockdown measures to slow the spread of the disease and
gain time to reorganize its health system [1]. In normal situations, healthcare
systems (HS) aspire to offer an effective and efficient provision of health services and availability of resources without compromising on quality. Simulation
methods have been widely used by healthcare researchers and practitioners as
decision support systems to improve the planning and management of hospitals
[13]. In an epidemic episode, the design and the support for making decisions
rapidly to reconfigure and repurpose the whole health sector while taking into
account worst-case scenarios, requires methodologies to model and simulate at
large scale.

ⓒ Springer Nature Switzerland AG 2020
K. Djemame et al. (Eds.): GECON 2020, LNCS 12441, pp. 89–103, 2020.
https://doi.org/10.1007/978-3-030-63058-4_9

Modelling epidemic episodes require an holistic approach that combines different perspectives [25]: Mathematical *spread of disease* (**SD**) models to describe the spread of the COVID-19 [15], that considers aspects such as the dependence of the impact of COVID-19 on the percentage of detected cases over the real total infected cases, the effect of different sanitary and infectiousness conditions of hospitalized people, and control measures such as the isolation of infected people, constrained mobility of people, and tracing of people by tests in order to increase the percentage of detected infected people, and the increase of sanitary resources to detect and treat affected people, which results in a decrease of people infected. The **SD** affects the *resource allocation* perspective (**RA**), that models the system as a discrete event system (DES) in which a finite set of concurrent processes share in a competitive way a finite set of resources. The patients flows through interconnected processes of treatments and cares defined in protocols defined for particular diseases. Doctors, nurses, beds, and equipments are the resources required to carry out the protocols. Scheduling, planning problems, and making decisions requires this perspective to support more efficient services with less cost, and to promote the interoperability between organizations for sharing resources and services. In turn, the spread of the disease strongly depends on the mobility of the population. *Mobility and transport* systems (**MT**) have been the focus of research in the simulation community with several agent-based traffic simulations in the literature [19]. Finally, *individual behaviors* (**IB**) related with economic and educational level, are many other environmental factors that affect the way each individual relates with the healthcare services. Individual behaviours are typically modelled as agent-based models to observe emergent behaviors by the simulation of different individuals.

Developing detailed models require the combination of these different perspectives, which result in the connection of different entities of simulation, and coupling them at different levels of abstraction. The contribution of this paper is the modelling and simulation of all perspectives as DES. It requires component and hierarchical constructs that allow the composition of complex behaviours conducted by a model driven engineering (MDE) approach, and the possibility to build distributed simulations that are able of scaling and dynamic load balancing. These important challenges have hampered the extensive use of distributed simulations, and the modelling of complex perspectives have required the use of mathematical models that describe the emergent behaviour without the need to describe low level details.

To have good models it is advisable to contemplate the execution environment in the abstraction of the system, and refine the models to low levels of abstraction. At each level of abstraction, the modeller should use a number of modelling artifacts to build the model. In this refinement process, a level of abstraction is reached in which the primitives necessary to define the model are not available, or the specification of this would require an enormous workforce. In this case, we need to incorporate the observed behaviour of low levels, as parameter of upper ones. For example, the simulation of data intensive applications over cloud resources can start with the specification of functional models, and later the integration of additional cloud resources to the functional model to obtain an operational model [22]. This is the approach followed in [12], where a Petrinet based performance model of Kubernetes is proposed. This model is finally annotated and configured with deterministic time, probability distributions, or functions obtained from monitoring data acquired from a concrete Kubernetes deployment, and the profiling of tasks executing on this infrastructure.

After this introduction that has shown the urgent need for modelling and simulation tools to support decision-making in the reorganization of health systems, Sect. 2 briefly reviews the related work. Section 3 summarizes our MDE approach based on formal models presented in previous papers, and puts it in the context of modelling health systems in situations of an epidemic episode. Then, Sect. 4 presents the basic primitives to model a health system and to define a modular and hierarchical model. In Sect. 5, we sketch models related with the perspectives related with epidemic episodes and show the process of elaboration of hierarchical models. Finally, conclusions are presented in Sect. 6.

2   Related Work

Modelling at different levels of abstraction implies to couple models at different scales, where microscopic levels interact with macroscopic levels and viceversa. *Recursive simulation* [16] provides a methodological approach. It consists in conducting simulations at the lower levels, which are launched to compute parameters useful for the higher base simulation. This is the approach followed in epidemiology [25], where models of individual behaviour to understand social behaviour are combined with health diffusion models to study the ease/disease spreading. In this case, different individual behaviours are simulated by DES models at the microscopic levels to provide parameters to the health diffusion models to observe the consequences at the macroscopic level. Complex models usually involve the combination of different models, such as in epidemiology where a system of differential equations defines the dynamics of the ease/disease spreading model. Differential equations models the emergent behavior of several interacting agents with different behaviors. Our work is compatible with these methodological approaches to combine different scale models and formalisms. However, we consider that it is possible to develop DES models of all these presented perspectives to obtain a more precise global model by coupling all perspective models, and allow the modeller to observe the effect of decisions in a more clear way. We consider out of the scope of this paper hybrid simulations and methodological approaches such as recursive simulation. To achieve our objective of a more precise model, our main focus is supporting the modelling and simulation of large scale DESs. Modelling and simulation at large scale is essential for improving the management of the own resources to support more efficient services and decision making, and providing high quality of services [21]. The synergic combination of simulation and formal models for functional, performance, and economical analysis are necessary for an efficient and reliable design and/or optimization.

Complex systems require large scale simulations that can be very demanding in terms of computational resources. This requirement has produced a growing interest in the use of Cloud for distributed simulation. However, important challenges has hampered the extensive use of distributed simulations, and therefore, the use of cloud computing by the simulation community. Current challenges of the discipline are presented in [11]. *Simulation Federations* promoted by the High Level Architecture (HLA) framework is the most extended approach to promote reusability and solve semantic interoperability in distributed simulations [7]. Model reuse and interoperability between them are prioritized at the cost of simulation efficiency, hidding computational resources to the programmer, and making difficult to prevent imbalances. Federation migration become a fundamental mechanism for large-scale distributed simulations. The other important approach to afford the complexity is the use of a MDE approach to increase productivity, and the role and semantic of languages used for modelling and supporting the MDE approach are relevant [23]. However, current approaches does not use formal languages, although in the 1990s, a significant number of works using PN were proposed [8,9]. A key aspect is the process to compile the PN specification to generate code for an efficient distributed interpretation of models, that support scalability and load balancing of workload during the simulation[2,3].

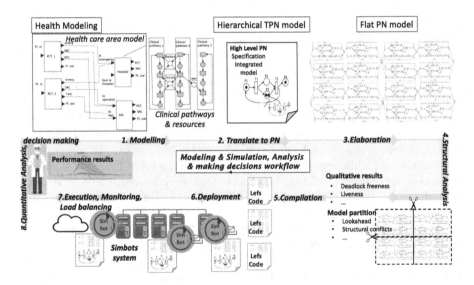

Fig. 1. Health systems modelling, distributed simulation, analysis and decision making workflow.

3   MDE for Developing Distributed Simulation of HS

Figure 1 summarizes the steps of our MDE approach based on formal models for the modelling and distributed simulation of large scale DES [2,3]: 1) Model complexity requires Domain Specific Languages to help the development of models in the scope of experts. Bernardi et al. [6] use UML activity diagram basic elements that are easy to understand for the medical doctors to define clinical guidelines and the way to transform them in Petri net models. Modular and hierarchical constructs allow to model complex organisations such health care areas that has been proposed as regional units of control of epidemic episodes. A health area includes Primary care teams (PCT), Specialized Attending Centers (SAC) and hospitals. The flow of patients throughout the structure of the area centers follows a sequence of treatments defined in medical protocols. These protocols uses the human and material resources of the centers [17]. 2) The definition of basic primitives promotes component reuse, which can be connected to configure according different health systems. Modular and hierarchical composition gives rise to a *hierarchical PN* model. 3) An *elaboration* process translates this high level PN specifications into a *flat model*, as it will be illustrated in Sect. 5. 4) The structural analysis of the flat model facilitates the initial partition of the model to distribute the simulation. Additionally, some structural properties of the PN can also be interpreted in medical terms such different protocols will not be blocked waiting for the same resource. 5) Model partitions are *compiled* into efficient code based on the idea of linear enabling function (LEF) presented in [3]. 6) *Partitions* are deployed in a system of *simbots*, the micro-kernels that provide the basic simulation services, including the simulation engine, the lefs code interpretation, and dynamic load balancing. 7) Finally, the results of simulation are collected for the decisions makers, which can decide redefine the model looking for a more efficient management of resources.

4   A PN Based Ontology for Modelling Complex Systems

Complex Systems are composed by a large number of components that are interrelated by complex processes. To manage the complexity, the modelling process of these systems require the stratification of process at different levels of abstraction, and the combination of multiple perspectives integrating them in a common simulation model. The simulation of the resultant model can scale if it can exploit concurrency and data dependencies, which require a careful analysis of the model to determine the existing opportunities to execute multiple activities at the same time, and to reduce data dependencies between the partitions of the model in a distributed simulation.

In this section, the basic modelling artifacts to define large scale DES models following a MDE approach based on the PN formalism is presented. In addition to facilitating the modelling of large complex DES, the objective is to generate an efficient scalable distribution of the model to handle a growing demand of computational resources. In order to define the abstractions we need systems models that have formal temporal, modular and hierarchical features and the availability of a scalable architecture. The formal temporal description of behaviour will be supported by **Timed PN**. The consideration of Timed PNs as formalism to represent behavior is based on its natural descriptive power of concurrency and the availability of analytic tools coming from the domain of Mathematical Programming and Graph Theory, which makes the formalism suitable to guide a MDE approach. Moreover, the formalism combine simulation and analysis techniques. **Object-orientation** supports computational mechanisms to implement modular and hierarchical systems [28]. Finally the availability of a scalable architecture for large-scale simulations requires and event driven execution model. The **actor model** based on asynchronous message passing will be the base for the design of large scale distributed simulations as unit of concurrency [5,14]. The actor model is an event driven model that scales to a large number of actors and removes the complexity of locking mechanisms. A single immutable interface that consists of a mailbox that buffers incoming messages, and a pattern based selection of messages to process them provides the flexibility for configuring different partitions.

PN is a formalism with simple primitives far from the level of abstraction required to model the complex behaviors in any application domain. In the same way, although object orientation support modular and hierarchical mechanisms, it is necessary to define first class primitives of the simulation modelling language to describe how a system is decomposed into subsystems.

4.1 Formalization of the Ontology-Driven Modelling and Simulation Framework

The resource allocation perspective is the most recurrent problem modelled and simulated to solve scheduling and planning problems, in the context of limited resource provisions [25]. A resource allocation system (RAS) is a discrete event system in which a finite set of concurrent processes shares in a competitive way a finite set of resources. By providing processes and resources as basic primitives it is possible to represent a large range of problems in different disciplines such as manufacturing [10], Software [26], Cloud [22], or healthcare [18] systems. Several analysis and control techniques in the PN literature are based on a structural element which characterizes deadlocks in many RAS models [26]. Multi-agent simulation follows a similar approach, where interacting autonomous processes interact in a specified environment and create an emergent behavior that reflects the dynamic behavior of the complex system under consideration [24]. To accomplish their tasks, agents interact in the context of competition/selection and scarcity of resource. Beyond processes and resources, the interaction between agents is supported by asynchronous communications channels, as they can be easily implemented on a wide-area network. Thus, we consider that most of the systems can be modelled by the the identification of three basic entities that compose a simulation model: *processes*, *resources* and *channels*.

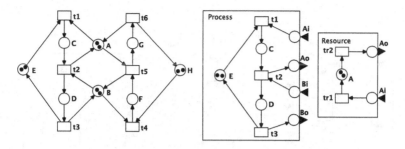

Fig. 2. Petri net and entities to model processes competing for resources.

RAS: Composition of Processes and Resources. In Fig. 2, the left PN shows sequential processes competing for resources. The first sequential process is represented by places C, D, E and transitions t1, t2, t3 that model an *automata*. This automata can represent a working process that describes the set of possible sequences of operations the system has to perform in order to manufacture a product, enact functional operations and transformations on data in a workflow, or follow clinical pathways developed and used by the medical staff in the hospital. Places F, G, H and transitions t4, t5, t6 represent the second sequential process. Tokens in places E represent two concurrent processes following the first sequential process, that can represent two parts that require the same working plan, two different data to be processed, or two patients to be attended in the hospital. The same happens with the two tokens in place H. Tokens in places A and B represent the availability of resources. By a system *resource* we mean an element of the system that is able to hold a product in a manufacturing system (i.e. for transport, operation, storage), a computational resource for processing a data, or a doctor or room to attend or host a patient. Figure 2 shows that two resources represented by a two tokens in places A and B can be used at each stage in the processes. The resource used when transition t1 is fired, is released by the process when the transition t2 is fired. Note that t1 and t5 are transitions in conflict, representing the two processes competing for the resources. If we have an arbitrarily large number of resources, the marking of these places does not limit the concurrent execution of the two modelled sequential processes, and then, these places can be removed. A place representing a resource with infinite capacity become an structural implicit place in Petri net terminology

Entities, Interface and Connections. Places, transitions and arcs are very low level primitives to represent a complex model. However processes and resources are the basics primitives to represent any RAS. In order to obtain the global model, basic primitives must be composed. These entities are the elements that describe the system modelling its interface by inputs and outputs. To enable the representation of the hierarchical modular model we adopts an ontological framework similar to the DEVs *System Entity Structure* (SES) [28], or the entities and architectures of VHDL. It is a declarative knowledge representation

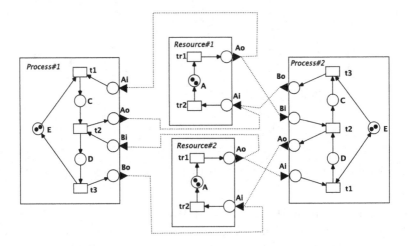

Fig. 3. Coupled component representing processes competing for resources.

scheme to structure models in terms of decompositions, coupling specifications and the generation of hierarchical simulation models. To build models from entities, the entity specification includes input and output ports that define the external interface of the component, and coupling relations. Coupling relations connect outputs with inputs. Hierarchical models are coupled models with components that may be atomic or coupled models. An entity can be an atomic entity without components, or a coupled entity with components.

Input, output ports, and interactions between components are translated to the PN model. PN models may be connected by merging transitions or places, and by means of new arcs [4]. Transition fusion can be interpreted as the execution of a joint activity, a *rendezvous* where each entity has only a partial view of the real activity and its constraints. Therefore, transition fusion represents channels of communication between processes. On the other side, a fusion of places can be interpreted as a resource that is shared between processes. The identification of processes, resources, and place fusion are the methodology to build RAS with PNs.

It is important to clarify that the semantics associated with the ports will be the result of the operations related to the fusion of transitions or places. Therefore the reader should not attempt to exactly translate the port concept presented in this paper with the port semantics in DEVS or VHDL. For instance, the DEVS and VHDL port have associated a type or value additionally to send or receive an event. In our model, transitions represent events or actions. The data received when the event is notified is related with the interpretation of the PN model. In the same way, the execution of the code associated with the fire of a transition is related with the semantic associated with the fire of a transition. Our main focus is the modelling and distributed execution of complex DES. Coupled processes are reluctant to scale in a distributed infrastructure. Orthogonal aspects such as time, or the representation of data and functions, can be implemented in any programming language and will be solved by the semantics of interpretation.

Figure 3 shows the process and resource entities to model behaviour represented by the left PN in Fig. 2. Graphical representation of entities and ports follows the DEVS notation, with boxes representing entities, and input and output arrows representing respectively input and output ports. Input ports are associated with places with not input arcs, and zero or one output arc. Output ports are associated with places with zero or one input arc, and not output arcs. The represented process uses resources in two stages, which requires to take the resources represented respectively by the A_i and B_i input ports, and release the resources represented respectively by the A_o and B_o output ports.

The resource is represented by only one place A with a token by each resource available. A resource entity must guarantee a conservative use of the resource. The resource in the figure has two transitions doing explicit the event of releasing the resource and the event of a process taking a resource. Alternatively, these additional transitions could be removed from the entity, and we could associate with the input and output port A_i and A_o to the place A.

Listing 1.1: JAVADEVS style code of entities and coupled entities.

```
1   // Atomic entities
    IOSubNetImpl subnet_p1= new IOSubNetImpl("process1");
3   subnet_p1.textualRepresentation("process");
    IOSubNetImpl subnet_p2= new IOSubNetImpl("process2");
5   subnet_p2.textualRepresentation("process");
    IOSubNetImpl subnet_r1= new IOSubNetImpl("resource1");
7   subnet_r1.textualRepresentation("resource");
    IOSubNetImpl subnet_r1= new IOSubNetImpl("resource2");
9   subnet_r1.textualRepresentation("resource");
    // Coupled entity
11  IOCoupledNetImpl GlobalNet =
         new IOCoupledNetImpl("processes_Resources");
13  netGlobal.add(process1);
    netGlobal.add(process2);
15  netGlobal.add(resource1);
    netGlobal.add(resource2);
17  // Coupling relations
    netGlobal.addCoupling(subnet_r1,"Ao",subnet_p1,"Ai");
19  netGlobal.addCoupling(subnet_p1,"Ao",subnet_r1,"Ai");
    netGlobal.addCoupling(subnet_r2,"Ao",subnet_p1,"Bi");
21  netGlobal.addCoupling(subnet_p1,"Bo",subnet_r1,"Bi");
    netGlobal.addCoupling(subnet_r1,"Ao",subnet_p2,"Ai");
23  netGlobal.addCoupling(subnet_p2,"Ao",subnet_r1,"Ai");
    netGlobal.addCoupling(subnet_r2,"Ao",subnet_p2,"Bi");
25  netGlobal.addCoupling(subnet_p2,"Bo",subnet_r1,"Bi");
```

A coupled entity is an aggregated entity composed by entities and coupling relationships. Listing 1.1 shows the code to declare the coupled component in a JAVADEVS style code. An IOSubNetImpl class is the Java implementation of an entity whose behaviour is specified by a PN. The PN specification is done in a textual file. Input and output places of the textual specification are mapped to input and output ports. In the code, lines 1 and 4 define the process entities called process1 and process2, and lines 6 and 8 define respectively the resources resource1 and resource2. Lines 3, 5, 7 and 9 show how to incorporate a textual PN specification to the entity. The name of input and output places defined in the textual specification are the names of input and output ports that define the entity interface.

The naming convention for hierarchical entities follows the usual dotted notation. Thus, the coupling relations between ports result in the fusion of places Process#1.Ai, Resource#1.Ao and Process#2.Bi that represent the competition for resources of Process#1 and Process#2.

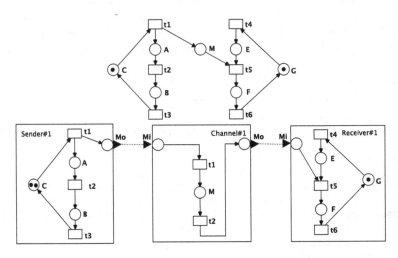

Fig. 4. Petri net and coupled entities to model processes communicating by a channel.

Channels: Composition of Processes by Asynchronous Messages. Systems are becoming progressively more complex since they are increasingly composed of connected entities. These systems are naturally understood and modelled as collection of interacting entities. These entities can be passive objects such as resources or active elements such as autonomous agents. These systems may be modelled as collections of interacting processes. Agent-based simulation, which adopts this approach, is one of the most relevant paradigms to design and implement distributed simulations [20]. Agents is a powerful metaphor, however there is not a clear definition of agent systems and most technologies related with intelligent agents are related with distributed systems [27], For this reason, although we refer to the agent terminology in this paper we will avoid to adopt it, considering our basic primitives are processes that communicate through a channel of communication.

Interactions implies the use of a *channel* that represents the synchronization of the internal behavior of entities. Transition fusion can represent that both processes engage simultaneously in the event represented by the transition. If buffering is required on a channel, this is achieved by interposing a buffer process between the two processes. If the buffer has a limited capacity, the channel can be modelled as a resource shared by sender and receiver. But in this case, it is an open loop, and there is not competition for the resource. Typically, the modeller thinks of the communication channel as a buffer of infinite capacity.

Top Fig. 4 shows two communicating processes and an asynchronous channel. Bottom part of figure shows the sender, receiver and an asynchronous channel components. Sender and receiver are connected by a channel component. The bottom coupled entity is defined connecting ports as illustrated in the figure. The coupling relation between ports `Sender#1.Mo` and `Channel#1.Mi` results in the fusion of places that represent the delivery of a message to the `Receiver#1` through the channel `Channel#1`, and the connection of `Channel#1.Mo` and `Receiver#1.Mi` port results in the fusion place that represent that the message is ready to be received.

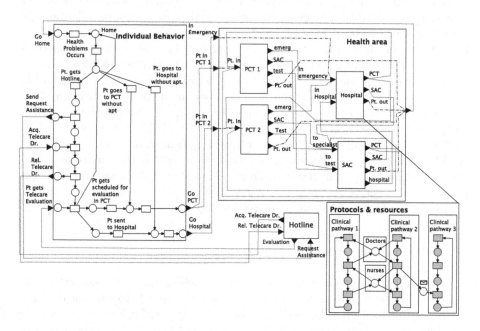

Fig. 5. PN and coupled entities to model processes communicating by a channel.

5   Elaboration Process of Modular and Hierarchical Petri Net Models for Simulation in the Cloud

A coupled entity has components and an interface defined by a set of input and output ports. Ports are mapped to ports of its components. This means that a coupled component can be part of another coupled component, and we can connect it with other parts of this upper coupled component. In this way, it is possible to define hierarchical composition of PN models. This hierarchical composition of PNs is illustrated in Fig. 5. The figure illustrate different coupled perspectives at different levels of abstraction of a HS to model an epidemic episode: the *individual behavior* that models patients that can decide to consult a *hotline*, or to go directly to use the services of the *health area*. The health area shows the connection of *PCTs*, *SAC* and the *hospital*. Each of these modules has its own *resources* and its defined *protocols* that guide the flow of patients. Medical records and test results are communicated between clinical pathways.

The result of the hierarchical composition of components result in a hierarchical TPN model. As it is illustrated in the Listing 1.1, components have a textual representation of the PN that specifies input and output ports. The definition of a coupled entity that aggregates entities and define coupling relationships results in a new textual flat specification that connect the textual representation of component by place fusion (step 3 of Fig. 1). The names of composed transitions and places are commonly structured as hierarchies to allow reuse of names in different contexts. The next code generation process is the compilation of the elaborated code. Entity information is essential to the partitioning process. For example, processes that share resources cannot be split because they include structural conflict, and the decision must be local in order to avoid an overhead of communications. On the other side, communication processes are the ideal processes for partitioning. A *Server name* is also essential to associate the hierarchical name that results from the elaboration of each transition, which represent an event, with the Lef code result of the compilation process. In this way, it is possible the user can interpret the logs resulting from simulations.

6   Conclusions and Future Work

This paper has proposed a framework for modelling different perspectives of healthcare systems and the process to translate the models to efficient code for distributed simulation. The novelty of our approach is the framework provide the basic primitives to model complex systems as communicating processes that compete for resources. The generation of efficient code for distributed simulation considering scalability and load balancing, allow domain experts to model all processes as discrete event systems, and simulate large scale models observing the coupled effect of different perspectives. In this way, the resulting global model provide an holistic experimental frame to derive results that could not be accurately addressed in any of the perspectives taken alone.

A prototype of the framework has been implemented. It provides the capability to build discrete event models and to simulate these models. The modelling language provides the basic primitives for composing models (processes, resources, and channels). The elaboration process is done in two steps, unfolding hierarchy and annotating semantic information important for the generated code, and then compiling the code as LEFs code to support scalability and load balancing.

Acknowledgments. This work was co-financed by the Aragonese Government and the European Regional Development Fund "Construyendo Europa desde Aragón" (COSMOS research group, ref. T35_17D); and by the Spanish program "Programa estatal del Generación de Conocimiento y Fortalecimiento Científico y Tecnológico del Sistema de I+D+i", project PGC2018-099815-B-100.

References

1. Reconfiguring health systems vital to tackling COVID-19 (2020). https://www.euro.who.int/en/countries/spain/news/news/2020/4/reconfiguring-health-systems-vital-to-tackling-covid-19
2. Arronategui, U., Bañares, J.Á., Colom, J.M.: Towards an architecture proposal for federation of distributed DES simulators. In: Djemame, K., Altmann, J., Bañares, J.Á., Agmon Ben-Yehuda, O., Naldi, M. (eds.) GECON 2019. LNCS, vol. 11819, pp. 97–110. Springer, Cham (2019). https://doi.org/10.1007/978-3-030-36027-6_9
3. Bañares, J.Á., Colom, J.M.: Model and simulation engines for distributed simulation of discrete event systems. In: Coppola, M., Carlini, E., D'Agostino, D., Altmann, J., Bañares, J.Á. (eds.) GECON 2018. LNCS, vol. 11113, pp. 77–91. Springer, Cham (2019). https://doi.org/10.1007/978-3-030-13342-9_7
4. Baumgarten, B.: On internal and external characterisations of PT-net building block behaviour. In: Rozenberg, G. (ed.) APN 1987. LNCS, vol. 340, pp. 44–61. Springer, Heidelberg (1988). https://doi.org/10.1007/3-540-50580-6_23
5. Beraldi, R., Nigro, L.: Distributed simulation of timed Petri nets. A modular approach using actors and Time Warp. IEEE Concurr. **7**(4), 52–62 (1999)
6. Bernardi, S., Colom, J.M., Albareda, J., Mahulea, C.: A model-based approach for the specification and verification of clinical guidelines. In: Proceedings of the 2014 IEEE Emerging Technology and Factory Automation, ETFA 2014, Barcelona, Spain, 16–19 September 2014, pp. 1–8 (2014)
7. Boukerche, A., Grande, R.E.D.: Optimized federate migration for large-scale HLA-based simulations. In: Proceedings of 12th IEEE/ACM International Symposium on Distributed Simulation and Real-Time Applications, pp. 227–235, October 2008
8. Chiola, G., Ferscha, A.: Distributed simulation of Petri nets. IEEE Concurr. **3**, 33–50 (1993)
9. Djemame, K., Gilles, D.C., Mackenzie, L.M., Bettaz, M.: Performance comparison of high-level algebraic nets distributed simulation protocols. J. Syst. Architect. **44**(6–7), 457–472 (1998)
10. Ezpeleta, J., Colom, J.M., Martínez, J.: A Petri net based deadlock prevention policy for flexible manufacturing systems. IEEE Trans. Robot. Autom. **11**(2), 173–184 (1995)
11. Fujimoto, R.M.: Research challenges in parallel and distributed simulation. ACM Trans. Model. Comput. Simul. **26**(4), 22:1–22:29 (2016)

12. Gracia, V.M., Tolosana-Calasanz, R., Bañares, J.Á., Arronategui, U., Rana, O.F.: Characterising resource management performance in kubernetes. Comput. Electr. Eng. **68**, 286–297 (2018)
13. Gunal, M.M.: A guide for building hospital simulation models. Health Syst. **1**(1), 17–25 (2012)
14. Haller, P.: On the integration of the actor model in mainstream technologies: the scala perspective. In: Agha, G.A., Bordini, R.H., Marron, A., Ricci, A. (eds.) Proceedings of the 2nd edition on Programming Systems, Languages and Applications Based on Actors, Agents, and Decentralized Control Abstractions, AGERE! 2012, 21–22 October 2012, Tucson, Arizona, USA, pp. 1–6. ACM (2012)
15. Ivorra, B., Fernández, M., Vela-Pérez, M., Ramos, A.: Mathematical modeling of the spread of the coronavirus disease 2019 (COVID-19) taking into account the undetected infections. The case of China. Commun. Nonlinear Sci. Numer. Simul. **88**, 105303 (2020)
16. Gilmer, J.B., Sullivan, F.J.: Issues in event analysis for recursive simulation. In: Proceedings of the 37th Winter Simulation Conference, Orlando, FL, USA, 4–7 December 2005, pp. 1234–1241. IEEE Computer Society (2005)
17. Mahulea, C., Garcia-Soriano, J., Colom, J.M.: Modular Petri net modeling of the Spanish health system. In: Proceedings of 2012 IEEE 17th International Conference on Emerging Technologies & Factory Automation, ETFA 2012, Krakow, Poland, 17–21 September 2012, pp. 1–8 (2012)
18. Mahulea, C., Garcia-Soriano, J., Colom, J.M.: Modular petri net modeling of the Spanish health system. In: Proceedings of 2012 IEEE 17th International Conference on Emerging Technologies & Factory Automation, ETFA 2012, Krakow, Poland, 17–21 September 2012, pp. 1–8. IEEE (2012)
19. Mastio, M., Zargayouna, M., Scemama, G., Rana, O.: Distributed agent-based traffic simulations. IEEE Intell. Transp. Syst. Mag. **10**(1), 145–156 (2018)
20. Mastio, M., Zargayouna, M., Scemama, G., Rana, O.: Two distribution methods for multiagent traffic simulations. Simul. Model. Pract. Theory **89**, 35–47 (2018)
21. Paščinski, U., Trnkoczy, J., Stankovski, V., Cigale, M., Gec, S.: QoS-aware orchestration of network intensive software utilities within software defined data centres. J. Grid Comput. **16**(1), 85–112 (2018)
22. Tolosana-Calasanz, R., Bañares, J.Á., Colom, J.M.: Model-driven development of data intensive applications over cloud resources. Futur. Gener. Comput. Syst. **87**, 888–909 (2018)
23. Topçu, O., Durak, U., Oğuztüzün, H., Yilmaz, L.: Distributed Simulation: A Model-Driven Engineering Approach. Springer International Publishing, Simulation Foundations, Methods and Applications (2016)
24. Topçu, O., Oğuztüzün, H.: Federate implementation: advanced. Guide to Distributed Simulation with HLA. SFMA, pp. 221–259. Springer, Cham (2017). https://doi.org/10.1007/978-3-319-61267-6_9
25. Traoré, M.K., Zacharewicz, G., Duboz, R., Zeigler, B.P.: Modeling and simulation framework for value-based healthcare systems. Simulation **95**(6), 481–497 (2019)
26. Tricas, F., Colom, J.M., Merelo Guervós, J.J.: Computing minimal siphons in Petri net models of resource allocation systems: an evolutionary approach. In: Proceedings of the International Workshop on Petri Nets and Software Engineering, Tunis, Tunisia, 23–24 June 2014, vol. 1160, pp. 307–322 (2014)

27. Wooldridge, M.J., Jennings, N.R.: Software engineering with agents: pitfalls and pratfalls. IEEE Internet Comput. **3**(3), 20–27 (1999)
28. Zeigler, B.P., Muzy, A., Kofman, E.: Theory of Modeling and Simulation: Discrete Event and Iterative System Computational Foundations, 3rd edn. Academic Press Inc., Cambridge (2018)

South Korea as the Role Model for Covid-19 Policies? An Analysis of the Effect of Government Policies on Infection Chain Structures

Alexander Haberling[1]([⊠]), Jakob Laurisch[2]([⊠]), and Jörn Altmann[3]([⊠])

[1] University of Mannheim, Mannheim, Germany
ahaberli@mail.uni-mannheim.de
[2] Dresden University of Technology, Dresden, Germany
jakob.laurisch@tu-dresden.de
[3] Seoul National University, Seoul, South Korea
jorn.altmann@acm.org

Abstract. The fast increase of Covid-19 cases led to high attention from local and international authorities to mitigate and reduce the propagation of the disease. Concerning the risks and the negative effects inflicted by the spread of the pandemic, many countries established a series of policies reinforcing public protection from the virus. With respect to these policies, this study characterizes the infection chain structure in Korea and identifies changes in the structure over time. Furthermore, using multiple linear regressions, the impact of government policy interventions on the infection chain structure is measured. The analysis shows a high fluctuation in infection chain structures at the beginning of the pandemic, which decreases with the implemented policies. The findings serve as a foundation for policymakers to evaluate the success of policies and strategies for reducing the diffusion of Covid-19 and to make optimized resource allocation decisions.

Keywords: Covid-19 · South Korea · Policy · Infection chain structure · Network analysis · Graph mining · Network diameter · Network diffusion · Time series analysis · Multiple linear regression

1 Introduction

The first cases of the novel corona-virus Sars-Cov-2 emerged near the end of 2019. After spreading rapidly through China, Korea, and many other countries, the World Health Organization (WHO) declared it a pandemic on March 11th, 2020 [13]. With an estimation of 7 billion infected people and 40 million deceased by the end of 2020 worldwide, assuming no countermeasures were implemented [10], national governments have been urged to find and implement effective and comprehensive responses [6,7]. As one of the countries praised for its successful

© Springer Nature Switzerland AG 2020
K. Djemame et al. (Eds.): GECON 2020, LNCS 12441, pp. 104–114, 2020.
https://doi.org/10.1007/978-3-030-63058-4_10

handling of the pandemic, Korea serves as a role model for pandemic policy worldwide.

The Korean Center for Disease Control & Prevention (KCDC) declared the first Covid-19 case in Korea on January 20th, 2020 [5]. During the following months, a variety of policies concerning immigration procedures, self-quarantine, mask distribution, and the educational sector were implemented [9]. Even though a lot of data was gathered by the KCDC, a comprehensive assessment of how effective the policies were to contain the Covid-19 pandemic is missing. This paper introduces a framework for characterizing the diffusion mechanisms of the pandemic and for measuring the effect of protective policies. By applying network analysis methods, the framework enhances existing methods to monitor the spread of diseases. In particular, this framework proposes a way to characterize infection chains by their network parameters, making resource allocation and decisions on adequate policies in time possible.

This paper shows that linking key events of a pandemic to changes in network parameters is possible. Additionally, a model analyzing the effect of legislative decisions on the network diameter is introduced. These provided tools enable policymakers and researchers to better understand and prevent the spread of Covid-19. The identification of growing infection chains helps to allocate resources (e.g., medical, computing, experts, medical staff) to areas where they are most needed and most effective.

1.1 Literature Review

To assess available measurement methods and understand legislation aimed at containing the disease, a literature review was conducted and resulted in the following observations. Eunha et al. [8] used publicly available patient data of South Korean cases to simulate a generalized growth model. Their results showed a reproduction number of 1.5, which quantifies the time-dependent variations in the average number of secondary cases generated per case, considering different intrinsic and extrinsic factors. They used an intrinsic growth rate of 0.6, describing the natural increase in population, and a scaling of growth parameter at 0.8, modeling exponential growth dynamics. Their findings also indicate a sub-exponential growth of Covid-19, four major clusters, and a crude case-fatality rate that was estimated to be increasing with older age. Chimmula and Lei [3] focused on the spread of the virus in Canada and made use of data provided by the John Hopkins University and Canadian health authorities. The development of a deep learning long short-term memory (LSTM), a recurrent neural network model frequently used for time-series predictions, enabled them to forecast the Covid-19 outbreak. Under certain conditions, they indicated a possible ending point of the outbreak at around June 2020.

With respect to policy research, Chang et al. [2] were concerned with the Covid-19 pandemic in Australia and calibrated an agent-based model to reproduce key characteristics of Covid-19 transmissions. Their results showed that intervention strategies such as travel restrictions, self-quarantining, and school closures were individually not bringing decisive benefits. Containment of the diffusion was only achieved when coupling several measures with a high level of social distancing compliance.

Wang et al. [11] conducted social network related research. They observed the network of relationships among patients and hospitals in the Chinese city Henan. Based on this, they estimated an average incubation time of 7.4 days, contrary to the 5–6 day estimate by the WHO [13], and identified 208 cases of cluster infections. As an recommendation for preventing the revival of the diffusion due to patients with long incubation times, the authors suggested a necessity for strong measures until the prevalence of the infection reduces dramatically.

1.2   Problem Description

Despite the impact of the inherent network structure of epidemics, only one research article could be found that analyzes the transmission structure of the underlying network of the Sars-CoV-2 virus, at the time of this research. The use of the network analysis methods to model Covid-19 diffusion mechanism is highly useful, as it allows identifying patterns of diffusion at an early stage. This knowledge allows governments to keep the Covid-19 diffusion under control and protect the society from further spreading of the virus.

Identifying patterns of diffusion of the virus and understanding how it can be contained with specific policies are the main objectives of this research.

In order to achieve that, infection chains are identified and their network structure is quantified with respect to Covid-19 policies. The resulting network measurements are analyzed over time, to identify the changes in the infection chain structure with respect to the policies in place and to identify the most effective policies.

The remaining paper is organized into three sections: the description of the methodology applied, the analysis of the data, and a brief discussion of the results.

2   Methodology

To quantify the infection chain structure, all network components of the network of infections are extracted. A component represents all infected people (i.e., cases) that can be linked with each other. Linking cases requires the analysis of past movements, activities, and interactions of infected people with other people. Figure 1 depicts an exemplary component (i.e., an infection chain). Components with only one infected person represent isolated cases, which could not be linked to other cases.

For the resulting directed trees, the component diameter, which is defined as the longest shortest path between any two nodes in a network, is calculated according to Eq. 1. With respect to the Covid-19 infections, the component diameter represents the upper limit for the length of the infection chain. Thereby, the length of the diameter is a representation of how far the virus spreads through the population without being detected. Components with a small diameter represent the successful early isolation of patients and the mitigation of further

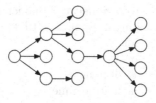

Fig. 1. Exemplary infection chain with diameter 6

infections. The earlier the infection chain is cut, the fewer victims will be claimed by the pandemic. The feasibility of using the chain diameter for policy evaluation is grounded in the imperfect nature of tracking Covid-19 cases. What is most likely one huge infection chain in reality is represented as many fractured chains in the available data sets. With this approach, deriving legislative actions from incomplete data is made possible.

As the network diameter represents the depth of the infection chain, it is preferred to other available network parameters (e.g., the average out-degree, which represents the width of the infection chain). The depth of the infection chain is important due to the rapid spreading of the virus, which requires authorities to be able to act quickly after the discovery of cases.

$$Diameter = max(d(u,v)|u,v \in C) \tag{1}$$

$d(u,v)$ = geodesic distance between the nodes u and v
C = the nodes in a network component

Changes in the infection chain structure over time are analyzed by calculating the average network diameter (Eq. 2) for each day. By averaging over the number of active chains, the changing amount of network components is taken into account for the calculation of the network diameter. This way, the diffusion of the pandemic can be compared over different time periods.

$$AverageDiameter_t = \frac{1}{N_t} * \sum_{i=1}^{N_t} Diameter_{i,t} \tag{2}$$

i = network component
t = time
N_t = number of active network components at time t

An estimation of correlations between Covid-19 related government policies and structural changes over time in the extracted network components is performed with multiple linear regressions following Eq. 3. This linear regression is designed to compare the focal policy with all other policies that are at work at the same time period.

$$y_{t+t^*} = \beta_0 + \beta_s * x_{s,t} + \beta_{\neg s} * \sum_{p,p \neq s}^{P} x_{p,t} + \epsilon_t \quad with \ s,p \in P \tag{3}$$

$$y = \text{average network diameter}$$
$$x = \text{status of policy} \in \{0, 1\}$$
$$p = \text{policy}$$
$$s = \text{focal policy}$$
$$P = \text{set of policies}$$
$$t^* = \text{incubation time}$$

Choosing the average component diameter at time $t + 14$ as the dependent variable accounts for the prescribed quarantine that most countries require for infected individuals [12]. To model the influence of virus-related legislation, the binary variable x_t indicates for each time step t whether a policy is active or not, with x_s representing the status of the focal policy and x_p representing all other policies. The model results in the estimation of β_s, representing the effect of the focal policy s on the average network diameter, $\beta_{\neg s}$, representing the effect of all other policies, and β_0, the y-intercept. Analyzing the values of these coefficients allows for the inference on the relative effect of s on the infection chain structure.

3   Analysis

3.1   Data Set

The data set used is provided by the KCDC [5] and the Data Science for Covid-19 (DS4C) project team [4]. It consists of various sub data sets that contain information on patient-level, as well as macro-level information on population movements, weather, and legislation. In this paper, two sub data sets on patient information and government policy, namely 'PatientInfo.csv' [4] and 'Policy.csv' [4] are used. The former is mostly restricted to patients outside of Daegu, since the local government of Daegu does not provide respective information [4].

The policy data set includes 53 policy decisions categorized in the subsections of 'Alert', 'Immigration', 'Health', 'Social', 'Education', 'Technology' and 'Administrative'. The data set on patient information contains the patient ID, the demographics of the patient, and the patient ID of the infecting patient for the period from January 26th, 2020 to May 12th, 2020.

Overall the patient data set contains information about 3519 patients and 829 transmissions from provinces all around South Korea, namely: Gyeongsangbuk-do, Gyeonggi-do, Seoul, Chungcheongnam-do, Busan, Gyeongsangnam-do, Incheon, Daegu, Gangwon-do, Sejong, Chungcheongbuk-do, Ulsan, Daejeon, Gwangju, Jeollabuk-do, Jeollanam-do, Jeju-do. The provinces are sorted in descending order of the number of cases.

3.2   Descriptive Network Analysis

The complete network extracted using the whole time window displays an average out-degree of 0.78 and is considered very sparse with a density of 0.0014%. It consists of 244 components, representing the infection chains. The average chain size is 4.37 with the largest chain containing 67 cases and the smallest chain 2 cases. The average diameter of the chains is 1.33 ranging from a diameter of 1 to 6. The variance of the diameter is 0.52, with a standard deviation of 0.72. Its median and mode fall on 1.

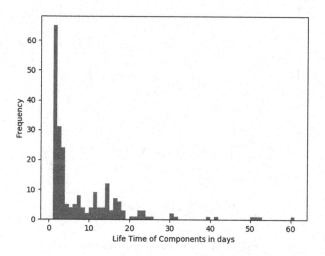

Fig. 2. Histogram of the component lifetime in days

The time between the first and the last confirmed infection of a component is considered its lifetime and averages around 6.99 days. The longest lifetime in the data set is 61 days, while the shortest is within a single day. Figure 2 provides more details on the distribution of the component lifetimes. The bin of the shown graph is 1.

Figure 3 displays the daily average diameter of all active chains. A infection chain is considered to be active during all days between the dates of its first and last confirmed case. Figure 4 displays the daily number of active chains and provides context to the dynamics of the daily average diameter.

The volatile growth in the early stages of the virus diffusion in Fig. 3 is followed by a steep decline. This can be explained by the prominent case of –patient 31–, the first patient labeled as a super spreader, accused of starting the cluster infections in the Shincheonji Church and Daegu [1], as well as by the increase in testing in Korea. Government efforts, involving a major increase in testing supplies and facilities, screening clinics, and the introduction of newly developed, more efficient, testing kits [1], enabled finding more infected people that were not related to previous components. As a result, the number of active chains increased rapidly (Fig. 4). In the following weeks, the daily average diameter levels off around a value of 1. The end of the time series is characterized by a sudden peak and an even steeper decline in the daily average Diameter. These outliers are also better understood by considering Fig. 4. The steep increase of the daily average diameter is caused by a steep decline in the number of active chains. The fewer chains are active, the less the daily average of these chains is

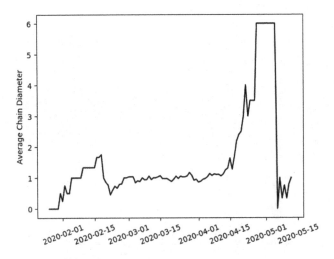

Fig. 3. Average diameter over time

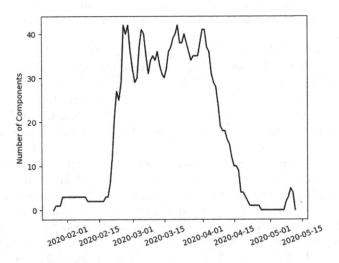

Fig. 4. Number of active components over time

regularized. At the highest point of Fig. 3 only one chain remains active. The chain with the highest diameter in the data set. The rock bottom is reached afterward, when this last active chain goes inactive, resulting in zero active components and, hence, a daily average diameter of zero.

The mean of all daily calculated average diameters is reported as 1.53 ranging from 6, when only the longest chain is active in a day, to 0 when no chain is active in a day. The variance is 2.3 with a standard deviation of 1.52. Both median and mode are 1.

3.3 Regression Analysis

To quantify the relationship between policy decisions and the daily average diameter, the regression model is employed. It assesses the effect of one policy (β_s) compared to the effect of all other policies ($\beta_{\neg s}$). This model has been estimated for all 53 policies listed in the data set.

In order to prevent the distortion of the regression estimation, the highly volatile end of the time frame was excluded. The time window used for the regression analysis spans from January 26th, 2020 to April 12th, 2020.

Table 1 displays the four legislative decisions that show a significant correlation with the daily average diameter, while the effects of the reference legislation do not. The estimated parameters of the four policies are identical, since all were passed on the same day and span the same time period. The negative β_s-coefficient of -0.1740 indicates a mitigating effect on the infection chain length.

Table 1. Regression models of significant focal policies

Policy	β_0	β_s	$\beta_{\neg s}$	R^2
Immigration HongKong	1.1207^{***}	-0.1740^*	0.0023	0.081
Immigration Macau	1.1207^{***}	-0.1740^*	0.0023	0.081
EM[1] kit authorization 1	1.1207^{***}	-0.1740^*	0.0023	0.081
Diagnosis app	1.1207^{***}	-0.1740^*	0.0023	0.081

[1]Emergency

Table 2 displays the models, in which the reference policies $\beta_{\neg s}$ are correlated with the average diameter. A negative β_s-coefficient of -0.4702 indicates a mitigating effect on the length of infection chains.

With these regressions, it was shown that it is possible to characterize Covid-19 infection chains with the help of network parameters. The dynamics of the daily average diameter was successfully linked to key events in Korea's Covid-19 course. In spite of major limitations (Sect. 4.2), the implemented model was useful to identify policies that show a mitigating effect on the daily average diameter and, thereby, on the length of infection chains.

Table 2. Regression Models of Significant Focal Policies and Significant Reference Policies

Policy	β_0	β_s	$\beta_{\neg s}$	R^2
Immigration China	1.3609^{***}	-0.4702^{***}	0.0047^*	0.438
EM[1] kit authorization 1	1.3609^{***}	-0.4702^{***}	0.0047^*	0.438

[1]Emergency

4   Conclusion

In this paper, Covid-19 infection chains are characterized by component diameters. Changes in the component structure are analyzed by taking the daily average diameter. The resulting time-series shows large fluctuation at the beginning of the observation period. For the majority of the observed time frames, the diameter fluctuates around the value of 1. The last weeks are characterized by two outliers. Using a multiple linear regression model, 4–6 policies are identified that show a mitigating effect on infection chain length, implicating a high influence on the prevention of spreading of the virus.

4.1   Contributions

The framework proposed in this paper provides the first step towards an in-depth analysis of the network properties of the infection chain structure of Covid-19 in Korea. It proposes a way to predict how the length of infection chains and, thereby, the state of diffusion of the pandemic is impacted through legislation.

This is useful for policymakers and researchers that want to understand the transmission and containment of the Covid-19 disease. It enables them to identify effective policies that could stop the rapid spread of the virus. These approaches could be used to compare the pandemic policies between countries and suggest measures for countries that struggle to contain the disease.

Furthermore, the results help designing mechanisms for allocating resources (e.g., medical, computing, experts, medical staff) to areas where there are components with large diameters. These components represent a large spike in demand for resources. Knowing the number of large components and their location will help to make better use of the available resources.

4.2   Limitations and Future Work

The research presented in this article comes with a few limitations that are listed in the following paragraphs. At the same time, these limitations allow for sophisticated extensions of this research.

First, the analysis of the network diameter over time is performed on the average value for every point in time t, the structure of the used data inheres a highly volatile daily average diameter in the last fraction of the time window (Sect. 3.1). When applying the regression model (3) to the whole time window, the volatility of these outliers will bias the estimated correlation of policies implemented in the later stage of the time series. Future efforts need to handle this bias by regularizing the daily average diameter in a different way.

Second, the lack of a control group, consisting of infection chains that are not affected by policies limits the regression model. The significance of focal policies can only be accessed relative to all other placed policies.

Third, the implemented model allows identifying legislation that is correlated with a shrinking infection chain length. However, policies that display a positive significant correlation might be of interest as well. When estimated with a control group, some of these policies might display a mitigating effect. For dealing with the lack of a control group based on empirical data, simulating the unhindered spread of the virus and, hence, creating a control group with no placed policies might also be a promising way.

Forth, for this paper, the only network measurement applied is the daily average component diameter. While it provides a good evaluation of the infection chain structure, further network measurements such as component size or degree centrality could provide additional information. Focusing on infection rates of chains by analyzing the average time needed for an infection to take place may grant interesting insights as well.

Fifth, the explainability of infection chain structure by other attributes, such as demographic information of the patients or the weather of the infection day, could provide a deeper understanding of the reproduction mechanisms of Covid-19 and allow controlling noise in the dependent variable.

Finally, it is important to take into account, that this study has been conducted in the midst of the Covid-19 pandemic, for which no long-term data on the infection development is available. With more data available in the future, analysis results will assumably improve.

Acknowledgements. We would also like to thank the reviewers of this article, who gave highly valuable feedback for improving our research. Furthermore, we are grateful for the initial discussions and contributions of Antoine Marie Zacharie Kundimana. This research has partly been supported by the Institute of Engineering Research at Seoul National University, which provided research facilities.

References

1. Center For Strategic & International Studies: A Timeline of South Korea's response to COVID-19. https://www.csis.org/analysis/timeline-south-koreas-response-covid-19. Accessed 5 Jun 2020
2. Chang, S.L., et al.: Modelling transmission and control of the Covid-19 pandemic in Australia. arXiv preprint arXiv:2003.10218 (2020)
3. Chimmula, V.K.R., Zhang, L.: Time series forecasting of Covid-19 transmission in Canada using LSTM networks. Chaos, Solitons Fractals **135**, 109864 (2020)
4. Kaggle: Data Science for Covid-19 (DS4C): DS4C Data science for COVID-19 in South Korea. https://www.kaggle.com/kimjihoo/coronavirusdataset. Accessed 5 Jun 2020

5. Korea centers for disease control & prevention. http://www.cdc.go.kr/cdc_eng. Accessed 5 Jun 2020
6. Perc, M., et al.: Forecasting Covid-19. Frontiers Phys. **8**, 127 (2020)
7. Sahasranaman, A., Kumar, N.: Network structure of Covid-19 spread and the Lacuna in India's testing strategy. Available at SSRN 3558548 (2020)
8. Shim, E., et al.: Transmission potential and severity of Covid-19 in South Korea. Int. J. Infect. Dis. **93**, 339–344 (2020)
9. The Government of the Republic of Korea: How Korea responded to a pandemic using ICT: Flattening the curve on COVID-19. http://www.undp.org/content/seoul_policy_center/en/home/presscenter/articles/2019/flattening-the-curve-on-covid-19.html. Accessed 7 Jun 2020
10. Walker, P., et al.: Report 12: the global impact of Covid-19 and strategies for mitigation and suppression. Imperial College London (2020)
11. Wang, P., et al.: Statistical and network analysis of 1212 Covid-19 patients in Henan, China. Int. J. Infect. Dis. **95**, 391–398 (2020)
12. World Health Organization: Coronavirus disease 2019 (Covid-19) situation report - 73. https://www.who.int/docs/default-source/coronaviruse/situation-reports/20200402-sitrep-73-Covid-19.pdf. Accessed 6 Jun 2020
13. World Health Organization: Rolling updates on coronavirus disease (COVID-19). https://www.who.int/emergencies/diseases/novel-coronavirus-2019/events-as-they-happen. Accessed 6 Jun 2020

Dependability and Sustainability

A Network Reliability Game

Patrick Maillé[1]([⊠])[iD] and Bruno Tuffin[2][iD]

[1] IMT Atlantique, IRISA, Rennes, France
patrick.maille@imt.fr
[2] Inria, Univ Rennes, CNRS, IRISA, Rennes, France
bruno.tuffin@inria.fr

Abstract. In an ad hoc network, accessing a point depends on the participation of other, intermediate, nodes. Each node behaving selfishly, we end up with a non-cooperative game where each node incurs a cost for providing a reliable connection but whose success depends not only on its own reliability investment but also on the investment of nodes which can be on a path to the access point. Our purpose here is to formally define and analyze such a game: existence of an equilibrium output, comparison with the optimal cooperative case.

Keywords: Reliability investment · Game theory · Interactions

1 Introduction: Problem Definition

We consider a topology with nodes wishing to be connected to a network access point. If from a node there is no direct connection to the access point, the connection has to be routed through other nodes. The feasibility/success/quality you experience as a node therefore depends on the quality you provide yourself, but also on the participation of peers to the network.

This type of problem has many applications. Typical, but non-exhaustive, ones are:

- An ad hoc network [9], which is a network without any fixed infrastructure where nodes serve as relays for their neighbors. Such an organization presents the advantages of being decentralized, and of incurring no deployment cost since relying on the collaboration and willingness to participate of nodes. Practical applications of those networks include army tactical ad hoc networks for a fast deployment and operation in a war context when no fix/wireless network exists, smartphone ad hoc networks not requiring the traditional wireless carriers, vehicular ad hoc networks for autonomous vehicles, sensor networks, etc. Investment/participation of nodes is a key issue for the success of those applications.
- Security/reliability issues: nodes in a network can be subject to (stochastic) failures reducing the path possibilities to the target. There may also be attacks on some nodes, rendering paths to the target through infected nodes not

K. Djemame et al. (Eds.): GECON 2020, LNCS 12441, pp. 117–125, 2020.
https://doi.org/10.1007/978-3-030-63058-4_11

practicable. Investing on security procedures limits the infection risks but incurs a cost; this trade-off and the impact on the whole system in the case of selfish nodes require attention.

The natural modeling framework is that of non-cooperative game theory [2,6]. In the literature, security and related investment games have been studied quite a lot; see for instance [4,5] and the references therein. Security and free riding have been studied in [10]. The closest paper to ours is [3], where a general framework for security investment is provided, with functional interactions between nodes. Our model fits that framework in general, but we focus here on something more specific, and our utility functions are different, hence the results in [3] need to be adapted.

Our contribution is the following: we design a graph model with nodes as players and links corresponding to possible direct connections between nodes. Each node is subject to failures and has to set up its reliability for a given cost. On the other hand, each node is interested in the existence (in probability) of a path to the target access node, meaning that its service quality also depends on the others' choices. Our specificity in this game-theoretic context is therefore the use of the so-called static reliability analysis which computes the probability of such a valid path. Numerous methods exist for this NP-hard problem, efficient Monte Carlo simulation being applied in the case of large networks [1,8]. We show how this problem can be analyzed, with specific results.

The remaining of the paper is organized as follows. Section 2 describes the formal mathematical model we are going to analyze and the goals of the paper. Section 3 presents two illustrative examples, helpful to grasp the stakes and difficulties at hand, as well as some results on the Price of Anarchy, measuring the loss of efficiency due to selfishness. The general results on the output of the game are presented in Sect. 4, and Sect. 5 concludes the paper by giving directions of future research.

2   Model

2.1   Graph Model

We consider an undirected connected graph $\mathcal{G} = (\mathcal{N}, \mathcal{L})$ where $\mathcal{N} = \{0, 1, \ldots, n\}$ is the set of nodes, and $\mathcal{L}$ is the set of links/possible connections between nodes. Node 0 is the unique access node, that all other nodes (players) wish to connect to. Links are assumed to always work, but nodes 1 to n are subject to (independent) failures, due to vulnerabilities, attacks, etc. The access node is assumed perfect. Let r_i be the probability to be up for Node i, and $q_i = 1 - r_i$. A configuration of the graph is given by a vector $X = (X_1, \ldots, X_n)$ where $X_i = 1$ if i is up and 0 if it is down. Retaining only the set $\mathcal{N}'$ of "up" nodes, we obtain a random partial graph $\mathcal{G}' = (\mathcal{N}', \mathcal{L})$.

Node i is interested in the probability R_i that in $\mathcal{G}'$ there is a path connecting i to 0. This type of problem has been extensively studied [1,8]; basically,

$$R_i = \sum_{x \in \{0,1\}^n} \Psi_i(x) \mathbb{P}[X = x] = \sum_{x \in \{0,1\}^n} \Psi_i(x) \prod_{j=1}^n (r_j x_j + q_j(1 - x_j))$$

where $\Psi_i(x)$ is 0 if there no path in the subgraph $\mathcal{G}'$ corresponding to configuration x (a vector $(x_1, ..., x_n)$ where $x_i = 1$ means Node i is up), and 1 if there is at least one such path. R_i is easy to compute analytically for small topologies, as a finite sum, but it is in general an NP-hard problem for which approximation methods, among which efficient simulation algorithms, must be used for large topologies. See [1,8] for a general description of the methodologies. Since it is not the purpose of the present paper, we assume that how to get a sufficiently accurate estimation is known.

2.2 Utility Functions

We assume that Node i has a valuation $f_i(R_i)$ for the service, depending on the probability to get a connection to the access point. Each function f_i is assumed increasing: the larger the quality/reliability, the more it is appreciated, and f_i is also assumed concave, a usual and reasonable assumption to express that getting a given reliability amount when you are at a low level is seen more valuable than when you are at a high level.

Node i is also assumed to experience a cost $c_i(r_i)$ to maintain a level r_i of reliability/security/quality of its own equipment. Function c_i is assumed increasing too, and strictly convex, with $c_i(0) = 0$ and $\lim_{r \to 1} c_i(r) = \infty$, again standard assumptions.

The utility u_i of Node i is then

$$u_i(r_1, \ldots, r_n) = f_i(R_i) - c_i(r_i)$$

where we recall that R_i is a function of $r = (r_1, \ldots, r_n)$.

We end up with a non-cooperative game where each node i plays with the level of investment resulting in (equivalent) reliability r_i, but his/her strategy impacts the valuation of other nodes.

2.3 Questions to Be Answered

From the definition of this problem, here are the questions we aim at answering:

- What is the outcome of the game? Does a Nash equilibrium exist? If yes, is it unique?
- How does the output compare with a cooperative situation? This is evaluated by computing the *Price of Anarchy* (PoA), measuring how the efficiency of a system degrades due to selfish behavior of its players, and defined as the ratio of the optimal social utility to the worst social utility at a Nash equilibrium (the social utility being the sum of utilities over all players).

3   Examples

3.1   A Simple Example with Non-Trivial Interactions Among Nodes

Consider the topology described in Fig. 1 where each node $i \in \{1, \ldots, 4\}$ wants to be connected to node 0. We let $c_i(x) = \alpha \frac{x}{1-x}$ for a constant $\alpha > 0$, and $f_i(x) = x$, which verifies the assumptions listed in the previous section.

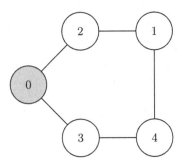

Fig. 1. A simple topology

Since Node i is on all paths to Node 0, reliability R_i can be expressed as $R_i = r_i R_i'$ where R_i' is the probability that there is a path from Node i to Node 0 when i is operational, and R_i' does not depend on r_i.

To compute the best response of Node i, we differentiate $u_i = r_i R_i' - \alpha \frac{r_i}{1-r_i}$ with respect to r_i. It gives the optimal value (with $x^+ = \max(x, 0)$)

$$r_i = \left[1 - \sqrt{\alpha/R_i'} \right]^+ . \tag{1}$$

For Nodes 2 and 3 at distance 1 of node 0, hence with $R_i' = 1$, we then get $r_i = 0$ if $\alpha \geq 1$ (that is, the investment cost is too high and the node prefers not to participate), and $1 - \sqrt{\alpha}$ otherwise.

Let us look at Nodes 1 and 4 now. Observe that we have $R_1' = r_2 + (1 - r_2) r_3 r_4$ and $R_4' = r_3 + (1 - r_3) r_2 r_1$. The utility of one node depends on the reliability choice of the other, therefore we have a game between nodes 1 and 4. Looking for the solution, we try to solve the system of equations

$$\begin{cases} \frac{\partial u_1}{\partial r_1} = r_2 + (1 - r_2) r_3 r_4 - \frac{\alpha}{(1-r_1)^2} = 0 \\ \frac{\partial u_4}{\partial r_4} = r_3 + (1 - r_3) r_2 r_1 - \frac{\alpha}{(1-r_4)^2} = 0, \end{cases}$$

giving $r_1 = 1 - \sqrt{\dfrac{\alpha}{r_2 + (1 - r_2) r_3 r_4}}$ and $r_4 = 1 - \sqrt{\dfrac{\alpha}{r_3 + (1 - r_3) r_2 r_1}}$. Solving it is intractable in general, but we can easily get numerical results. Examples of solutions in terms of α are given in Table 1. The lower the cost, the higher the reliability.

Table 1. Some numerical results in terms of α for the example of Sect. 3.1

α	$r_2 = r_3$	$r_1 = r_4$
0.3	0.4522774425	0.2330400670
0.1	0.6837722340	0.6517825785
0.01	0.9	0.8990317600
0.001	0.9683772234	0.9683460395
0.0001	0.99	0.9899990048

For this example with homogeneous utility valuations and costs, it is interesting to see that all r_i are converging to 1 as $\alpha \to 0$: the lower the investment cost, the better it is to participate because there is a gain at no cost.

But we can say more when α tends to 0:

$$r_1 = r_4 = 1 - \sqrt{\alpha}/\sqrt{(1 - \sqrt{\alpha})(1 + r_1\sqrt{\alpha})} = 1 - \sqrt{\alpha}(1 + o(1))$$

where the $o(\cdot)$ is for $\alpha \to 0$. This yields $r_1 = r_2 + o(\sqrt{\alpha})$. Hence the r_i are asymptotically equivalent, even in relative terms if we consider the difference with respect to 1 (the failure probabilities) since $1 - r_1 = \sqrt{\alpha} + o(\sqrt{\alpha}) = 1 - r_2 + o(1 - r_2)$, i.e., $\frac{1-r_1}{1-r_2} = 1 + o(1)$.

Finally, we can look at what would happen if the nodes were collaborating, that is, if they were trying to maximize the social utility defined as

$$\sum_{i=1}^{4} u_i = r_2 + r_3 + r_1(r_2 + (1 - r_2)r_3r_4) + r_4(r_3 + (1 - r_3)r_2r_1) - \alpha \sum_{i=1}^{4} \frac{r_i}{1 - r_i}.$$

Getting the global optimum for $(r_1, \ldots, r_4) \in [0, 1]^4$ seems intractable, but we can easily get numerical values again. Table 2 displays for the same values of α as in Table 1 the maximum value of $\sum_{i=1}^{4} u_i$, the corresponding r_is, and the Price of Anarchy, that is that optimal value divided by the value of $\sum_{i=1}^{4} u_i$ at equilibrium. Note that the PoA is necessarily larger than 1. It is interesting to note that the Price of Anarchy is close to one. It also seems to converge to 1 as $\alpha \to 0$. In other words, selfishness of nodes does lead to negligible losses with respect to the cooperative case, particularly as α is close to 0.

3.2 A Simple Example with Unbounded Price of Anarchy

We introduce here another simple example, where the interactions among nodes do not really form a game (only one node affects the others), but the example illustrates what can happen in terms of the Price of Anarchy.

Let us consider the topology of Fig. 2, with only Node 1 directly connected to the target node, and Nodes 2 to n only connected to Node 1. The Nash equilibrium is easy to compute, since the actions of Nodes 2 to n only affect

Table 2. Social Optimum and Price of Anarchy in terms of α for the example of Sect. 3.1

α	Optimum $(r_1 = r_4, r_2 = r_3)$	$\sum_{i=1}^4 u_i$	PoA
0.3	(0.3445638958, 0.5265329288)	0.4924406891	1.06014
0.1	(0.6842015722, 0.7383790483)	1.670241284	1.021059
0.01	(0.9027739526, 0.90999676)	3.208617313	1.000922
0.001	(0.9687904071, 0.969673)	3.747335781	1.0000352
0.0001	(0.9900470095, 0.9900)	3.920006440	1.000000122

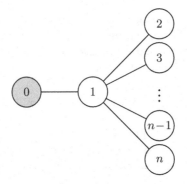

Fig. 2. A specific topology with $n+1$ nodes

themselves and not Node 1. For Node 1, from (1) the Nash equilibrium (NE) strategy is simply

$$r_1 = \left[1 - \sqrt{\alpha}\right]^+ := x^{\text{NE}}.$$

Then Nodes 2 to n all see $R_i' = r_1$, and therefore they all set, again from (1)

$$r_2 = \cdots = r_n = \left[1 - \sqrt{\frac{\alpha}{\left[1 - \sqrt{\alpha}\right]^+}}\right]^+ := y^{\text{NE}}.$$

Now, let us investigate the globally optimal choices. By symmetry, Nodes 2 to n should set the same reliability level y, and if we denote by x the reliability of Node 1, the objective function is

$$\sum_{i=1}^n u_i = x - \alpha \frac{x}{1 - x} + (n - 1)\left(xy - \alpha \frac{y}{1 - y}\right), \tag{2}$$

which gives $y = \left[1 - \sqrt{\frac{\alpha}{x}}\right]^+$, and can be plugged into (2) to compute the optimal x (we do this numerically to avoid cumbersome algebra). But we can already notice that the Price of Anarchy is unbounded in general: if we take $\alpha = 0.49$, at equilibrium Node 1 selects $r_i = 1 - \sqrt{\alpha} = 0.3$ which leads all the other nodes to select $r_i = 0$, so the social utility is $u_1^{NE} = 0.09$. On the other hand, the optimal social utility is at least the one we would reach with $r_1 = 0.9$ and $r_2 = r_3 = ... = r_n = 0.3$, which equals $-3.57 + 0.06n$, hence the Price of Anarchy is at least $\frac{2}{3}n - 40$, which increases linearly with n.

To treat our example for a more general set of parameters, Fig. 3 shows the equilibrium and globally optimal strategies of Node 1, and of Nodes 2 to n. The corresponding costs are computed according to (2), and are compared through the Price of Anarchy. As in the previous example, the Price of Anarchy tends to 1 when α tends to 0 (if the cost of reliability is null, all nodes should select r_i close to 1, both at equilibrium and at the socially optimal outcome).

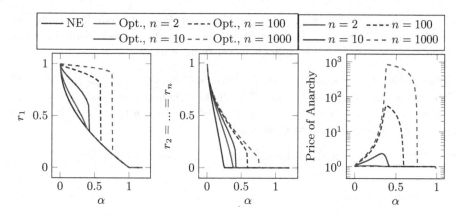

Fig. 3. Equilibrium and globally optimal strategies for Node 1 *(left)* and for the other nodes *(center)*, and Price of Anarchy *(right)*, for the instance of Fig. 2.

4   Analytical Results

While the previous section was dealing with instructive examples, we provide here general results towards the analysis of Nash equilibria and the resulting outcome.

A first result, observed on the examples in the previous section, is about the nodes directly connected to the access point (Node 0):

Proposition 1. *For nodes at distance 1 from Node 0, the decision does not depend on other nodes.*

Proof. It comes from the fact that for such nodes, $R'_i = 1$ because there is a direct link between i and 0.

We now get interested in the Nash equilibria of the game. Since Nash equilibria are fixed-points of best-response correspondences, we first provide results on best-responses.

Proposition 2. *If f_i is concave and c_i is strictly convex, Node i has a unique best response in $[0, 1)$.*

Proof. Note that R_i is a linear function of r_i (actually $R_i = r_i R_i'$ with R_i' the reliability of the random subgraph where both nodes 0 and i are perfect, and R_i' does not depend on r_i). As a consequence $u_i(r_1, \dots, r_n)$ is strictly concave in r_i, hence the result.

Proposition 3. *The game has at least one Nash Equilibrium.*

Proof. It is a direct consequence of Rosen's theorem with concave utility functions, with action sets on a compact, here $[0, 1]$ for each player.

This is similar to what was shown in [3], something expected. Regarding the equilibrium uniqueness, we can apply existing results to express a sufficient condition, but that condition is difficult to verify in practice:

Proposition 4. *Let $U(r)$ be the Jacobian matrix $U(x) = (\frac{\partial u_i(r)}{\partial r_j \partial r_i})_{1 \le i,j \le n}$. Let $U^t(r)$ be the transpose matrix of $U(r)$. If the symmetric matrix $U(r) + U^t(r)$ is negative definite (that is, for all $r \in [0,1]^n$ we have $y^t(U(r) + U^t(r))y < 0$ $\forall y \ne 0$) the Nash equilibrium is unique.*

Proof. It is a sufficient condition of Rosen's uniqueness result [7].

5   Conclusions

In this paper, we have introduced a specific model for the interactions among participants (nodes) in an ad-hoc network in terms of reliability investments, when all nodes want a reliable access to a given point. When nodes are selfish, the non-cooperative game can be difficult to analyze, but we have proved that, under reasonable conditions, it always has an equilibrium. We have highlighted the contrast with globally optimized decisions, for which the investments of nodes close to the sink are higher than in the non-cooperative setting, due to the positive externality they create. We have shown that the loss of efficiency due to user selfishness, measured through the Price of Anarchy, can be arbitrarily large in general, but is in practice small for many settings (in particular, when reliability is cheap). This suggests some careful consideration is needed before deciding whether some coordination should be enforced.

References

1. Cancela, H., El Khadiri, M., Rubino, G.: Rare events analysis by Monte Carlo techniques in static models. In: Rubino, G., Tuffin, B. (eds.) Rare Event Simulation using Monte Carlo Methods, pp. 145–170, John Wiley & Sons (2009)
2. Nan, J.-X., Zhang, L., Li, D.-F.: The method for solving bi-matrix games with intuitionistic fuzzy set payoffs. In: Li, D.-F. (ed.) EAGT 2019. CCIS, vol. 1082, pp. 131–150. Springer, Singapore (2019). https://doi.org/10.1007/978-981-15-0657-4_9

3. Jiang, L., Anantharam, V., Walrand, J.: How bad are selfish investments in network security? IEEE/ACM Trans. Netw. **19**(2), 549–560 (2011)
4. Maillé, P., Reichl, P., Tuffin, B.: Interplay between security providers, consumers, and attackers: a weighted congestion game approach. In: GameSec - Second International Conference on Decision and Game Theory for Security. College Park, MD, Maryland, United States, pp. 67–86 (2011)
5. Maillé, P., Reichl, P., Tuffin, B.: Of threats and costs: a game-theoretic approach to security risk management. In: Gülpınar, N., Harrison, P., Rüstem, B. (eds.) Performance Models and Risk Management in Communications Systems. SOIA, vol. 46, pp. 33–53. Springer, New York (2011). https://doi.org/10.1007/978-1-4419-0534-5_2
6. Osborne, M., Rubinstein, A.: A Course in Game Theory. MIT Press (1994)
7. Rosen, J.B.: Existence and uniqueness of equilibrium points for concave n-person games. Econometrica **33**, 520–534 (1965)
8. Rubino, G.: Network reliability evaluation. In: Bagchi, K., Walrand, J. (eds.) State-of-the art in performance modeling and simulation. Gordon & Breach Books (1998)
9. Toh, C.: Wireless ATM and Ad-Hoc Networks: Protocols and Architectures. Kluwer Academic Publisherb Group (1997)
10. Varian, H.: System reliability and free riding. In: Camp, L.J., Lewis, S. (eds.) Economics of Information Security, pp. 1–15. Springer, US, Boston, MA (2004)

NuPow: Managing Power on NUMA Multiprocessors with Domain-Level Voltage and Frequency Control

Changmin Ahn⑩, Seungyul Lee⑩, Chanseok Kang⑩,
and Bernhard Egger$^{(\boxtimes)}$⑩

Seoul National University, Seoul, Republic of Korea
{changmin,seungyul,chanseok,bernhard}@csap.snu.ac.kr

Abstract. Power management and task placement pose two of the greatest challenges for future many-core processors in data centers. With hundreds of cores on a single die, cores experience varying memory latencies and cannot individually regulate voltage and frequency, therefore calling for new approaches to scheduling and power management. This work presents NuPow, a hierarchical scheduling and power management framework for architectures with multiple cores per voltage and frequency domain and non-uniform memory access (NUMA) properties. NuPow considers the conflicting goals of grouping virtual machines (VMs) with similar load patterns while also placing them as close as possible to the accessed data. Implemented and evaluated on existing hardware, NuPow achieves significantly better performance per watt compared to competing approaches.

Keywords: Many-core processors · Power management · NUMA

1 Introduction

The past decade has brought a shift from high-performance single-core processors to chip multiprocessors (CMPs) integrating from a few tens up to a thousand cores into one processor die [2,6,10,30]. Increasing the number of cores leads to larger memory bandwidth requirements; CMPs thus support multiple memory controllers that are connected to the cores by a network-on-chip (NoC) [3]. Depending on the location of the issuing core and the accessed memory controller, large differences in access latency are observed, resulting in a NUMA architecture on a single chip.

Chip-level power and thermal constraints have become one of the primary design constraints and performance limiters [2]. To reduce overall chip energy consumption, processors support dynamic voltage and frequency scaling (DVFS) of clocked resources. Depending on the utilization of the cores, the voltage and the frequency of a core is set to minimize the power consumption while meeting given performance requirements [5]. The hardware required to allow per-core

© Springer Nature Switzerland AG 2020
K. Djemame et al. (Eds.): GECON 2020, LNCS 12441, pp. 126–141, 2020.
https://doi.org/10.1007/978-3-030-63058-4_12

voltage regulation on CMPs with tens or hundreds of cores is becoming too costly [21]; instead, multiple-voltage multiple-frequency (MVMF) designs have been proposed that require all cores within a domain to operate at the same level [9,13,14,32]. In the following, we refer to CMPs that support per-core DVFS control as *core MVMF* CMPs and to those that only allow per-domain DVFS control as *domain MVMF* CMPs.

Managing power on CMPs has received considerable attention. Existing work foremost focuses on minimizing power consumption or optimizing performance for a given power budget [11,17,24,27,31]. Solutions for domain MVMF CMPs combine DVFS with thread migration [7,16,18,20,31] to allow for better tailored DVFS settings by co-locating threads with similar performance requirements in the same domain. Power management techniques for existing CMPs fall short for a number of reasons when applied to future CMPs with hundreds or thousands of cores. Most works assume core MVMF CMPs which limits their applicability to domain MVMF CMPs. In addition and to the best of our knowledge, no work considers the NUMA properties of CMPs when managing power for domain MVMF CMPs, resulting in core mappings that are not optimal with respect to the locality of the data accessed by individual threads.

This paper presents NuPow, a hierarchical power management technique that has been built from ground up for domain MVMF CMPs with NUMA properties. NuPow can be applied to SMP systems as well as non-coherent memory architectures running individual VMs. We demonstrate the feasibility of the technique by providing and evaluating a working implementation on the Intel Single-Chip Cloud Computer (SCC) [14]. Even though this prototype chip is a decade old, its architecture resembles that of proposed CMPs with hundreds of cores; the Intel SCC can thus serve as a concept vehicle to demonstrate the effectiveness of the presented approach. All experiments and measurements are performed on the architecture itself; i.e., are not simulated and include all overhead incurred by DVFS transitions, cold cache misses, VM migration, and the different power management controllers. We compare the proposed technique to a DVFS-only approach [16] and a method that combines DVFS with VM migration [20]. Executing load patterns observed in Google's data centers [33], we achieve, on average, a 51, 33, and 10% higher performance-per-watt ratio over standard Linux, DVFS-only, and NUMA-unaware DVFS with VM relocation at no performance degradation.

2   Motivation and Related Work

2.1   Characteristics of Chip Multiprocessors

Technology scaling, thermal limitations, and the insight that doubling the logic in a processor core only delivers about 40% more performance have led to the introduction of chip multiprocessors with tens or hundreds of cores on one processor die [3,4]. Architectural characteristics of today's and future many-core CMPs impose new restrictions on the design and implementation of operating systems, in particular, with respect to task scheduling and power management.

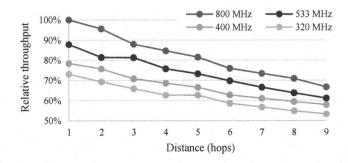

Fig. 1. Measured normalized memory throughput in dependence on the distance (hops) from the accessed memory controller for different core frequencies on the Intel SCC.

The cores of a CMP are typically organized in a two-dimensional array. The Kilocore processor, for example, arranges its 1000 cores on a 32x32 grid [2]. A network-on-chip connects the cores and is used both for inter-core communication and accesses to memory and external devices such as network or storage controllers. The flow of data packets through the NoC is controlled by routers; this routing comes with a small delay. As a consequence, the distance and topology of the NoC between the source and the destination can have a significant effect on the access latency of individual cores to memory. Figure 1 shows the results of measuring the relative memory throughput on the Intel SCC in dependence on the number of hops between the issuing core and the accessed memory controller for various core operating frequencies. At the highest frequency of 800MHz, memory throughput drops by 33% when the core is located farthest away from the memory controller, demonstrating the necessity of NUMA-aware task placement.

2.2 Power Management on CMPs

A vast body of research has shown DVFS to be an effective technique to limit power dissipation on core MVMF CMPs. The core observation behind DVFS is that the clock frequency of a core can be lowered without affecting performance when the core is idle or observes stalls caused by frequent memory accesses. Equipping every core with a voltage regulator, however, is becoming too costly [21], so domain-level multiple-voltage/multiple-frequency CMP designs are being proposed. In such domain MVMF designs, all cores in the same domain share the same voltage and frequency.

The NUMA properties of modern CMP architectures and the constraints with regards to power management require new approaches that combine task scheduling with domain MVMF-aware power management. From a power management perspective only, VMs with similar performance requirements should be scheduled together on cores in the same voltage and frequency domains in order to achieve optimal power savings. On the other hand, the NUMA characteristics of the chip require the scheduler to place VMs as close as possible to the accessed memory controllers. Furthermore, the scheduler and the power manager may need to adhere to user-defined performance goals such as minimizing power under constant performance, maintaining Quality of Service (QoS), even heat dissipation, or maximizing throughput for a given power budget. This paper introduces NuPow, a cooperative and hierarchical power management framework for domain MVMF CMPs that balances the independent goals of NUMA-aware scheduling and MVMF power management to achieve better energy efficiency.

2.3   Related Work

There exists a large body of work focusing on NUMA-aware work scheduling and the design and implementation of power management techniques for CMPs. One line of related work considers heterogeneous CMP. Kumar [22] proposes CMPs composed of cores different power characteristics. Ghiasi [12] proposes CMPs with cores executing at different frequencies. Both works show that such systems offer improved power consumption and thermal management. NuPow modifies the voltages and frequencies of the cores dynamically, without being bound to a specific hardware heterogeneity. Another line of research has focused on exploiting idle periods. Meisner proposes PowerNap [25] and DreamWeaver [26] that require hardware support for quick transitions between on- and off-states; the latter improves the former by batching wake-up events to increase the sleep periods. NuPow is orthogonal to such approaches.

Several power management techniques have been presented for existing core MVMF CMPs [7,8,15–17,19,23,24,27,31,34]. Li [23] analytically models to what extent parallel applications can be parallelized under a given power-budget. Isci [17] applies different DVFS policies under a power budget and shows that the best policy performs almost on par with an oracle policy. Meng [27] presents an adaptive power saving strategy that adheres to a chip-wide power budget by run-time adaptation of configurable processor cores. Rangan [31] proposes ThreadMotion, a technique for global shared-memory processors that moves threads between cores with different power and performance characteristics in order to improve power consumption. Hardware support is required to make thread migration more beneficial than DVFS. Cai [7] presents Thread Shuffling that migrates the hardware contexts of a single parallel application to exploit non-critical threads; non-critical threads can then be executed at reduced speed. Ma [24] proposes a solution aiming at a mixed group of single-threaded and multi-threaded applications and ignores NUMA properties of the CMP. Imamura [15] uses artificial neural networks to control power management and task placement, and Deng [8], finally, applies DVFS to multiple memory controllers. Their work is orthogonal to NuPow.

Techniques for domain MVMF CMPs typically propose hierarchical power management techniques [1,19,28]. Jha [19] classifies and migrates tasks based on DVFS sensitivity and cache behavior. That work and the approach of Yang [34], who focuses on multi-stage applications, aim at obtaining the best performance for a given power budget and ignore NUMA properties. Ali [1] exploits the low-power states of Intel processors to schedule virtual machines in a NUMA-aware manner. Unlike NuPow, these approaches assume global shared memory and a shared-memory kernel.

The works most closely related to NuPow are Ioannou [16] and Kang [20]. The former work applies DVFS to a static task assignment, the latter combines task migration with DVFS to obtain a significantly higher performance/watt ratio. Neither work considers the NUMA properties of CMPs. Both techniques are evaluated on the Intel SCC which allows for a direct comparison with NuPow on identical hardware.

3   Hierarchical Power Management

NuPow's cooperative hierarchical power manager combines VM relocation with DVFS to achieve optimal power efficiency for domain MVMF CMPs with NUMA properties.

3.1   VM Relocation

Virtual machines with similar performance characteristics need to be grouped together in frequency/voltage domains to allow for optimal DVFS settings and, as a consequence, improved power efficiency. If a VM with a high load is executed on a core co-located with lightly-loaded VMs in one domain, the entire domain needs to run at a higher power setting to satisfy the performance requirements of the busy VM. NuPow relocates VMs to group VMs with similar computational requirements such that individual domains can run at an optimal voltage/frequency setting. Taking data locality into consideration complicates the situation. Placing a VM away from the memory controllers where its data resides increases access latency and, in turn, requires a higher operation frequency to maintain throughput. In the opposite case, moving a VM closer to its data leads to lower access latency and may allow to run the core at a lower frequency.

3.2   Distributed Power Management

NuPow distributes the power management to a hierarchy of controllers that match the structure of the underlying MVMF architecture. Located at the lowest level are *core controllers* that manage a single core. Each frequency and voltage domain is controlled by a *frequency* or *voltage controller*, respectively, and a global *chip controller* sits on top of the hierarchy. The hierarchical structure and communication pattern improves the NuPow's scalability and is a natural fit to the task to be performed at each level.

- The **core controllers** monitor the performance characteristics of their core, predict performance requirements, and periodically report this data to the superordinate frequency controllers. Measured are IPC (Instructions Per Cycle) and the number of memory operations to determine the memory boundness of a VM. The required performance is extrapolated based on weighted collected data.

- The **frequency controllers** gather the performance data from the core controllers within their domain and forward the processed data to their superordinate voltage controllers. The frequency controllers also set the clock frequency of their domain.
- The **voltage controllers** collect, process, and forward data from the subordinate frequency controllers to the chip controller. The voltage controllers are also in charge of setting the operating voltage of their domains.
- The **chip controller** aggregates the data from the subordinate voltage controllers to compute an VM placement that considers the NUMA affinity of the VMs and allows for more optimal DVFS settings at the voltage and frequency domain levels.

4   DVFS and VM Relocation Policies

To allow cloud service providers to offer an undiminished quality of service while minimizing energy consumption, the focus of NuPow in this paper lies on optimizing the *performance per watt* ratio of the overall chip while maintaining throughput. The power management is implemented in the chip controller. DVFS and relocation algorithms are periodically invoked. Though the former depends on the latter, the DVFS and relocation policy are separated to support different combinations of relocation and DVFS policies.

4.1   DVFS Policies

NuPow supports all DVFS policies proposed for hierarchical power management by Ioannou [16] and Kang [20]. We compare NuPow against the two works using the `Tile` DVFS policy. `Tile` DVFS sets the voltage to the highest voltage requested by any of its frequency domains but allows each frequency domain to run at the optimal frequency that does not sacrifice performance.

4.2   Phase Ordering and Frequency Considerations

To achieve maximum power savings, VM relocation should occur before applying DVFS because a good placement of VMs allows for better voltage/frequency settings. The frequency of VM relocation and voltage/frequency changes depends on the cost of the individual operations. The total relocation time is not affected by the number of relocated VMs because the relocations occur in parallel. Voltage changes incur a not insignificant overhead because all cores in the affected domain are stopped during the voltage adjustment. Frequency changes, on the other hand, are almost instantaneous and can be performed more often.

4.3   Relocation of Virtual Machines

A naïve algorithm assigns the VM in order of their performance requirements to the domains. While the resulting placement is optimal in terms of power

Algorithm 1. Power-optimizing VM Placement

```
 1: function COMPUTERELOCATIONMAP(Δm)
 2:    vms ← set of all VMs with required voltage/frequency
 3:    for each v ∈ {v_high, · · · , v_lowest} do
 4:       vdom_v ← ⌈|{vm ∈ vms|vm.v = v}|/#vdom⌉
 5:       for each vd ∈ vdom_v do
 6:          vd.vms ← add VMs that require voltage v wrt to their data placement
 7:          vd.loc ← compute location on chip minimizing distance to data of VM
 8:          fdom ← compute required frequencies for domains in vd
 9:          for each f ∈ {f_high, · · · , f_lowest} do
10:             fdom_f ← {x ∈ vdom|voltage(x) = v}
11:             for each fd ∈ vd do
12:                fd.vms ← add VMs that require frequency f wrt to their data placement
13:                fd.loc ← compute location within vd minimizing distance to data of VM
14:             assign unplaced VMs in descending order of required frequency to free cores in vd
15:          if ENERGY(new placement)·(1 + Δm) < ENERGY(current placement) then
16:             return new placement
```

savings, it fails to consider the NUMA-properties of the NoC and the overhead of relocation. The relocation of a VM is very quick; measurements on a real system yield an overhead of $\leq 3\,\text{ms}$ [20]. Each time a VM is relocated to a different core, however, the VM will experience cold misses in the local caches that, in turn, lead to a loss of performance as well as increased memory traffic. A good algorithm has to balance the benefit of relocating a workload against the overhead incurred by relocation.

NuPow's relocation algorithm computes an optimized placement of VMs onto the cores that allows for an overall lower chip power consumption. Since we do not trade performance for power savings, the computational load of a VM determines the minimally required voltage and frequency of the core it is placed on. The goal of the algorithm is to minimize the number of domains that run at each domain/frequency and placing these domains on the chip in a NUMA-optimal way. Algorithm 1 shows the pseudo-code of the placement algorithm. The algorithm iterates over all available voltages and frequencies (lines 3, 9). For each voltage v, the VMs requiring that voltage are assigned to a voltage domain (line 6) and that domain is placed on a free domain such that the total distance of all VMs contained within to their data is minimized (line 7). The same step is then repeated within the voltage domain for all frequencies (lines 8–13). If there are free cores within the domain after this process, yet unplaced VMs are assigned in descending order of their required frequency (line 14). After all VMs have been placed, the energy consumption (Sect. 4.4) of the new placement is predicted and compared to that of the current placement. If the difference is larger than a given threshold Δm, the new placement is enacted (lines 15–16). The threshold Δm ensures that the expected energy savings are significant to avoid relocating VMs with little expected benefit.

4.4   Energy Model

The power consumption of CMOS logic comprises dynamic, short-circuit, and leakage power [29]. Voltage and frequency have a significant effect on dynamic power:

$$P \propto V^2 f \tag{1}$$

For a VM assignment with given voltage/frequency levels for the different domains, the energy consumption over the next epoch t can be approximated by

$$E_{status\_quo} = t \cdot \sum_{v \in vd} \sum_{f \in fd(v)} P(V_{current}(v), F_{current}(f)) \tag{2}$$

where $V_{current}(v)$ and $F_{current}(f)$ return the current voltage and frequency of a given voltage or frequency domain.

Relocating VMs may allow for better DVFS settings but incurs an overhead. The relocation overhead, O_{reloc}, is the overhead caused by the actual relocation and the (worst-case) time required to fill the empty cache on the newly assigned core. The memory overhead, O_{mem}, captures the sensitivity of a workload to the location of the assigned core on the CMP. The expected energy consumption to perform the same work after migration is then given by

$$E_{reloc} = P_{reloc} \cdot (t + O_{reloc} + O_{mem}) \tag{3}$$

$$P_{reloc} = \sum_{v \in vd} \sum_{f \in fd(v)} P(V_{relocated}(v), F_{relocated}(f)) \tag{4}$$

$$O_{reloc} = t_{relocation} + t_{cache\_fill}(F_{relocated}(f)) \tag{5}$$

$$O_{mem} = t \cdot \frac{throughput_{status\_quo}}{throughput_{relocated}} \tag{6}$$

where P_{reloc} is computed from offline power consumption data for each frequency level. The maximum throughput at each frequency and core location is profiled once offline; the actually required throughput of an application depends on the core's last-level cache misses and is measured by the core controllers.

5   Implementation

5.1   The Intel Single-Chip Cloud Computer

NuPow is implemented and evaluated on the Intel Single-chip Cloud Computer (SCC). The Intel SCC consists of 48 independent cores interconnected by a routed NoC. No cache coherence is provided for the core-local L1 and L2 caches. Each pair of cores forms a *tile*; the 24 tiles are organized on a 6x4 grid. Four memory controllers in the four corners of the chip provide access to up to 64 GB of memory. An FPGA provides the interface between the CMP and the management PC (MCPC). Figure 2 shows a block diagram of the SCC.

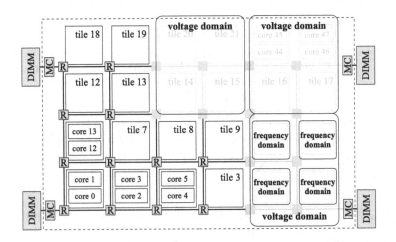

Fig. 2. Intel SCC block diagram

DVFS Capabilities. The SCC allows control over voltage and frequency for cores and the NoC. The right upper hand of Fig. 2 illustrates frequency and voltage domains on the SCC. In total, there are six voltage domains comprising four frequency domains à two cores each. The SCC supports seven different supply voltage levels, however, only four are of practical interest: $1.1V$ to run at a frequency of 800 MHz, $0.9V$ to run at 533 MHz, $0.8V$ for 400 MHz, and $0.7V$ for frequencies between 320 and 100 MHz.

Power Measurement. The SCC provides a number of on-chip voltage and ampere meters. The total consumed power is computed by multiplying the supply voltage with the supply current for the entire SCC chip. Experimental results always report total chip power, i.e., include the overhead caused by the different domain controllers.

5.2   Virtual Machine Relocation

On a cache-coherent shared memory CMP, VMs can be migrated simply by pinning them onto a specific core. The Intel SCC does not support a cache-coherent shared memory space; instead all 48 cores are assigned separate memory spaces. Copying the volatile state of a VM to the memory of the designated core would incur a prohibitively large overhead; instead NuPow employs zero-copy migration by changing the core's memory mappings to point to the VM's data. This, in effect, relocates not just the VM but also the hypervisor running on the core. The interested reader is referred to Kang [20] for technical details on the relocation process.

5.3   Domain Controller Implementation

The domain controllers (core, frequency, voltage, and chip) are present in the system software running on core; the physical core ID determines which controllers

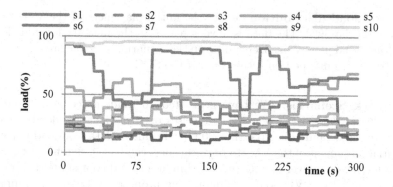

Fig. 3. Example of ten distinct workload patterns.

are (de-)activated in a running kernel. After relocation, the kernels check if the core they are running on requires activation/deactivation of one of the four controllers. Core controllers are active on every kernel. The 24 frequency controller are activated on the cores with an odd core ID. The six voltage controllers run on the lower-left core of each domain. The chip controller is located on core 30.

6   Experimental Setup

6.1   Hardware

All experiments are conducted on the Intel SCC [14]. Each core runs a modified version of the Intel SCC Linux. The on-chip voltage and ampere meters are queried with a frequency of 10'000Hz. All results report the power consumed by all 48 cores and the NoC. In particular, since NuPow is implemented entirely in software and is executed on the cores of the SCC, the result include the power consumed by NuPow.

6.2   Benchmarks

A benchmark scenario is defined by (1) a number of workload patterns and (2) a distribution of the workloads to cores.

(1) A **workload pattern** represents a load pattern experienced by a single VM and is composed of CPU load and memory load. Figure 3 shows an example of 10 different CPU workloads patterns s1-s10. The workload patterns of the datacenter scenarios are based on data gathered in Google data centers [33]. We have extracted the workloads of 100 randomly selected physical nodes in the system over a period of 3,000 s. Time is scaled by factor 10, i.e., a workload pattern runs for 300 s. This is not in our favor since rapidly changing load patterns put more stress on relocation. We also employ three synthetically generated workload patterns to demonstrate the potential of the presented approach.

(2) A **workload distribution** defines the initial placement of the VMs to the cores on the SCC. The data is always placed in the memory located closest to the initial placement. Depending on the scenario, between 2 to 40 different patterns are mapped onto the cores of the SCC.

Benchmark Scenarios. We have generated 26 random scenarios from the Google cluster data. Each scenario comprises of w distinct workload patterns that are selected randomly from the 100 Google cluster data workload patterns. The initial placement of the VMs to physical cores can have a significant effect on the effectiveness of power management techniques that do not support workload migration (i.e., the DVFS only technique the proposed approach is compared against), so each reported result is the arithmetic average of three individual runs with three distinct initial random placements.

6.3 Comparison of Results

The baseline of the experiments is obtained by running the benchmark scenario on the SCC at full speed (800 MHz) with no power management. NuPow is compared against the DVFS only approach of Ioannou [16] and the DVFS+migration technique with its locality-unaware buyer-seller algorithm described by Kang [20] denoted Buyer-Seller. The hierarchical framework and the DVFS policies for all three methods are identical. We evaluated the different core migration algorithms using the Tile DVFS policies (Sect. 4.1). For all methods and benchmarks scenarios, the migration benefit threshold Δm is set to 10%. Migrations are evaluated and performed once every 3 s. All benchmark scenarios are executed to completion.

7 Results

7.1 Varying Number of Workloads

We first evaluate six distinct real-world datacenter scenarios G1–G6 with respect to a varying number of assigned workloads from 8 to 40. The workload pattern G1 contains four, G2–G5 seven, and G6 10 distinct workload patterns that are randomly assigned to the number of workloads (i.e., for the 8-workload case and G1 we make 8 random selections from the pool containing the four workload patterns). The initial location of the workloads on the chip can affect the result; we create three different random assignments and report the average of running each of the three assignments three times; i.e., each individual result represents the average of nine runs.

Figure 4 displays the results for the datacenter scenarios G1 to G6 with 8, 16, 24, 32, and 40 workloads running simultaneously. The y-axis shows the performance per watt of NuPow relative to DVFS only. We observe that NuPow shows better relative improvements if the number of active workloads (i.e., active cores) is between 16 and 32 cores. In the case of 8 workloads, DVFS only manages to

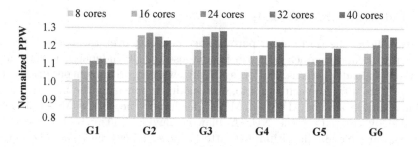

Fig. 4. Normalized performance per watt of NuPow relative to DVFS only.

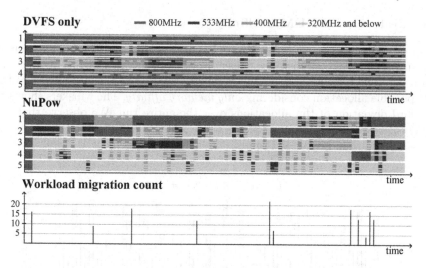

Fig. 5. Frequency map comparing DVFS only with NuPow for the G6 workload.

do quite a good job (51% over no power management) despite its inability to migrate workloads because the low occupation still provides sufficient opportunities to apply DVFS. On the other end of the spectrum with 40 cores there are less opportunities for power savings with or without migration. The best case are moderately loaded CMPs where NuPow outperforms DVFS only by 25% on average.

The effect of workload migration is visualized in Fig. 5. The topmost graph shows the frequency map of DVFS only with the Tile policy for the different voltage domains. The middle graph shows the frequency map for the same workload with the proposed Greedy algorithm. While DVFS only is required to run most domains at a high frequency for most of the time, we observe that NuPow is able to group workloads with similar utilization into a few domains and apply aggressive DVFS on the lightly loaded domains. The bottom graph in Fig. 5, finally, shows the number of workload migrations over time.

7.2   Independent Workloads

Figure 6 shows the normalized performance-per-watt over the baseline for 20 datacenter scenarios. Each scenario is composed of 40 independent randomly selected workloads patterns. NuPow's NUMA-aware algorithm outperforms DVFS only by 20 to 40% for each scenario, once again emphasizing the importance of workload migration for MVMF CMPs. The importance of NUMA-awareness is visible by comparing the NUMA-unaware `Buyer-Seller` to the proposed NUMA-aware `Greedy` algorithm: the latter achieves a between 7 and 12% better performance per watt with an average of a 10% better energy efficiency.

7.3   Evaluation of NUMA Affinity

Figure 7 compares the NUMA-unaware `Buyer-Seller` algorithm against `NuPow` in terms of the weighted distance of each workload's memory load to its memory controller. The data is show for the same 20 scenarios and is normalized to the best possible allocation considering *only memory affinity*. The whiskers show the standard deviation of the allocations over the entire run. We observe that the NUMA-aware `NuPow` algorithm places the workloads significantly closer to the accessed data than `Buyer-Seller`.

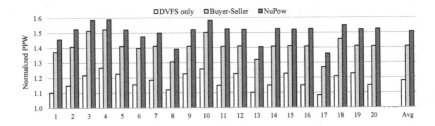

Fig. 6. Normalized performance per watt for 20 distince datacenter scenarios.

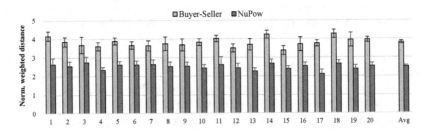

Fig. 7. Weighted memory distance comparing `Buyer-Seller` and `NuPow`.

8 Conclusion

We have presented NuPow, a NUMA-aware cooperative hierarchical power management technique for many-core systems with multiple-voltage/multiple-frequency islands. Combined with dynamic monitoring of each core's performance metrics, this technique allows the power manager to group virtual machines with similar performance requirements together so that traditional DVFS policies can apply DVFS settings closer to the optimal setting while at the same time locate memory-bound workloads closer to their data. In order to remain scalable, the power manager is implemented in a hierarchical fashion, logically re-creating the hierarchy imposed by the hardware through the different power management domains. NuPow has been implemented and evaluated on the Intel Single-Chip Cloud Computer. Experiments with a wide range of real world workload benchmark scenarios show that, on average, the proposed technique outperforms existing DVFS policies by 33% and by 10% compared to a NUMA-unaware approach.

Acknowledgements. This work was supported by the National Research Foundation of Korea (NRF) funded by the Korean government, in part, by grants NRF-2015K1A3A1A14021288, 2016R1A2B4009193, by the BK21 Plus for Pioneers in Innovative Computing (Dept. of Computer Science and Engineering, SNU, grant 21A20151113068), and by the Promising-Pioneering Researcher Program of Seoul National University in 2015. ICT at Seoul National University provided research facilities for this study.

References

1. Ali, Q., Zheng, H., Mann, T., Srinivasan, R.: Power aware NUMA scheduler in vmware's esxi hypervisor. In: Proceedings of the 2015 IEEE International Symposium on Workload Characterization, IISWC 2015, Washington, DC, USA (2015)
2. Bohnenstiehl, B., et al.: KiloCore: a 32-nm 1000-processor computational array. IEEE J. Solid-State Circ. **52**(4), 891–902 (2017)
3. Borkar, S.: Thousand core chips: a technology perspective. In: Proceedings of the 44th Annual Design Automation Conference, DAC 2007 (2007)
4. Borkar, S., Chien, A.A.: The future of microprocessors. CACM **54**(5), 67–77 (2011)
5. Burd, T.D., Brodersen, R.W.: Energy efficient CMOS microprocessor design. In: Proceedings of the Twenty-Eighth Hawaii International Conference on System Sciences, vol. 1 (1995)
6. Butts, M.: Synchronization through communication in a massively parallel processor array. IEEE Micro **27**(5), 32–40 (2007)
7. Cai, Q., González, J., Magklis, G., Chaparro, P., González, A.: Thread shuffling: combining DVFS and thread migration to reduce energy consumptions for multi-core systems. In: Proceedings of the 17th IEEE/ACM International Symposium on Low-power Electronics and Design, ISLPED 2011 (2011)
8. Deng, Q., Meisner, D., Bhattacharjee, A., Wenisch, T.F., Bianchini, R.: Multiscale: memory system DVFS with multiple memory controllers. In: Proceedings of the 2012 ACM/IEEE International Symposium on Low Power Electronics and Design, ISLPED 2012 (2012)

9. Dighe, S., et al.: Within-die variation-aware dynamic-voltage-frequency-scaling with optimal core allocation and thread hopping for the 80-core teraflops processor. IEEE J. Solid-State Circ. **46**(1), 184–193 (2011)
10. Duran, A., Klemm, M.: The intel many integrated core architecture. In: 2012 International Conference on High Performance Computing and Simulation (HPCS) (2012)
11. Fu, X., Wang, X.: Utilization-controlled task consolidation for power optimization in multi-core real-time systems. In: 2011 IEEE 17th International Conference on Embedded and Real-Time Computing Systems and Applications, vol. 1 (2011)
12. Ghiasi, S.: Aide de camp: asymmetric multi-core design for dynamic thermal management. Ph.D. thesis, Boulder, CO, USA (2004). aAI3136618
13. Herbert, S., Marculescu, D.: Analysis of dynamic voltage/frequency scaling in chip-multiprocessors. In: 2007 ACM/IEEE International Symposium on Low Power Electronics and Design (ISLPED) (2007)
14. Howard, J., et al.: A 48-core IA-32 message-passing processor with DVFS in 45nm CMOS. In: 2010 IEEE International Solid-State Circuits Conference Digest of Technical Papers (ISSCC) (2010)
15. Imamura, S., Sasaki, H., Inoue, K., Nikolopoulos, D.S.: Power-capped DVFS and thread allocation with ANN models on modern NUMA systems. In: 2014 IEEE 32nd International Conference on Computer Design (ICCD) (2014)
16. Ioannou, N., Kauschke, M., Gries, M., Cintra, M.: Phase-based application-driven hierarchical power management on the single-chip cloud computer. In: Proceedings of the 2011 International Conference on Parallel Architectures and Compilation Techniques, PACT 2011 (2011)
17. Isci, C., Buyuktosunoglu, A., Cher, C.Y., Bose, P., Martonosi, M.: An analysis of efficient multi-core global power management policies: maximizing performance for a given power budget. In: Proceedings of the 39th Annual IEEE/ACM International Symposium on Microarchitecture, MICRO 39 (2006)
18. Jain, V.: Fast process migration on intel SCC using lookup tables (LUTs). Technical report Masters thesis, Arizona State University, May 2013
19. Jha, S.S., Heirman, W., Falcón, A., Tubella, J., González, A., Eeckhout, L.: Shared resource aware scheduling on power-constrained tiled many-core processors. J. Parallel Distrib. Comput. **100**, 30–41 (2017)
20. Kang, C., Lee, S., Lee, Y.J., Lee, J., Egger, B.: Scheduling for better energy efficiency onÂ many-core chips. In: Job Scheduling Strategies for Parallel Processing: 19th and 20th International Workshops, JSSPP 2015, Hyderabad, India, 26 May 2015 and JSSPP 2016, Chicago, IL, USA, 27 May 2016, Revised Selected Papers (2017)
21. Kim, W., Gupta, M.S., Wei, G.Y., Brooks, D.: System level analysis of fast, per-core DVFS using on-chip switching regulators. In: IEEE 14th International Symposium on High Performance Computer Architecture (HPCA 2008) (2008)
22. Kumar, R., Tullsen, D.M., Ranganathan, P., Jouppi, N.P., Farkas, K.I.: Single-ISA heterogeneous multi-core architectures for multithreaded workload performance. In: Proceedings of the 31st Annual International Symposium on Computer Architecture, ISCA 2004 (2004)
23. Li, J., Martínez, J.F.: Power-performance implications of thread-level parallelism on chip multiprocessors. In: IEEE International Symposium on Performance Analysis of Systems and Software (ISPASS 2005) (2005)
24. Ma, K., Li, X., Chen, M., Wang, X.: Scalable power control for many-core architectures running multi-threaded applications. In: Proceedings of the 38th Annual International Symposium on Computer Architecture, ISCA 2011 (2011)

25. Meisner, D., Gold, B.T., Wenisch, T.F.: Powernap: eliminating server idle power. In: Proceedings of the 14th International Conference on Architectural Support for Programming Languages and Operating Systems. ASPLOS XIV (2009)
26. Meisner, D., Wenisch, T.F.: Dreamweaver: architectural support for deep sleep. In: Proceedings of the Seventeenth International Conference on Architectural Support for Programming Languages and Operating Systems. ASPLOS XVII (2012)
27. Meng, K., Joseph, R., Dick, R.P., Shang, L.: Multi-optimization power management for chip multiprocessors. In: Proceedings of the 17th International Conference on Parallel Architectures and Compilation Techniques, PACT 2008 (2008)
28. Mishra, A.K., Srikantaiah, S., Kandemir, M., Das, C.R.: CPM in CMPS: coordinated power management in chip-multiprocessors. In: Proceedings of the 2010 ACM/IEEE International Conference for High Performance Computing, Networking, Storage and Analysis, SC 2010 (2010)
29. Mudge, T.: Power: a first-class architectural design constraint. Computer **34**(4), 52–58 (2001)
30. Olofsson, A.: Epiphany-V: A 1024 processor 64-bit RISC System-On-Chip. https://arxiv.org/abs/1610.01832 (2016). Accessed July 2020
31. Rangan, K.K., Wei, G.Y., Brooks, D.: Thread motion: fine-grained power management for multi-core systems. In: Proceedings of the 36th Annual International Symposium on Computer Architecture, ISCA 2009 (2009)
32. Rotem, E., Mendelson, A., Ginosar, R., Weiser, U.: Multiple clock and voltage domains for chip multi processors. In: Proceedings of the 42nd Annual IEEE/ACM International Symposium on Microarchitecture. MICRO 42 (2009)
33. Wilkes, J.: More Google cluster data. Google Research Blog (2011). http://googleresearch.blogspot.com/2011/11/more-google-cluster-data.html. Accessed July 2020
34. Yang, H., Chen, Q., Riaz, M., Luan, Z., Tang, L., Mars, J.: Powerchief: intelligent power allocation for multi-stage applications to improve responsiveness on power constrained CMP. In: Proceedings of the 44th Annual International Symposium on Computer Architecture, ISCA 2017 (2017)

Multi-tier Power-Saving Method in Cloud Storage Systems for Content Sharing Services

Horleang Choeng, Koji Hasebe$^{(\boxtimes)}$, Hirotake Abe, and Kazuhiko Kato

Department of Computer Science, University of Tsukuba,
1-1-1, Tennodai, Tsukuba 305-8573, Japan
horleang@osss.cs.tsukuba.ac.jp, {hasebe,habe,kato}@cs.tsukuba.ac.jp

Abstract. Fast-growing cloud computing has a mass impact on power consumption in datacenters. In our previous study, we presented a power-saving method for cloud storage systems, where the stored data were periodically rearranged in a disk array in the order of access frequency. The disk containing unpopular files can often be switched to power-saving mode, enabling power conservation. However, if such unpopular files became popular at some point, the disk containing those files spin up that leads to increase power consumption. To remedy this drawback, in this paper, we present a multi-tier power-saving method for cloud storage systems. The idea behind our method is to divide the disk array into multiple tiers. The first tier containing popular files is always active for fast response, while lower tiers pack unpopular files for power conservation. To maintain such a hierarchical structure, files are periodically migrated to the neighboring tiers according to the access frequency. To evaluate the effectiveness of our proposed method, we measured the performance in simulations and a prototype implementation using real access traces of approximately 60,000 time-series images with a duration of 3,000 h. In the experiments, we observed that our method consumed approximately 22% less energy than the system without any file migration among disks. At the same time, our method maintained a preferred response time with an overall average of 86 ms based on our prototype implementation.

Keywords: Power-saving · Storage system · Cloud computing · Content sharing service

1 Introduction

Cloud computing has grown rapidly over the last few decades, resulting in a dramatic increase in power consumption of datacenters. According to a report [15], in 2014, datacenters in the US consumed approximately 1.8% of the total electricity consumption. As a high percentage of the total computing energy is consumed by storage systems, a number of attempts to reduce storage power consumption. Many of these studies were essentially based on the commonly

© Springer Nature Switzerland AG 2020
K. Djemame et al. (Eds.): GECON 2020, LNCS 12441, pp. 142–154, 2020.
https://doi.org/10.1007/978-3-030-63058-4_13

employed technique of skewing the workload toward a small subset of disks, thereby enabling the other disks to remain in standby (i.e., low-power) mode. Massive Arrays of Idle Disks (MAID) [5] is one of the first efforts at this approach. MAID distributed the workload to a subset of disks used as a cache to preserve data. Popular Data Concentration (PDC) [12] periodically rearranged the data based on their new access frequencies in a disk array.

In our previous study [11], we proposed a method based on the idea of PDC. Our method efficiently gathered unpopular files in to a part of the disk array in an environment where large amounts of files were continuously uploaded. However, most of the uploaded files were rarely accessed as time elapsed, but accesses reoccurred occasionally and seemed to happen randomly. The algorithm proposed in our previous study failed to move the files that became popular again from the unpopular disks to the active disks.

To remedy this drawback, in this paper, we propose a multi-tier power-saving method for cloud storage systems for cloud content sharing services. Our method divides the disk array into multiple tiers. The top tier, consisting of always active working disks, stores popular files for fast response, while the lower tiers, consisting of archiving disks, pack unpopular files for power conservation. To maintain this hierarchical structure, files are periodically migrated to the neighboring tiers according to the access frequency.

To evaluate the effectiveness of our proposed method, we measured the performance in both simulations and a prototype implementation using real access traces of approximately 60,000 time-series public photographs on 500px [1] for 3,000 h. In the experiments, we measured the performance of power-saving and response time in a system consisting of two tiers. The results showed that our method consumed approximately 22% less energy than a system without any file migration among disks. Moreover, we observed that our method maintained a preferred response time with an overall average of 86ms based on our prototype implementation.

The rest of this paper is organized as follows. Section 2 presents related work. Section 3 gives the details of the system design. Section 4 introduces the power consumption model for our evaluation. Sections 5 and 6 present the results of our simulations and evaluation using an implementation. Finally, Sect. 7 concludes the paper and presents future work.

2   Related Work

There have been a number of studies on saving power consumption in storage systems (cf. also [4] for a comprehensive survey of this research area). These techniques can be classified into the following three categories according to variations in their approach.

The first category focuses on popularity and concentrates popular data on specific disks. Massive Array of Idle Disks (MAID) [5] provides specific disks that are used as a cache to store frequently accessed data, thereby reducing accesses to other disks. PDC [12] periodically reallocates data in the storage array according to the latest access frequencies.

The second category uses NVRAM to extend the standby mode period by caching data to a write store. A typical example is Pergamum [10], which uses NVRAM to buffer write accesses and store data signatures and thus reduce the number of direct accesses to the disks.

The final category considers redundancy (i.e., data replication). In DIverted Accesses (DIV) [6], original and redundant data are separated onto different disks, thereby allowing I/O requests to be concentrated onto the disks that contain the original data. Hibernator [13] applies the idea of PDC to RAID and Dynamic Rotations Per Minute (DRPM) [14]. RIMAC [18] provides two-layered caches, one for storing data and the other for parity conservation. Power-Aware RAID (PARAID) [17] is another power-saving technique for RAID. It allocates the replicas in a specific way so that data are collected or spread to adapt to changes in operational workloads.

Many of these methods mentioned above were targeted at small-scale storage systems. Recently, applications of these techniques to datacenter-scale storage systems have been actively investigated. As a typical example, GreenHDFS [7] divides Hadoop Distributed File Systems (HDFS) into hot and cold zones. Another example is a study that used data replication extended from Green-Cloud [9] for energy-efficient [3]. This method can reduce power consumption, bandwidth usage, and communication delays substantially.

Our previous study [11] also aims to save power consumption in large-scale storage systems. That study specifically focuses on the issue of how to efficiently aggregate workloads in an environment where large amounts of files are continually uploaded, as typified by the storage systems for cloud content sharing services. However, as mentioned in the previous section, in that study, files that became less popular over time became popular again at some point, and it was impossible to remove it from an unpopular disk. This paper extends the method of [11] while solving this problem.

3   System Design

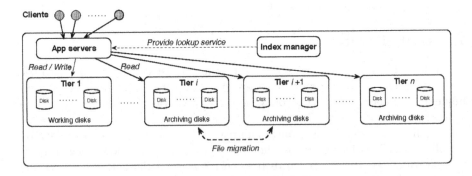

Fig. 1. System design.

Our target systems consist of hundreds to thousands of disks, application servers, I/O servers, and an index manager. Figure 1 illustrates the overall design, where the I/O servers are omitted for readability. Each disk is physically connected to an I/O server and is logically classified into one of the groups (tiers): Tier 1 to Tier n, and the empty disk pool. The disks in the top tier (Tier 1) are called working disks, while the rest are called archiving disks. We assume that our system continuously uploads the files, such as those in real content sharing service platforms. The application servers manage all I/O requests from the clients. The index manager provides a lookup service for file accesses to any working and archiving disks. An application server always writes the files uploaded by the clients to one of the top tier. After uploading, the index manager assigns each file a unique ID and records it with the disk index in which the file is stored.

The number of working disks increases one-by-one as clients sequentially upload files up to an initial number. If the number of working disks reaches the maximum, any access to a full working disk leads to file migration. At this point, an archiving disk is added. Then, some of the most unpopular files are migrated to an archiving disk supplied by the empty disks. The index manager records the file name and disk index in the archiving disks to which the file is migrated. If the files are not migrated, the disk index is the corresponding disk itself. File migration is conducted between neighboring tiers as follows (for $1 \leq n \leq n-1$).

Migration from the i-th Tier to i+1-th Tier: This migration happens in two cases: (1) whenever any disk in the first tier becomes full after clients uploaded the files, and (2) whenever any disk in the i-th tier becomes full after the files are migrated from the neighboring disks.

Migration from i+1-th Tier to i-th Tier: This migration happens if the frequency of accesses of a file in the i-th tier reaches the predetermined threshold. The file is moved to a disk in the $i + 1$-th tier and then sent to the client.

Here we note that the number of accesses to be migrated is critical because it affects the whole system. The reason is that if the file is migrated with every access, we can reduce many accesses to the archiving disks, but it fills the working disk faster, leading to another migration later. We observed the percentage of power-saving based on the number of accesses to be migrated, which is described in Sect. 5. The application server ensures that the total number of files in the working disks is no more than 30% of the total files of the whole system. If the volume exceeds its threshold, a new working disk is added to the first tier, enabling the scalability of the system. At the start of the upload, all files are stored in the working disks, and the archiving disk does not exist. When the migration occurs, a disk is pulled from the empty disks and named as the archiving disk to supply the need to store the migrated files. Another disk is added whenever a destination archiving disk is full.

4   Power Consumption Model

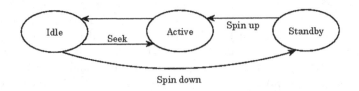

Fig. 2. State transitions for three-state disk drive.

A modern disk drive enables dynamic power management, meaning that there are transitions among the three states called active, idle, and standby modes. Figure 2 illustrates the state transitions. Data transfer occurs in the active mode. When a disk is awaiting I/O requests, it is transitioned to the idle mode, where the disk continues to rotate. A disk in idle mode is transitioned to the standby mode after a fixed threshold time (the idleness threshold) has elapsed since the last access. In the standby mode, the spindle is at rest, and the heads are parked, resulting in power savings.

Table 1. HDD parameter setting.

Symbol	Description	Value
D_{si}	Disk capacity	1,000 GB
D_{ra}	Average data transfer rate	125 MB/s
P_{id}	Power consumption in idle mode	3.36w
P_{sb}	Power consumption in standby mode	0.63w
P_{ac}	Power consumption in active mode	5.9w
P_{sk}	Power consumption to seek	5.9w
P_{up}	Power consumption to spin up	24w
T_{sk}^{rd}	Average seek time for read	8.5 ms
T_{sk}^{wr}	Average seek time for write	9.5 ms
T_{tr}	Rotational latency	4.16 ms
T_{up}	Spin up time	10 s
T_q	Time for current processing I/O requests	–
T_{tf}	Data transfer time	–
T_{th}	Idleness threshold	85.6 s

Table 1 summarizes the model parameters and the values that we used in our evaluations. These settings are based on the specifications of the Seagate Desktop

HDD ST1000DM004 [2]. In the table, the values for T_q and T_{tf} are unspecified because they depend on the finishing time of the previous I/O request and the size of the data transferred, respectively. In our model, the power consumption of a disk drive executing an I/O request is estimated as the sum of the power required for transferring data and the power required for state transition. For example, the total power consumed by a disk in standby mode spinning up and performing I/O requests is $T_{up} \cdot P_{up} + T_{acs} \cdot P_{ac}$ [mJ], where T_{acs} denotes the access time explained below. The response time of access to a disk depends on the current mode of the disk. When we set T_{acs} as the access time (I/O request processing time), T_{sk} as the seek time, T_{rt} as the rotational latency, and T_{tf} as the transfer time, we have an equation as

$$T_{acs} = T_{sk} + T_{rt} + T_{tf}.$$

The response time of accesses in each mode is given by

$$T_{rp} = \begin{cases} T_{acs} & \text{(if it is in idle mode),} \\ T_{acs} + T_{up} & \text{(if it is in standby mode),} \\ T_{acs} + T_q & \text{(if it is in active mode).} \end{cases}$$

It is critical to set the idleness threshold to a suitable value if we wish to reduce the power consumption using dynamic power management. A too-small threshold could result in a frequent spin-up, requiring considerable power (denoted by P_{up}). Conversely, a too-long threshold could prohibit state transitions from idle to standby mode, which could further reduce power consumption. To set a suitable idleness threshold, we use the well-known break-even time technique, i.e., we determine the amount of time a disk must be in standby mode to conserve the same energy consumed by transitioning the disk down and back to the active mode. More precisely, the break-even time (denoted by T_{be}) can be calculated as follows. First, T_{be} can be decomposed into

$$T_{be} = T_{up} + T_{sb}^{min}.$$

Here, T_{sb}^{min} is the minimum length of the standby mode after completing the previous I/O request satisfying the following equation:

$$P_{sb} \cdot T_{sb}^{min} + P_{up} \cdot T_{up} = P_{id}(T_{sb}^{min} + T_{up}).$$

This equation means that the total power required to be in standby mode and spin-up (described as the left-hand side) is equal to the total power required to remain in the idle mode (described as the right-hand side). From these results, we obtain

$$T_{be} = \frac{P_{up} \cdot T_{up} - P_{sb} \cdot T_{up}}{P_{id} - P_{sb}}.$$

In our model, $T_{be} = 85.6$ sec, which we used as the idleness threshold in our evaluations.

5 Simulation

5.1 Preparation

Photographs for Simulation. For simulations, we used 63,204 time-series images from 500px [1], which is an online photo sharing service. All photographs include the cumulative number of accesses, "likes" (the number showing the popularity of the photographs voted by users), comments, and tag information of every hour for 3,000 h. We analyzed the bias of the popularity of each photograph to evaluate the relationship with the time since they were uploaded.

Analysis of Photographs for Simulation. Figure 3 shows the hourly average number of accesses of images over 3,000 h. Here, the horizontal and vertical axes represent the elapsed time and the average number of access per hour, respectively. Consequently, we can assume that many accesses tend to concentrate on some specific images. Figure 4 shows the distribution of total accesses of each image after 3,000 h elapsed. The maximum access is 182,669 times, while the minimum access is only two times. The rate of total accesses in the top 1% of total images holds almost half of the total accesses, while the rate of accesses in the top 30% of the total images holds almost 90% of the total accesses. Consequently, we can assume that most of the accesses to the images belong to the top 30% of the total images. Therefore, we consider that by storing 30% of the images in the working disks, and the rest (around 70%) in the archiving disks, we can reduce the power consumption of the whole system. Most (90%) of the accesses will likely be concentrated on the working disks, and the workload in archiving disks is at rest, resulting in power consumption reduction.

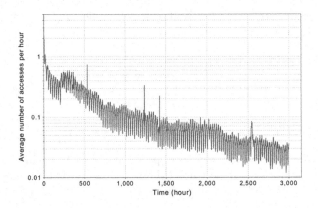

Fig. 3. Hourly average number of access of images.

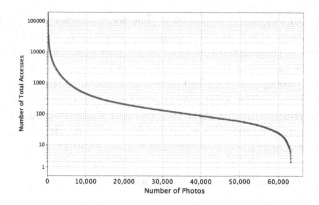

Fig. 4. Distribution of total accesses after 3,000 h.

Parameters and Setting. Based on our system design in Sect. 3 and the power consumption model in Sect. 4, we developed a simulator. The number of accesses mimics the access traces of the images mentioned in Sect. 5.1. Table 2 describes the workload setting. In our simulations, the working disks initially consist of eight disks, while the archiving disks consist of zero disks supplied from empty disks (21 disks were used at the end of the simulations). The number of archiving disks increased one-by-one, depending on the file migration from the working disks.

Table 2. Workload setting.

Type	Value
File size	5 MB
Write	26 images per minute
Read data	500px's image access pattern
Simulation duration	3,000 h

5.2   Simulation Results

We observed the power consumption of our system and compared it to a simple system in which the same set of files are uploaded to an array of disks (increasing one-by-one) without any file migration, named no-migrating system. The number and type of disks in this no-migrating system are the same as those in the proposed system. Because our proposed method focuses on file migration between disks in different tiers (working disk and archiving disk), it is critical to define the two main factors for migration. The first factor is unpopular files. In our experiments, we assume that unpopular files are those with less access frequency or with the oldest access time. The second factor is to determine the number of accesses of files needed to migrate back to any working disk because the performance of the system would worsen if many migrations occur. We experimented on these two main factors to determine the best migration method for our proposed system. Table 3 illustrates the result of our experiment on the percentage of power-saving, where WD and AD represent working and archiving disks, respectively. The results show that the best result for power consumption is when we migrate the oldest accessed files from working disks to archiving disk and when the number of access to old files is more than 10 times.

Table 3. Experiment on percentage of power-saving.

WD→AD	AD→ WD				
	1 access	3 accesses	5 accesses	10 accesses	20 accesses
Number of accesses	17.8%	19.4%	21.3%	22.1%	22.1%
Old accessed time	18.6%	20.0%	22.2%	23%	21.9%

Figure 5 shows the change in the percentage of power consumption of the best results we described above. Here, the horizontal and vertical axes represent the elapsed time and the percentage of power-saving. We started measuring the power consumption between the proposed method and a no-migrating system after the migration process started. Our proposed system conducted file migration, while the files stored in the no-migrating system are static. According to our results, our method performed better with a maximum of 29% less power consumption. Also, over the 3,000 h, this method consumed approximately 22% less energy than the no-migrating system.

Since simulation is not enough to evaluate our proposed system, we conducted a prototype implementation, described in Sect. 6.

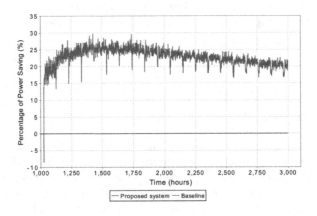

Fig. 5. The change of percentage of power-saving.

6 Experiments on Implementation

6.1 Parameters and Setting

We observed the response time in an environment where the system workload was the same as that in the simulation described in Sect. 5. Our prototype consisted of a client server and an application server connected to an array of 12 disks, each of which was equipped with a single 3 TB hard disk drive. We assumed that the capacity of each disk is 1 TB to match our simulation. Because of the limitation of our experimental environment, we mimicked the simulation of our target system in the following way. All the disks were created as RAID 0 and were connected to the app server. The app server consisted of an index manager mapping the location of each disk and file. We evaluated the response time by measuring the time from sending requests until the data were delivered to the clients. To avoid the effect of the cache, we disabled the cache in each disk before experimenting and erased the memory cache every 30 sec during the experiment. Since the controller of our RAID 0 disks can only set the spin-down and spin-up time (for a power-saving mode) to a minimum of 30 min, we mimicked the spin-down and spin-up time as the same as those in the simulation. In other words, we mimicked the spin-up time by letting the server wait before accessing the disk. Also, as described in Table 1, we set the idleness threshold and the spin-up time to 85.6 sec and 10,000 sec, respectively. Our server network bandwidth is a 1,000 BASE-T network. We selected three disks as working disks and the rest of the nine disks as archiving disks. The files we placed on these disks were the same as those after 3,000 h have passed in the simulation. We measured the response time of every access for one hour from this point. At the beginning of this experiment, the number of read and write requests sent to the application servers was approximately 240,000 requests.

6.2 Implementation Result

Figure 6 and Fig. 7 show the change in the maximum and average, respectively. The horizontal axis represents the duration of implementation, while the vertical axis shows the response time. We can see in Fig. 6 that some files had a response time of more than 10,000 ms, indicating that the files were accessed when the disks were in power-saving mode. Furthermore, we observed that the files with a response time over 10,000ms were all stored in the first two archiving disks, meaning that our proposed method can enable the disk to switch to power-saving mode. We experimented with the response time of the no-migrating system to compare it with that in the proposed system. We observed that the overall average response time of the no-migrating system is 52 ms. Meanwhile, the overall average of the response time of the proposed system is only 86 ms (Fig. 7). Although the proposed system performed slower than the no-migrating system, we still prefer the proposed system because we can reduce power consumption by approximately 22%.

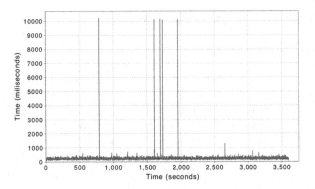

Fig. 6. Maximum response time.

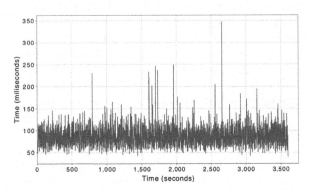

Fig. 7. Average response time.

7   Conclusion and Future Work

In this study, we proposed a multi-tier power-saving method in storage systems, targeting cloud content sharing services. The main objective of this study was to reduce the number of accesses in disks that are in power-saving mode. We presented a method that performed data migration between two subsets of an array. One subset, working disks, was always in the active mode, and the other subset, archiving disks, switched to power-saving mode whenever there was no access after a threshold of time. By migrating the files between archiving disks and working disks, we could reduce the number of accesses, enabling power conservation. To evaluate our proposed system, we conducted a simulation by mimicking the actual social service using approximately 60,000 time-series images. The simulation showed that our system consumed a maximum of 29% and an average of 22% less energy compared to the system with no file migration among the disks. Furthermore, our prototype showed that although there is file migration among the disks, our system still could offer a preferred response time of 86ms in the overall average.

In future work, it is critical to investigate migration factors because we only focused on the oldest accessed time and number of accesses. Recently, some studies apply machine learning to predict the number of views of a file before it is uploaded [8,16]. These studies could precisely predict the popularity of files by using the file itself, its content, and its social context. It would be interesting if we could apply this technique to our system by predicting the popularity of files to find the unpopular files to migrate to the archiving disks.

References

1. https://web.500px.com
2. https://www.seagate.com/www-content/product-content/barracuda-fam/desktop-hdd/barracuda-7200-14/en-us/docs/100686584y.pdf
3. Boru, D., Kliazovich, D., Granelli, F., Bouvry, P., Zomaya, A.Y.: Energy-efficient data replication in cloud computing datacenters. Cluster Comput. **18**(1), 385–402 (2015). https://doi.org/10.1007/s10586-014-0404-x
4. Bostoen, T., Mullender, S., Berbers, Y.: Power-reduction techniques for data-center storage systems. ACM Comput. Surv. (CSUR) **45**(3), 33 (2013)
5. Colarelli, D., Grunwald, D.: Massive arrays of idle disks for storage archives. In: SC 2002: Proceedings of the 2002 ACM/IEEE Conference on Supercomputing, pp. 47–47. IEEE (2002)
6. E. Pinheiro, R.B., Dubnicki, C.: Exploiting redundancy to conserve energy in storage systems. In: Proceedings ACM SIGMETRICS Conference on Measurement and Modeling of Computer Systems, pp. 15–26 (2006)
7. Kaushik, R.T., Bhandarkar, M.: Greenhdfs: towards an energy-conserving, storage-efficient, hybrid Hadoop compute cluster. In: Proceedings of the USENIX Annual Technical Conference, vol. 109, p. 34 (2010)
8. Khosla, A., Das Sarma, A., Hamid, R.: What makes an image popular? In: Proceedings of the 23rd International Conference on World Wide Web, pp. 867–876. ACM (2014)
9. Kliazovich, D., Bouvry, P., Khan, S.U.: Greencloud: a packet-level simulator of energy-aware cloud computing data centers. J. Supercomput. **62**(3), 1263–1283 (2012). https://doi.org/10.1007/s11227-010-0504-1
10. M. Storer, K. Greenan, E.M., Voruganti, K.: Pergamum: replacing tape with energy efficient reliable, disk-based archival storage. In: Proceedings USENIX Conference on File and Storage Technologies (2008)
11. Okoshi, J., Hasebe, K., Kato, K.: Power-saving in storage systems for internet hosting services with data access prediction. In: 2013 International Green Computing Conference Proceedings, pp. 1–10. IEEE (2013)
12. Pinheiro, E., Bianchini, R.: Energy conservation techniques for disk array-based servers. In: Proceedings of the 18th Annual International Conference on Supercomputing, pp. 68–78. ACM (2004)
13. Zhu, Q., Chen, Z., Tan, L., Zhou, Y., Keeton, K., Wilkes, J.: Hibernator: helping disk arrays sleep through the winter. In: Proceedings ACM symposium on Operating Systems Principles, pp. 177–190 (2005)
14. Gurumurthi, S., Sivasubramaniam, A., Kandemir, M., Franke, H.: DRPM: dynamic speed control for power management in server class disks. In: ACM SIGARCH Computer Architecture News (2003)
15. Shehabi, A., et al.: United states data center energy usage report (2016)

16. Trzciński, T., Rokita, P.: Predicting popularity of online videos using support vector regression. IEEE Trans. Multimedia **19**(11), 2561–2570 (2017)
17. Weddle, C., Oldham, M., Qian, J., Wang, A.I.A., Reiher, P., Kuenning, G.: PARAID: a gear-shifting power-aware RAID. ACM Trans. Storage (TOS) **3**(3), 13 (2007)
18. Yao, X., Wang, J.: RIMAC: a novel redundancy-based hierarchical cache architecture for energy efficient, high performance storage systems. In: Proceedings ACM SIGOPS/EuroSys European Conference on Computer Systems, pp. 249–262 (2006)

Instant Virtual Machine Live Migration

Changyeon Jo⬤, Hyunik Kim⬤, and Bernhard Egger$^{(\boxtimes)}$⬤

Seoul National University, Seoul, Republic of Korea
{changyeon,hyunik,bernhard}@csap.snu.ac.kr

Abstract. Live migration of virtual machines (VMs) is an important tool for data center operators to achieve maintenance, power management, and load balancing. The relatively high cost of live migration makes it difficult to employ live migration for rapid load balancing or power management operations, leaving much of its promised benefits unused. The advance of fast network interconnects has led to the development of distributed shared memory (DSM) that allows a cluster of nodes to utilize remote memory with relatively low overhead. In this paper, we explore VM live migration over DSM. We present and evaluate a novel live migration algorithm on our own DSM implementation. The evaluation of live migrating various VMs executing real-life workloads shows that live migration over DSM can reduce the total migration time by 70% and the total amount of transferred data by 65% on average. The absolute average total migration time of only 1.1 s demonstrates the potential of live migration over DSM to lead to better load balancing, energy management, and total cost of ownership.

Keywords: Virtualization · Distributed shared memory · Live virtual machine migration · Cloud computing

1 Introduction

The growing size of datasets in modern memory-intensive workloads presents unique challenges to cloud computing infrastructure and the underlying system software. To process such workloads, Amazon EC2, for example, offers instances with up to 24 TiB of RAM [2]. In this context, two challenges are of particular interest: (1) the total memory footprint of such workloads does not fit into the physical memory of a single machine, and (2) the working set size fluctuates strongly over time. While the first challenge could be addressed by paging to secondary storage, such a system would need to encompass both a large physical memory and abundant fast secondary storage - both measures that render it difficult to efficiently utilize memory resources and that increase the total cost of ownership (TCO) of a data center.

Distributed shared memory (DSM) has long been proposed as a remedy to solve the problem of limited local memory. DSM provides a unified address space across a cluster of physical machines that can be accessed by any machine, whether the accessed memory is local or remote. This allows to allocate more memory for

© Springer Nature Switzerland AG 2020
K. Djemame et al. (Eds.): GECON 2020, LNCS 12441, pp. 155–170, 2020.
https://doi.org/10.1007/978-3-030-63058-4_14

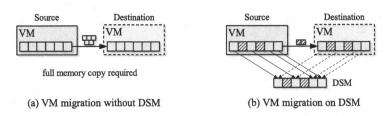

(a) VM migration without DSM   (b) VM migration on DSM

Fig. 1. DSM live migration

running workloads than is physically available on the host it is running on. DSM also enables elastic use of memory across physical node boundaries which helps to raise the overall memory utilization and lower the TCO of a cluster. Despite the many advantages of deploying DSM in data centers, however, DSM has been deemed impractical in production environments due to its significantly longer latency to access remote memory. The recent advances in fast network interconnects are rapidly closing the gap between local and remote memory accesses. For example, an off-the-shelf commodity Mellanox ConnectX-6 network interface card (NIC) achieves sub-microsecond access latencies and 100 Gbit/s bandwidth over remote direct memory access (RDMA). This modern high-performance networking hardware revives the idea of DSM in the era of cloud computing, and recent research shows that DSM can provide on-par performance compared to running applications entirely in local memory [8,9,13,15,17,20].

In addition to DSM achieving higher utilization of memory resources, it also enables novel optimizations for virtualized environments. Live migration of a virtual machine, i.e., the act of moving the execution context along with all volatile data of a VM from one physical host to another while the VM is running, not only enables data center operators to perform maintenance on physical machines, but also to balance the load between physical hosts [19]. If a physical machine is running low on resources, some VMs are live-migrated away to avoid a resource overload and provide a better service. On the other hand, consolidation of VMs from lightly-loaded hosts on fewer nodes can help lower the energy consumption and TCO of a data center.

This paper focuses on live migration of VMs in a DSM environment. While traditional approaches copy the entire volatile state of a VM - including its main memory and paged out data on secondary storage - from the source to the destination host, the novel approach presented in this work employs the local memory as a cache for DSM. When migrating a VM, only the local cache of the VM's volatile data needs to be migrated since all other memory is directly accessible through the DSM (Fig. 1).

We first present the design and implementation of DSM that is tailored to virtual environments. The DSM uses RDMA to reduce remote memory access latency and runs VMs without a significant performance degradation even under a highly memory-constrained environment. We then discuss a novel VM migration algorithm employing DSM to reduce the total migration time by sending only the contents of the local memory to the destination. An evaluation of VMs

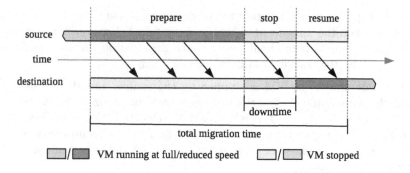

Fig. 2. VM live migration overview.

running modern memory-intensive applications demonstrates that, on average, the presented approach is able to reduce the total migration time by 70% and can migrate large-memory VMs almost instantly.

The contributions of this paper are as follows:

(1) A high-performance DSM for virtualized environments that runs applications without a noticeable performance degradation on DSM.
(2) A novel DSM-based VM live migration algorithm that does not require an entire memory copy.
(3) An implementation and evaluation of the techniques in QEMU/KVM.
(4) Results that show almost instant live migration of VMs running various realistic workloads.

2   Background of VM Live Migration and DSM

This section briefly introduces VM live migration and distributed shared memory.

2.1   VM Live Migration

Live migration is a technique that moves a running VM from one physical host to another without stopping the execution of the VM. The main action of live migration consists of copying the entire volatile state of the VM, including its memory, from the source machine to the destination host. The memory of a VM can be copied before or after moving the execution state (VCPU register values, device driver states) to the destination host. The VM is only briefly stopped during the transfer of the execution state. Figure 2 shows the different phases of live migration.

Prepare: In this phase, the source starts to copy the volatile state of the VM (mostly the data in the memory) from the source to the destination host. Since the VM keeps running on the source, it may alter memory that has already been transferred to the host, therefore *pre-copy*-based live migration algorithms iteratively copy the modified state to the destination host. Pre-copy enters the *Stop* phase when the amount of dirtied memory falls below a certain threshold. The VM experiences a minimal performance degradation during the *Prepare* phase caused by the tracking of dirtied memory pages.

Stop: In this phase, the VM is stopped on the source, and the states of the VM on the source and the destination host are synchronized. When the synchronization completes, the VM is resumed on the destination host. The length of the *Stop* phase depends on the amount of data to be synchronized, and the minimization of this phase is typically an important optimization goal of live migration algorithms.

Resume: This phase only exists in live migration algorithms that do not transfer the entire state in the *Prepare* and *Stop* phase. During the *Resume* phase, the destination host fetches the remaining volatile state from the source host in the background. Data accessed by the VM that still resides on the source is reactively fetched from the source which typically leads to a heavy performance degradation of the VM. *Post-copy*-based live migration operate in this manner. The advantage of this technique is that it effectively reduces the total amount of data to be transferred by skipping the iterative pre-copy phase; however, accesses to data still residing on the source can severely degrade the performance of the VM.

2.2   Performance Metrics of VM Live Migration

To accommodate large in-memory workloads, cloud service providers have begun to offer VMs with tens to thousands GiBs of memory [2,6,7]. Despite the increased network bandwidth, migrating such large amounts of data not only takes a long time but also consumes a large amount of network bandwidth; optimization of several performance metrics is thus of importance. The major performance metrics of VM live migration are:

- The **total migration time** denotes the time from start to end of the migration.
- The **downtime** represents the duration of the *stop* phase, i.e., period during which the VM is unavailable to the user.
- The **total transferred data** measures the total amount of data transferred from source to destination.
- **Performance degradation** is a measure representing the performance degradation experienced by the VM during live migration such as reduced throughput or increased service latency.

2.3   Distributed Shared Memory

Distributed shared memory (DSM) provides a global shared address space for all machines in the same cluster. DSM provides an easy-to-use communication mechanism for distributed applications. It also enables the execution of applications with a large working set that does not fit into the memory of a single machine (Fig. 3).

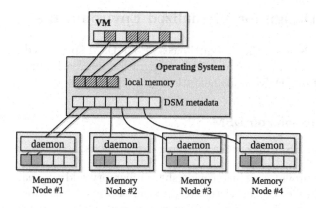

Fig. 3. DSM design

DSM can be implemented using hardware-based or software-based approaches. In this paper, we focus on software-based DSM. A common practice of software-based approaches is to implement DSM using virtual memory. The virtual-to-physical address translation process enables interception of accesses to locations outside the local memory of a machine and redirection to the DSM. The overhead of remote accesses is minimized by designating a portion of the local memory as a cache for DSM.

The main obstacles of deploying DSM are the comparatively slow remote memory accesses and the high cost of maintaining a coherent view of DSM in the presence of local caches. To overcome the first obstacle, we employ RDMA (Remote Direct Memory Access) to minimize the software overhead of a remote memory access. The second obstacle is avoided by the observation that VMs do not share memory and thus no explicit coherence management is necessary.

2.4 Why DSM for Virtual Machines?

The major cloud service providers now provide large memory VM instances with up to 24 TiB of memory [1,6,7]. DSM is an efficient way to implement such large memory instances. DSM allows the machines of a cluster to share memory and thus helps increasing the overall memory utilization of the cluster. In addition, modern data-intensive workloads exhibit dynamically changing working set sizes, which implies that a relatively small local memory on the server is sufficient to run the application without a significant performance degradation. The live migration cost of large-memory VMs provides another motivation for deploying DSM in virtualized environments. Large-memory VMs tend to experience significantly higher migration costs and have been reported as a reason for service disruption in production clusters [3,19]. DSM can reduce the cost of VM migration by significanly reducing the amount of memory to be copied, which makes deploying DSM further attractive. We expect that cloud service providers will start deploying DSM in their datacenters in the near future.

3 DSM Design for Virtualized Environments

This section discusses the design choices of our DSM specialized for virtualized environments and presents a novel live migration approach aimed at exploiting the benefit of our DSM implementation.

3.1 Assumptions on DSM

The presented DSM makes the following assumptions:

- The DSM provides a cluster-wide shared memory address space.
- The DSM relies on the virtual-to-physical address translation mechanism of the host operating system to allow transparent access to remote memory.
- The working set of an application is copied into local memory for direct access and to hide the remote memory access latency through a transparent caching mechanism.
- The DSM does not provide transparent cache coherence. Coherent memory is supported but requires explicit API calls before synchronization points. This greatly simplifies the design of the DSM and achieves far better performance than software-based transparent cache coherence.

Unlike traditional DSM designs, we assume that only one application (a VM) exclusively accesses its DSM-backed memory address space and data sharing is only enabled upon request. These properties are sufficient to execute VMs on DSM and allow VMs to run with little performance degradation. Any DSM implementation that shares the same characteristics can be easily modified to support the presented live migration algorithm in this paper.

3.2 DSM Components

This section briefly introduces the design of the DSM, how to allocate memory to a VM (or an application), and the discusses the components of the DSM.

User Interface. The DSM is implemented as a kernel module and exposed to user space as a character device. The virtual machine monitor (VMM) or regular applications use this device to reserve the desired amount of distributed shared memory. The memory is mapped into the virtual address space of the VM by the VMM. To the VM, the entire memory space appears as local physical memory, i.e., the VM is not aware that it is running on top of DSM.

OS Service. Our DSM kernel module provides the illusion of a single address space covering both local and remote memory. It transparently manages an area of local memory as a cache for recently accessed DSM. Accesses to remote memory cause a page fault which is handled by the DSM kernel module. The accessed page is fetched from the remote node and brought into local memory. If the local

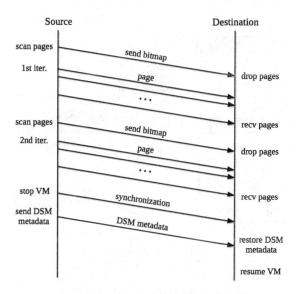

Fig. 4. DSM live migration timeline

cache is full, a victim page is selected and written back to remote memory to make room for the new page. Another task of the OS service is to balance memory requests across the cluster. The service communicates with the memory nodes and distributes memory allocation requests nodes with low memory pressure.

Memory Nodes. All nodes in the cluster act both as providers and consumers of DSM. A consumer node may send several requests to different nodes that then reserve the requested amount in their local memories. A centralized approach with one or separate pool of memory nodes (called as memory disaggregation and gaining popularity in the recent days) is also possible and does not change the semantics of the presented DSM and live migration algorithm as long as all remote memory is accessible from both the source and destination host.

3.3   DSM-Optimized Live Migration Algorithm

In traditional environments, the volatile state of a VM is local to a host and thus needs to be copied to the destination in its entirety to enable live migration. In a DSM environment, however, all memory except the data cached in local nodes is visible from any node in the cluster. This allows us to design a novel live migration approach that eliminates most of the state transfer in the *Prepare* phase. Figure 4 shows a timeline of the events in DSM-optimized live migration. We first explain the necessary steps of the live migration algorithm on the source node.

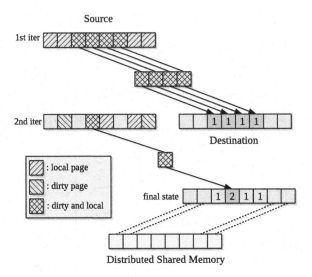

Fig. 5. DSM live migration example

Step 1: Preparation. The source node notifies the destination node of the imminent migration. The destination host performs the necessary initialization such as starting an empty process for the VM. This step takes only a negligible amount time with respect to the total migration time.

Step 2: Iterative Pre-copy. The first task of the iterative pre-copy algorithm usually encompasses sending the entire memory once to the destination. The presented DSM-optimized algorithm, however, only needs to send the pages that exist in the local cache. Memory residing in a remote node does not need to be transferred since the data can be accessed directly from the destination node. Note that in post-copy mode, this step is executed after the following step 3.

Figure 5 shows an example of iterative pre-copy under DSM. In the first iteration, the VMM marks all pages as dirty in order to transfer the entire memory to the destination. For a VM using DSM, however, only a subset of all pages exists in the local memory. The example shows that four pages with index 2 to 5 are cached in local memory. In the first iteration, all pages are marked dirty. The set of pages to be sent to the destination is given by the intersection of the dirty and the local pages. During the data transfer of the first iteration, the VM keeps running and modifies pages 2, 4, and 8. In the second iteration, again the intersection of all local pages (pages 4, 5, and 7) and dirty pages (pages 2, 4, and 8), that is, page 4, is sent to the destination. Pages 2 and 8 were modified but have already been synchronized with their remote copy, so they do not need to be transferred. In these two iterations, a total of five pages need to be transferred to the destination with our DSM-optimized algorithm. The original pre-copy algorithm would have to send 11 pages (8 in the first, 3 in the second iteration) in total.

Step 3: Synchronization. In the synchronization phase, the VM is stopped, so no pages are dirtied at the source anymore. The dirtied and local pages are sent in a last iteration along with the VM's CPU and device state. In this step, the DSM-optimized algorithm also transfers the DSM metadata to the destination host. The DSM metadata for a VM contains the location of all remote memory pages and is required on the destination node to access the remote data of the VM.

Step 4: Cleanup. In this last step, the VM is terminated on the source host.

Destination Node. The tasks of the destination are simpler than those on the source node. Two additional steps are required to correctly complete the DSM-optimized VM migration. At the beginning of every iteration, the destination receives the status of DSM-local pages from the source. The destination computes the intersection of DSM-local pages from the source and DSM-local pages on the destination. Then the destination purges all DSM-local pages that do not belong to the intersection an can thus be restored from remote memory. The purged pages are reused to hold new DSM-local pages sent from the source; this allows us to limit the amount of local memory required for VM live migration on the destination node. Second, in the stop phase, the destination receives the DSM metadata from the source node and maps it into the address space of the VM on the destination host to enable access to its data.

4   Implementation

This section gives some implementation details of the DSM and the modifications to QEMU/KVM required to support the DSM-optimized live migration algorithm.

4.1   Linux Kernel DSM

Our DSM is implemented in a Linux kernel module. The kernel module maps the DSM as a character device node into user-space. DSM-backed memory is obtained by invoking the `mmap` system call on that device node. The returned virtual address range represents a distributed memory region. This virtual address range is not mapped to any memory initially. Accesses to unmapped addresses trigger a pagefault that is handled by our DSM module. The module maps the accessed page to local or remote memory.

Resolving a Pagefault. The early pagefaults are resolved by allocating memory from local memory. We request a 4 KB page from the kernel, map the page to the faulted address, and let the application continue. As the VM continues to access more pages in its virtual address space, the size of the locally allocated pages will eventually hit the set limit allowed for caching DSM data. From this point on, the kernel module starts to page out pages that have not been accessed recently to remote memory. To do so, it first finds a node with sufficient free memory to back up the part of the data in the local memory, then reserves the required amount on that node, and finally copies the victim page(s) to the remote node. If a pagefault is to a paged-out address, the kernel fetches the data from the remote node, places it in a local page, updates the page tables, and then lets the VM continue.

Background processes running on all nodes of the DSM periodically exchange information about the available free memory. Donor nodes are selected on-demand using the worst-fit policy. The minimum memory request size is 64 MB to reduce the overhead of DSM metadata. The donor node allocates a contiguous address range in its memory, and the kernel module maps a part of the VM's virtual address space to this area. Victim pages are selected by an approximate-LRU algorithm implementing a CLOCK policy [4].

Memory Server. Each memory node in the DSM cluster runs a daemon to serve memory requests from other nodes. Each memory server is connected to all other nodes. Memory allocation requests are handled using remote procedure calls (RPC). In response to an allocation request, the memory server locally allocates memory using `malloc` and registers the area for `RDMA`. After the registration is complete, the memory server replies to the request by sending the allocated memory's DSM metadata which is used by the requesting node for later accesses.

4.2   Userspace DSM Library

To allow the implementation of our DSM-optimized live migration technique in userspace, a userspace library is available that provides the necessary API. The API implements the following functionality: (1) set local DSM cache size, (2) read status of local DSM page, (3) make a DSM region persistent, (4) drop specific pages of a DSM region, and (5) provide access to DSM metadata. The library is used by the DSM-optimized algorithm presented in Sect. 3.3.

4.3   DSM Live Migration Implementation in QEMU/KVM

We implement the DSM-optimized VM live migration technique in the most popular VM hypervisor, QEMU/KVM [5]. QEMU/KVM has been widely adopted in production clouds, hence adding the new feature to QEMU/KVM will allow for an easy adoption of the new approach into existing data centers. The functions enabling live migration over DSM are implemented in a library so the technique can be easily accessed by other hypervisors such as VMware and Xen.

Starting a VM on DSM. QEMU/KVM internally allocates a contiguous address range from anonymous memory using `mmap`. Modifying QEMU/KVM to use DSM-backed memory is trivial: the only necessary change is to provide a file descriptor to the DSM device node instead of a NULL pointer to signal anonymous memory. The DSM kernel modules transparently handles all accesses to memory of a VM, local or remote, so VM itself requires no modification and can make use of DSM-backed memory transparently.

DSM Live Migration in QEMU. QEMU/KVM supports many live migration techniques out-of-the-box with a clean API. Adding a new live migration technique requires describing the parameters of the new live migration technique, then QEMU automatically generates the boilerplate code. The DSM-optimized live migration algorithm is implemented with around 350 lines of code. The code mainly invokes the DSM userspace API to retrieve a page's status, to obtain a list of dirtied pages and compute the pages to be transferred, and to send a few messages from the source to the destination to synchronize the live migration steps between the source and the destination.

5   Evaluation

This section evaluates the DSM-optimized live migration technique and compares it with DSM-unaware pre-copy as available in QEMU/KVM.

5.1   Test Environment

The source and destination nodes are equipped with an Intel(R) Xeon(R) Silver 4114 2.20 GHz processor (10-core, 20-thread) and 64 GiB of local memory. Each machine runs Ubuntu 18.04 with Linux kernel version 5.3.7. The machines are connected by a ConnectX-4 56g Infiniband NIC with a theoretical bandwidth of 56 Gbit/s and a latency of 0.6 μs. The DSM and VM live migration traffic share the same Infiniband connection and can interfere. The VM network is physically separated and uses a 1 Gbit/s Ethernet NIC. QEMU/KVM version 4.2 provides the hypervisor, and the VMs run Ubuntu 18.04 as their guest OS. The VMs use network-attached storage to access their disk images. VM disk I/O traffic is routed through the VM network. All VMs used in the experiments are equipped with 4-VCPU and 8 GB of local memory. The local memory is limited by our DSM depending on the evaluated scenario.

5.2   Workloads Used in the Evaluation

The presented live migration technique over DSM is evaluated with a wide range of applications from high-performance parallel processing benchmark suites (Parsec, NPB, and Spark) and the CIFAR10 Tensorflow inference benchmark. All applications run with four threads to fully utilize all available cores. The total memory footprint of the applications is 2.5 GB on average. The average working set size (measured by scanning the access bit in the page table) over a 60 s window is 1.2 GB on average with a standard deviation of 877 MB. The workloads have dynamically changing working sets and the memory footprints are large enough to stress the DSM.

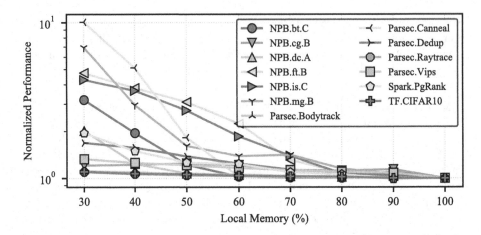

Fig. 6. Application performance on DSM

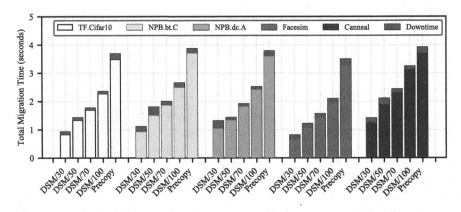

Fig. 7. Total migration time of the DSM approach and the baseline

5.3 Application Performance on DSM

We first show that DSM is a viable option for a virtualized environment by evaluating application performance degradation in dependence of the allocated local memory. We tested application performance in a VM by limiting the DSM local memory size against the application's total memory footprint. The baseline is obtained by running the VM entirely in local memory; sufficient memory is available such that no paging occurs. Figure 6 shows the application performance of DSM-backed-storage normalized to the baseline; note the log-scale of the Y axis.

The results in Fig. 6 show that all applications run without noticeable performance degradation with 80% of local memory. Even in the extreme case of only providing 30% of the total memory footprint as local memory, more than half of all applications show a high tolerance with a slowdown of under 2. Note that the tested applications are all memory-bound, so we expect that less memory-intensive applications such as smaller databases and web service application will show even better tolerance than the evaluated applications.

5.4 Performance of DSM-Optimized Live Migration

Next, we present the results of our DSM-optimized live migration algorithm applied to VMs running the applications from Sect. 5.3. The DSM-optimized approach is compared to the pre-copy algorithm implemented in QEMU/KVM. QEMU/KVM supports optional data compression to reduce the amount of transferred data. However, we found that data compression is counterproductive since the compression algorithm cannot saturate the fast network links. As a consequence, data compression is not enabled for the baseline and our DSM-optimized migration technique.

Figure 7 the total migration time of the presented DSM-optimized live migration algorithm compared to QEMU/KVM's pre-copy algorithm. The y-axis represents the absolute total migration time in seconds, the x-axis five representative applications with at 30%, 50%, 70%, and 100% of the total application memory footprint in local memory. The Infiniband NIC is used in IPoIB (IP over Infiniband) mode and the TCP protocol for the data transfer. The result shows that the presented approach clearly outperforms the baseline. The more memory is remote, the better performs the DSM-optimized live migration. For example, with 30% local memory, the source needs to send at most 30% of the total VM's memory in one iteration. Note that our approach also outperforms QEMU's pre-copy with 100% of VM memory kept locally. This seemingly counterintuitive result stems from the way zero pages are handled. Zero pages are pages whose contents are only 0s; QEMU excludes such pages to reduce the amount of data transferred. While QEMU has to inspect every page to determine whether it is a zero page or not, this information is readily available in our DSM, which considerably speeds up the detection of zero pages and leads to overall better performance. On average, our approach reduces the total migration time by 70 and the downtime by 8%. The total amount of transferred data is reduced by 65% at a 30% local memory ratio setting.

Overall, these results are very promising and show the potential of DSM-backed virtualization. Live migration needs to be fast when a node experiences a shortage of resources. It is reasonable to assume that in this case, the ratio of local memory has already been reduced at least for some VMs; and migrating such VMs away from the overloaded outperforms standard live migration by a factor 2–4.

6 Related Work

VM live migration and DSM have more than a decade of history. In this section, we introduce previous work and highlight our contribution.

VM Live Migration. Clark [11] first presented the *pre-copy* approach and showed that a VM can be migrated seamlessly with its workload After the inception of pre-copy, many follow-up works have presented optimization techniques to make live migration more efficient. Hines [14] presented the *post-copy* approach which trades VM performance for a reduction in the transferred data and a shorter downtime. Many works have shown optimization techniques for live migration performance that can be applied to both pre-copy and post-copy. In difference to this work, most of the published research focuses on VMs with a small amount of memory of up to 10 GiB. VM workloads have changed significantly along with hardware improvements, ubiquitous parallel processing, and much larger working set sizes than a decade ago. We argue that it is the right time to think about a fundamentally different approach for VM live migration; such as, for example, the DSM approach presented in this paper.

Distributed Shared Memory. DSM also has a long history in the computer systems, and many different designs have been proposed. In this paper, we focus on executing VMs or unmodified processes on a mix of local and remote memory to improve overall utilization of memory resources. One early work on this topic is NSwap [16]. As the name implies, it implements a swap device using remote memory as secondary storage. It is a special kind of DSM that does not support cache coherence, naming, and data sharing but provides a simple way of space sharing of the cluster of memory. Many follow-up works show some promising aspects of using remote memory as an extension of local memory, however, none of them were realized in a production environment due to the slow networks and insufficient computation power of that time. Similar ideas have been revived with the significant advances in networking hardware in recent days [8, 9, 12, 13, 15, 20]. The performance gap between local and remote memory access is now quite close [10, 18], and we expect this trend to continue with optical networks.

Many recent works on this topic show promising results of running applications on a mix of local and remote memory; in difference to this work, they focus on native applications and not virtual machines. Certain types of application have been shown to perform well even in highly memory-constrained environments; a results that makes DSM for virtual environments even more promising.

7   Conclusion

This paper has presented a design for distributed shared memory tailored at virtualized environments. A novel DSM-optimized live migration algorithm makes use of the DSM's properties to improve several metrics of VM migration. The presented approach is able to significantly reduce both the total migration time and the downtime of large memory VMs and enables almost instant VM live migration for moderately-sized VMs.

Acknowledgments. This work was supported by the National Research Foundation of Korea (NRF) funded by the Korean government, in part, by grants NRF-2015K1A3A1A14021288, 2016R1A2B4009193, by the BK21 Plus for Pioneers in Innovative Computing (Dept. of Computer Science and Engineering, SNU, grant 21A20151113068), and by the Promising-Pioneering Researcher Program of Seoul National University in 2015. ICT at Seoul National University provided research facilities for this study.

References

1. Amazon EC2 instance types - amazon web services. https://aws.amazon.com/ec2/instance-types/. Accessed July 2020
2. Amazon EC2 instance types - memory optimized - high memory. https://aws.amazon.com/ec2/instance-types/#Memory_Optimized. Accessed July 2020
3. Google cloud platform blog: Now shipping: ultramem machine types with up to 4TB of ram. https://cloudplatform.googleblog.com/2018/07/now-shipping-ultramem-machine-types-with-up-to-4tb-of-ram.html. Accessed July 2020
4. Page replacement algorithm - Wikipedia. https://en.wikipedia.org/wiki/Page_replacement_algorithm. Accessed July 2020
5. QEMU. https://www.qemu.org/. Accessed July 2020
6. Virtual machine series—Microsoft Azure. https://azure.microsoft.com/en-us/pricing/details/virtual-machines/series/. Accessed July 2020
7. VM instances pricing—compute engine documentation — google cloud. https://cloud.google.com/compute/vm-instance-pricing. Accessed July 2020
8. Aguilera, M.K., et al.: Remote regions: a simple abstraction for remote memory. In: 2018 USENIX Annual Technical Conference (USENIX ATC 2018) (2018)
9. Amaro, E., et al.: Can far memory improve job throughput? In: Proceedings of the Fifteenth European Conference on Computer Systems. EuroSys 2020. Association for Computing Machinery, New York (2020). https://doi.org/10.1145/3342195.3387522
10. Binnig, C., Crotty, A., Galakatos, A., Kraska, T., Zamanian, E.: The end of slow networks: it's time for a redesign. Proc. VLDB Endow. **9**(7) (2016). https://doi.org/10.14778/2904483.2904485
11. Clark, C., et al.: Live migration of virtual machines. In: Proceedings of the 2nd Conference on Symposium on Networked Systems Design and Implementation - Volume 2, NSDI 2005 (2005)
12. Gao, P.X., et al.: Network requirements for resource disaggregation. In: 12th USENIX Symposium on Operating Systems Design and Implementation (OSDI 2016) (2016)
13. Gu, J., Lee, Y., Zhang, Y., Chowdhury, M., Shin, K.G.: Efficient memory disaggregation with infiniswap. In: 14th USENIX Symposium on Networked Systems Design and Implementation (NSDI 2017) (2017)
14. Hines, M.R., Gopalan, K.: Post-copy based live virtual machine migration using adaptive pre-paging and dynamic self-ballooning. In: Proceedings of the 2009 ACM SIGPLAN/SIGOPS International Conference on Virtual Execution Environments, VEE 2009. Association for Computing Machinery, New York (2009). https://doi.org/10.1145/1508293.1508301
15. Koh, K., Kim, K., Jeon, S., Huh, J.: Disaggregated cloud memory with elastic block management. IEEE Trans. Comput. **68**(1), 39–52 (2018)

16. Newhall, T., Finney, S., Ganchev, K., Spiegel, M.: Nswap: a network swapping module for Linux clusters. In: Kosch, H., Böszörményi, L., Hellwagner, H. (eds.) Euro-Par 2003. LNCS, vol. 2790, pp. 1160–1169. Springer, Heidelberg (2003). https://doi.org/10.1007/978-3-540-45209-6_157
17. Nitu, V., Teabe, B., Tchana, A., Isci, C., Hagimont, D.: Welcome to zombieland: practical and energy-efficient memory disaggregation in a datacenter. In: Proceedings of the Thirteenth EuroSys Conference, EuroSys 2018. Association for Computing Machinery, New York (2018). https://doi.org/10.1145/3190508.3190537
18. Rumble, S.M., Ongaro, D., Stutsman, R., Rosenblum, M., Ousterhout, J.K.: It's time for low latency. In: HotOS, vol. 13 (2011)
19. Ruprecht, A., et al.: VM live migration at scale. In: Proceedings of the 14th ACM SIGPLAN/SIGOPS International Conference on Virtual Execution Environments, VEE 2018. Association for Computing Machinery, New York (2018). https://doi.org/10.1145/3186411.3186415
20. Shan, Y., Huang, Y., Chen, Y., Zhang, Y.: Legoos: a disseminated, distributed OS for hardware resource disaggregation. In: 13th USENIX Symposium on Operating Systems Design and Implementation (OSDI 2018) (2018)

Economic Computing and Storage

Towards Economical Live Migration
in Data Centers

Youngsu Cho[iD], Changyeon Jo[iD], Hyunik Kim[iD], and Bernhard Egger[✉][iD]

Seoul National University, Seoul, Republic of Korea
{youngsu,changyeon,hyunik,bernhard}@csap.snu.ac.kr

Abstract. Live migration of virtual machines (VMs) enables maintenance, load balancing, and power management in data centers. The cost
of live migration on several key metrics combined with strict service-level
objectives (SLOs), however, typically limits its practical application to
situations where the underlying physical host has to undergo maintenance. As a consequence, the potential benefits of live migration with
respect to increased resource usage and lower power consumption remain
largely untouched. In this paper, we argue that live migration-aware
SLOs combined with smart live migration algorithm selection provides
an economically viable model for live migration in data centers. Based on
a model predicting key parameters of VM live migration, an optimization
algorithm selects the live migration technique that is expected to meet
client SLOs while at the same time to optimize target metrics given by
the data center operator. A comparison with the state-of-the-art shows
that the presented guided live migration technique selection achieves significantly fewer SLO violations while, at the same time, minimizing the
effect of live migration on the infrastructure.

Keywords: Live migration · Live migration modeling · Data center

1 Introduction

Millions of virtual machines run in data centers of large Infrastructure as a Service (IaaS) providers. Virtualization enables service providers to achieve a higher
utilization of their infrastructure whilst providing isolation between the multiple
co-located tenants [4]. A key technology to achieve high availability and resource
utilization in warehouse-scale computing (WSC) is live migration. Live migration transfers a running VM from one host to another and enables operators to
balance the load between hosts, to perform maintenance on hard- and software,
and to reduce the data center's energy consumption by consolidating VMs onto
fewer machines. Various cloud resource management systems propose employing live migration for consolidation and load balancing [13,26,29,35], however,
live migration in commercial data centers is still mostly used for maintenance
only. Google, for example, migrates over a million VMs every month to perform
maintenance on hard- and software in its data centers [11,28].

© Springer Nature Switzerland AG 2020
K. Djemame et al. (Eds.): GECON 2020, LNCS 12441, pp. 173–188, 2020.
https://doi.org/10.1007/978-3-030-63058-4_15

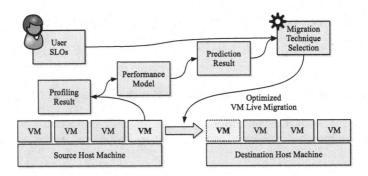

Fig. 1. High-level organization of the presented framework.

Despite the economical benefits of reduced energy consumption and higher resource utilization, a number of reasons wide-spread adoption of live migration a means to load balancing and power savings in data centers. First, live migration causes a small performance reduction of the migrated VM. This makes it difficult to fulfill end-user SLOs guaranteeing a certain throughput and high availability. Second, live migration increases the network traffic and CPU load in the data center. Violated SLOs and additional resource usage both incur a short-term financial cost to the operators while the mid- to long-term benefits are harder to quantify [34]. The resulting immobility of VMs is one of the root causes for resource underutilization in data centers as is evident from Alibaba and Google clusters utilization data that shows large opportunities for improvement [2,4,12].

This paper makes the case that new SLOs that take into account the characteristics of live migration combined with smart live migration open new opportunities for economical live migration in WSC. SLOs that permit a certain performance degradation enable live migration of such VMs without incurring a financial penalty. This allows data center operators to apply live migration more frequently and achieve higher resource utilization and a lower total cost of ownership (TCO). This, in turn, allows for new VM pricing models and increased competitiveness.

The main obstacle to live migration-aware SLOs the inability to accurately quantify the effect of live migration on the VM and the data center. The performance degradation of a VM during live migration depends on multiple factors that include the employed live migration technique, the size of the VM, and the workload running in the VM. Similarly, the effect on resources of the data center such as consumed network bandwidth and CPU utilization needs to be quantifiable.

To this end, this work presents a framework for economic live migration in data centers; Figure 1 shows its high-level organization. At the core of the framework is a model that predicts several key metrics related to live migration under consideration of the live migration technique, the VM, and the data center. The framework considers the SLOs of the VMs and migrates VMs whose migration is expected to fulfill the SLOs of all involved VMs. The model is able to predict five

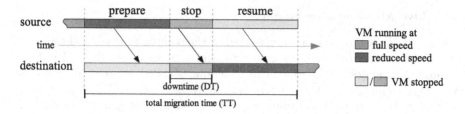

Fig. 2. Live migration phases.

key metrics for the nine most common live migration techniques in a heterogeneous data center. The proposed live migration-aware SLOs define the maximum duration and performance degradation an end-user is willing to accept during live migration. The presented framework is evaluated in a small heterogeneous data center. The framework is able to migrate VMs with far fewer SLO violations than any single static live migration technique, demonstrating that, when applied judiciously, live migration has the potential to lead to more flexibility, higher resource utilization, and a lower TCO in commercial data centers.

The remainder of this paper is organized as follows. Section 2 discusses live migration and its metrics. Sections 3 and 4 presents the model and the end-user SLOs. Section 5 details the experimental setup and evaluates the presented framework. Section 6 discusses relevant related work, and Sect. 7 concludes this paper.

2   Background

2.1   The Anatomy of Live Migration

Migrating a VM from one physical host to another requires transferring the entire volatile state of the VM. The volatile state of a VM includes its memory contents, the execution context, and device buffers. With typical VM memory sizes from four to tens of gigabytes the transfer of the main memory dominates the migration overhead [7].

Live migration can be divided into three distinct phases (Fig. 2): *prepare*, *stop-and-copy*, and *resume*. In the *prepare* phase, part of the VM's memory is transferred to the destination host, while the VM keeps running on the source. It is possible that the VM experiences a performance degradation that is caused by the additional resource consumption of the migration technique. The *prepare* phase is succeeded by the *stop-and-copy* phase during which the VM is completely stopped and the execution control is transferred from the source to the destination host. In the *resume* phase, finally, the VM is restarted on the destination and the remaining volatile state is fetched from the source host. Some migration techniques do not copy the entire volatile state in the prepare phase. This can lead to a severe performance degradation during the resume phase.

2.2   Live Migration Techniques

Live migration techniques can be classified by the point in time when the memory of a VM is transferred. One extreme is to send all data before the VM instance is moved to the destination host; this technique is called *pre-copy* [6]. Since the VM keeps running while the memory is being transferred, dirtied memory pages (i.e., pages that are modified while a transfer is ongoing) need to be copied more than once. Pre-copy iteratively copies dirtied memory pages to the destination host until the amount of dirtied pages reaches a given threshold. The VM is then stopped on the source host and the remaining dirty pages and the VM context are transferred to the destination. Finally, the VM is restarted on the destination host. Since the entire volatile state of the VM has been transferred, pre-copy has a very short resume phase.

At the other end of the spectrum lies *post-copy* [14] that immediately transfers the minimal context and restarts the VM on the destination host. The VM's main memory is fetched in the background and on-demand from the source host. Post-copy transfers each memory page exactly once, however, the long resume phase can lead to severe performance degradation in the VM. As usual in engineering, the optimum is seldom found at the extremes; several hybrid live migration techniques have been proposed that split the transfer of the volatile state between the prepare and the resume phase.

In addition to the decision when to transfer the volatile state, there exist several orthogonal optimizations that improve the performance of live migration. *CPU throttling* limits the performance of the VM's CPUs to reduce the rate of dirtied memory. While this optimization can improve the performance of the pre-copy technique, it may also lead to significant performance degradation in the VM. Data compression is another optimization aiming at reducing the amount data to be transferred. Typically, two variants are supported: data compression and delta compression. *Data compression* uses a standard block compression algorithm to compress the data before sending it over the network. Data compression works especially well if the entropy of the data is low, however, the computational overhead incurred by the compression algorithm may cause a performance reduction of the migrated and the co-located VMs. *Delta compression* tries to solve this problem by using the computationally light delta compression algorithm. The significant memory requirements of this algorithm may prohibit its application in situations when live migration is initated because the source host is low on memory.

This paper explores the two basic algorithms, pre-copy and post-copy, and seven combinations of pre-copy with the optimizations CPU throttling, data compression, and data compression as shown in Table 1. The presented framework is implemented in the KVM/QEMU virtual machine manager (VMM) [5] that supports all of these algorithms out-of-the-box. A number of alternative optimization techniques for live migration have been proposed [15,17,19,20,23,31] but are not considered in this work because they are not supported by the virtualization layer employed in industrial data centers.

Table 1. Evaluated migration techniques

Abbreviation	Description
PRE	Pre-copy
POST	Post-copy
DLTC	Pre-copy with delta compression
DTC	Pre-copy with data compression
DLTC.DTC	Pre-copy with delta compression followed by data compression
THR	Throttled pre-copy
THR.DLTC	Throttled pre-copy with delta compression
THR.DTC	Throttled pre-copy with data compression
THR.DLTC.DTC	Throttled pre-copy with delta compression followed by data compression

3   Live Migration Model

The model employed in this paper is able to predict the performance of several live migration metrics (Sect. 3.1) for each of the nine live migration techniques (Sect. 2.2) for a given VM. The model takes as input the relevant parameters of the workload running inside a VM, information about the involved source and destination hosts, and the available network bandwidth. These parameters are gathered prior to the migration during a brief profiling phase. The model extends the state-of-the-art in live migration modeling [18]. In contrast to [18], the presented model has been extended to support heterogeneous physical nodes and more live migration techniques. The extended model distinguishes between different CPU vendors and types, and the CPU clock frequency.

Given the wide range of live migration techniques, physical hosts, and characteristics of VMs, the model is machine-trained. A large database of several 100'000 live migrations performed in our research cluster using all migration techniques is used as the training data set. Each record contains the characteristics of the VM obtained through black-box profiling, the state of the involved physical hosts, the live migration technique, as well as the actual metrics observed during the migration. In addition to real-world benchmarks and to better cover the large parameter space, the training dataset also contains data obtained from migrating VMs running synthetic workloads. Support vector regression (SVR) [30]) is employed to train the model parameters. A separate model is trained for each combination of the live migration technique, the predicted metric, and the type of the source and destination hosts.

3.1   Live Migration Metrics

Table 2 lists the seven VM live migration metrics measured and predicted in this paper. Metrics of interest to the end-user include the downtime DT, the

Table 2. Measured and modeled live migration metrics.

Metric	Description
Total migration time (TT)	Total elapsed time from start to completion of a migration
Downtime (DT)	Time duration of the *stop-and-copy* phase, i.e., the time during which the VM is stopped
Transferred data (TD)	Total amount of transferred from the source to the destination host
CPU utilization (CPU)	Additional CPU load incurred on the source host during migration
Memory utilization (MEM)	Amount of memory consumed by the live migration algorithm
Performance degradation (PERF)	Performance degradation experienced by migrated VM measured in instructions per second (IPS)
Degradation time (DegT)	Duration of migrated VM's performance degradation

performance degradation $PERF$, and the duration of the degradation $DegT$. Metrics of interest to the data center operator are the total migration time TT, the amount of transferred data TD, and the CPU and memory utilization incurred by the live migration (CPU and MEM). For all seven metrics lower is better.

3.2 Analytically Modeling Performance Degradation

End-user SLOs considered in this work are the *minimally guaranteed CPU performance* and the *duration of the degradation* while a VM is migrated. Users running a throughput-oriented workload may be willing to accept a 90% degradation in performance for a short duration while end-users for latency-critical workloads may prefer an SLO guaranteeing a minimal 10% performance degradation for a longer period of time. Other SLOs such as the frequency of migration are part of future work.

Live migration-aware SLOs are not only of interest to end-users but also to data center operators. VMs that accept a performance degradation during live migration can be offered at a lower price than VMs that are required by SLOs to provide strict tail-latencies. This flexibility allows the data center operators to classify VMs into *stationary VMs* that cannot be migrated and *mobile VMs* whose SLOs allow migration. These mobile VMs can then be targeted for migrations for the purpose of load balancing, increasing utilization and consolidation in a warehouse.

An analysis of real-world workload patterns reveals that predicting the maximal performance degradation based on profiled performance is difficult [7].

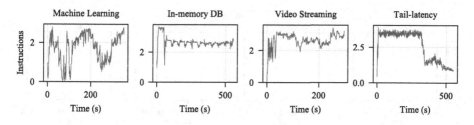

Fig. 3. Workload IPS pattern

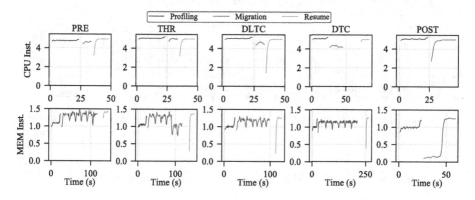

Fig. 4. VM performance in dependence of the migration technique.

Figure 3 shows that workloads exhibit large IPS variations as execution transitions between different phases. Since it is impossible to know whether the profiled IPS was obtained during an idle or a high-load period, predicting the IPS based on such data is not a viable approach. This paper thus predicts the relative performance degradation *PERF* and the duration of the degradation *DurT* based on analytical models that are fine-tuned by measuring performance degradation of synthetic benchmarks during live migration with all techniques and between all combinations of hosts.

Figure 4 plots the IPS of a CPU-intensive (upper row) and memory-intensive (lower row) workload for different migration techniques. The plots reveal that the performance during migration is strongly affected by the host CPU load, the VM CPU utilization, the VM memory size, the working set size, and the page dirty rate. The effect of CPU throttling on performance is visible for memory-intensive workloads migrated using the THRottling technique. Similarly, the severe performance degradation caused by the POST-copy technique is pronounced especially for memory-intensive workloads.

To predict the *guaranteed minimal performance* and the *duration of the degradation* for a workload, live migration technique, and involved hosts, the workload generator is executed with four intensity levels ranging from 0 (CPU bound) to 3 (memory bound) with different working set size and page dirty rates. The results of these experiments are consolidated into a Linear Regression model that allows

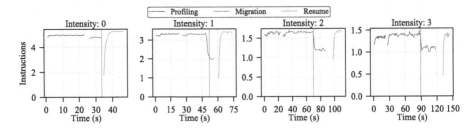

Fig. 5. Estimated start of performance degradation for THR (purple line).

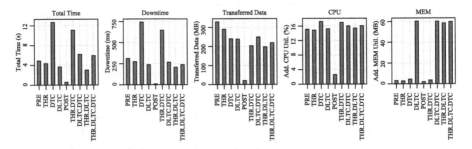

Fig. 6. 10-fold cross validation of the model (geo mean absolute error)

to compute the guaranteed minimal performance of a VM. Figure 5 shows the estimated starting point of throttling for the different memory intensities indicated by the magenta vertical line.

3.3 Predicting Key Live Migration Metrics Using Machine-Learned Models

The remaining five parameters (total migration time, downtime, transferred data, CPU and memory utilization) are predicted by the machine-learned SVR model. The model is trained with around 90'000 live migration instances for each technique and physical host type. In addition to the 20 input features from prior work [18], the model also takes the processor type of the source and destination host as additional inputs to account for the heterogeneity of the physical hosts involved. Figure 6 displays the result of 10-fold cross validation of the presented model trained using a SVR Bagging regressor; details of model training are given in prior work [18]. The accuracy of the model is slightly below that of prior work - which is expected due to the higher number of features caused by heterogeneous hosts and the nine predived live migration techniques.

4   Service Level Objectives and Migration Technique Selection

Existing Service Level Agreements in commercial data centers focus foremost on service uptime [3,10] and allow for little performance variation [8]. As a consequence, virtual machines are *stationary*: once placed on a host, a VM is immobile and migrated only when the host has to undergo maintenance [9]. Stationary VMs stifle efficient load balancing and consolidation, both operations that are beneficial for data center operators to lower the TCO. One of the main reasons of the reluctance to pro-actively live migrate VMs is that the effects of live migration on the migrated VM and the data center are difficult to quantify. The model presented in the preceding section demonstrates that is it possible to predict several key metrics of live migration in an accurate and low-overhead manner. To benefit from this ability to accurately predict the effect of live migration, is necessary to rethink existing migration policies and service level agreements (SLAs).

The ability to predict downtime, guaranteed performance, the duration of the performance degradation of live migration allows service providers to offer what we call SLOs for *mobile* VMs. Service level objectives can be defined from the perspective of the end-user and the service provider. The former are part of the SLA between the end-user and the service provider and typically cause a financial loss when violated. The latter are objectives whose optimization leads to a lower TCO due to reduced resource usage; their violation, however, does not directly lead to contractual violations with financial reparations.

SLOs that enable mobile VMs are beneficial for both the service provider and the end-user. The service provider benefits from a pool of movable VMs that can be migrated to achieve load balancing or node consolidation. The end-user benefits from cheaper VMs since mobile VMs are expected to be priced below stationary VMs.

5 Evaluation

5.1 Cluster Configuration and VM Workloads

VMs are deployed on our internal research cluster comprising eight heterogeneous physical nodes. Four nodes are equipped with a quad-core Intel Skylake i5-6600 processor and 16 GB of physical memory. The other four nodes contain an octa-core AMD FX-8300 processor and 16 GB of physical memory. The nodes are interconnected with three separate networks, one for application traffic, one for migration traffic, and one for remote storage traffic. The nodes run Ubuntu 16.04 with the QEMU-KVM 2.8.5 hypervisor that supports all evaluated live migration techniques from Table 1. Each VM is configured with 1 VCPU and 2 GBs of memory. The migration network has a bandwidth of 1Gbit/s.

The workloads executed in the VMs include Intel-Hadoop Hibench [16], Tailbench [21], YCSB memcached [36], and Mplayer [33]. The Hibench benchmark suite contains several micro-benchmarks and machine learning workloads that are widely used in cloud services. Tailbench consists of latency-critical workloads, and the YCSB Memcached benchmark is designed to evaluate the performance of in-memory database workloads. Mplayer, finally, represents a video-streaming workload.

Table 3. SLOs for mobile VMs.

Policy name	User SLO	Provider SLO	Opt.Goal	Description
Min TT	–	–	TT	Minimize total time
High Performance	DT $\leq$ 1s	CPU 100%	DT	Minimize downtime under strict limits for downtime and performance
	PERF $\geq$ 95%	MEM 512MB		
	DegT $\leq$ 5s			
Least Traffic	DT $\leq$ 2s	CPU 100%	TD	Minimize transferred data with relaxed downtime and performance limits
	PERF $\geq$ 60%	MEM 512MB		
	DegT $\leq$ 20s			
Least Operation Cost	DT $\leq$ 3s	CPU 100%	TT	Minimize migration time with performance guarantees
	PERF $\geq$ 75%	MEM 512MB		
Reduced Downtime	DT $\leq$ 1s	TT 60s	DT	Minimize downtime while limiting migration time and performance degradation
	PERF $\geq$ 50%			
	DegT $\leq$ 30s			
Traffic Overload	PERF $\geq$ 80%	TD 3GB	TD	Limit transferred data while maintaining performance
	DegT $\leq$ 60s			

5.2 Migration Polices

Table 3 lists the SLO policies evaluated in this paper. All policies except *Min TT* contain user and provider SLOs that must be met. The optimization goal lists the metric that is to be minimized if several live migration techniques are expected to meet all SLOs. The policies are constructed to cover several scenarios. *Min TT* migrates VMs as fast as possible by minimizing the total migration time *TT*; this policy is useful if the machine has to undergo an emergency shutdown. The other five policies contain more or less stringent SLOs for both the user and the provider with different optimization goals to cover various scenarios.

5.3 Live Migration Sequence and Technique Selection

The experiments evaluate a sequence of 480 migrations that occurred in real-live on the cluster. In every case, the state of the cluster is recreated as faithfully as possible with the same number of co-located VMs running the same workloads, nevertheless, differences in the actual resource utilization are possible due to different execution phases within the workloads. When replaying the migration sequence, the management framework (Fig. 1) first profiles all VMs on the source host as discussed in [18]. Next, the profiles are fed into the model to predict

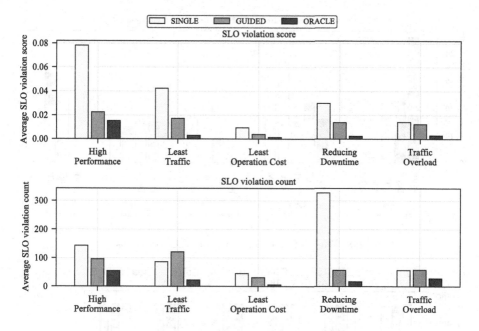

Fig. 7. Avg. relative SLO violations and total violation count for different technique selections.

the metrics for all VMs and live migration techniques. If several techniques are expected to meet all SLOs, the technique that minimizes the optimization goal is chosen. If all techniques are predicted to violate one or more SLOs, the technique with the smallest average relative violations is chosen. Note that in a real-world scenario, the framework may choose not to migrate a VM in such a case; since this paper aims to demonstrate that the number of SLO violations can be minimized with the presented model, the framework always migrates a VM.

5.4 Analysis of SLO Violations

Figure 7 shows the average relative score of SLO violations (i.e., the average severity of the violations) and total number of SLO violations for the different live migration techniques. The *Min TT* scenario is not shown because it has no SLOs. The white bar shows the *single* static live migration technique that incurs the minimal relative SLO violation score, the presented model-*guided* technique, and results for an *oracle* model that can predict all metrics without any error. We observe that the guided approach clearly outperforms the choice of a single technique by a large margin and comes relatively close to the oracle model. *Guided* outperforms *static* in all cases except the absolute number of SLO violations for the *Least Traffic* policy. While the *post-copy* technique is the single best technique that minimizes the number of SLO violations, the violations are much more severe than those incurred by the *guided* approach.

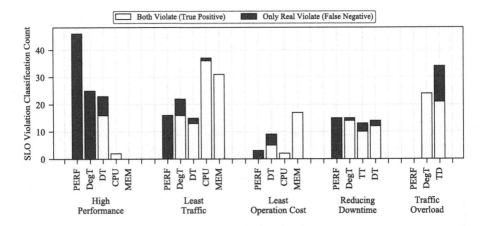

Fig. 8. Effect of modeling error on SLO violations.

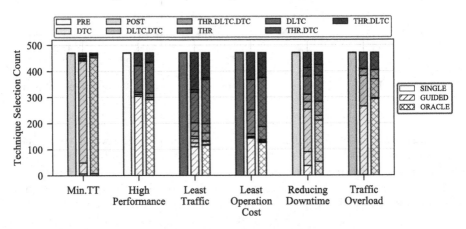

Fig. 9. The ratio of the selected techniques by the guided approach.

While the model shows an average error of 10% over all predicted metrics, an interesting question is how this prediction error manifests in terms of absolute SLO violations. Figure 8 shows the results. The white bar denotes true positives, i.e., the selected technique was predicted to violate an SLO and actually did so, while the blue bar shows false negatives (violation occurred despite no violation predicted). Only false negatives are a concern since true positives were expected to occur. The results reveal that the prediction of performance under stringent constraints is difficult for the proposed model and leaves room for improvement in future work. Note, however, that to the best of our knowledge, there exists no model that can predict performance and the duration of the performance with higher accuracy than the model presented in this work.

5.5 Importance of Model-Guided Live Migration Technique Selection

Figure 9 finally plots the selected live migration techniques for *single, guided,* and *oracle* technique selection for the different migration policies from Table 3. The figure reveals that selecting the appropriate technique depends less on the migration policy but rather on the workload running inside the VM and the state of the source host. In other words, this results clearly demonstrates the necessity of model-guided live migration technique selection to reduce not only the total number of SLO violations but also the severity of those violations.

6 Related Work

Since the introduction of various live migration techniques over the last decade, a number of researchers have tackled the problem of employing the different techniques properly. Koto [22], Nathan [25], and Svard [32] all propose guidelines for live migration technique selection that are, however, difficult to deploy in real systems due to the lack of a systematic way of choosing them. Similarly, there exist a number of works that model the performance of live migration techniques. Analytical models require complex calibration when deployed and are thus not of much practical use in heterogeneous data centers. Jo [18] has presented the first machine learning-based attempt to live migration modeling. That work only considers five techniques and four metrics but served as the basis for the model developed in this paper.

A number of migration frameworks have been presented that aim at resolving or avoiding hot-spots. Sandpiper [35] is an early dynamic migration system which is mitigating hotspots in the cluster on-demand. It periodically builds a per-node resource utilization profile and predicts hotspot occurrence in advance using a simple time-series prediction technique. Sandpiper uses a simple heuristics that selects the VM to migrate and only employs the pre-copy migration technique. CloudScale [27] presents a resource prediction technique to avoid SLO violations before they manifest. It increases resource capping when a peak resource demand is expected in the near future. CloudScale's design can tolerate a certain amount of resource demand misprediction by not fully committing all available resources. VMs are only migrated when no resources are available on the node. While CloudScale takes the migration overhead into consideration to prevent possible SLO violations during live migration and employs a simple linear regression model to predict live migration cost. It has been shown, however, that a simple linear model is unable to predict the migration cost of a VM with high accuracy [1,18,24].

This work is based on prior work by Jo [18] that focuses on developing machine-learned models to predict six live migration metrics (total time, downtime, transferred data, CPU and memory utilization, and performance degradation). The modeling of live migration metrics is similar to prior work. This work uses the same machine-learned approach to model five of the six metrics, but supports nine instead of five migration techniques and heterogeneous data centers. Also, it was found that performance degradation and the new metric performance degradation duration are better predicted with analytical models. Other than prior work, this paper proposes and evaluates new live migration-aware SLOs that enable data centers to classify VMs into stationary and mobile to achieve flexible migration of VMs and thus better resource utilization.

7   Conclusion

Strict SLOs and the uncertainty of the effect of live migration prevent data centers from employing live migration to achieve better load balancing and higher resource utilization. This paper demonstrates that the combination of live migration-aware SLOs and an accurate model predicting several key metrics of live migration allows for an economically more efficient use of live migration in data centers while minimizing the number of SLA violations. An evaluation with six policies and 480 live migrations shows that the presented migration-aware SLOs and smart live migration framework is able to significantly reduce the total number of SLO violations and the relative violation of these SLO compared to any static single migration technique.

The live migration dataset, the model, and the source code of the framework are available at https://csap.snu.ac.kr/software.

Acknowledgements. This work was supported by the National Research Foundation of Korea (NRF) funded by the Korean government, in part, by grants NRF-2015K1A3A1A14021288, 2016R1A2B4009193, by the BK21 Plus for Pioneers in Innovative Computing (Dept. of Computer Science and Engineering, SNU, grant 21A20151113068), and by the Promising-Pioneering Researcher Program of Seoul National University in 2015. ICT at Seoul National University provided research facilities for this study.

References

1. Akoush, S., Sohan, R., Rice, A., Moore, A.W., Hopper, A.: Predicting the performance of virtual machine migration. In: Proceedings of the 2010 IEEE International Symposium on Modeling, Analysis and Simulation of Computer and Telecommunication Systems, MASCOTS 2010, pp. 37–46. IEEE Computer Society, Washington (2010). https://doi.org/10.1109/MASCOTS.2010.13
2. https://github.com/alibaba/clusterdata (2018). Accessed June 2020
3. https://aws.amazon.com/legal/service-level-agreements/ (2020). Accessed June 2020
4. Barroso, L.A., Hölzle, U., Ranganathan, P.: The datacenter as a computer: designing warehouse-scale machines. Synth. Lect. Comput. Archit. **13**(3) (2018)
5. Bellard, F.: QEMU, a fast and portable dynamic translator. In: USENIX Annual Technical Conference, FREENIX Track, vol. 41, p. 46 (2005)
6. Clark, C., et al.: Live migration of virtual machines. In: Proceedings of the 2nd Conference on Symposium on Networked Systems Design & Implementation - Volume 2, NSDI 2005, pp. 273–286. USENIX Association, Berkeley (2005). http://dl.acm.org/citation.cfm?id=1251203.1251223

7. Egger, B., Gustafsson, E., Jo, C., Son, J.: Efficiently restoring virtual machines. Int. J. Parallel Prog. **43**(3), 421–439 (2013). https://doi.org/10.1007/s10766-013-0295-0

8. https://cloud.google.com/compute/docs/benchmarks-linux (2020). Accessed June 2020

9. https://cloud.google.com/compute/docs/instances/live-migration (2020). Accessed June 2020

10. https://cloud.google.com/terms/sla/ (2020). Accessed June 2020

11. https://goo.gl/Ui3HFd (2018). Accessed June 2020

12. https://github.com/google/cluster-data (2019). Accessed June 2020

13. Hermenier, F., Lorca, X., Menaud, J.M., Muller, G., Lawall, J.: Entropy: a consolidation manager for clusters. In: Proceedings of the 2009 ACM SIGPLAN/SIGOPS International Conference on Virtual Execution Environments, VEE 2009, pp. 41–50. ACM, New York (2009). https://doi.org/10.1145/1508293.1508300

14. Hines, M.R., Gopalan, K.: Post-copy based live virtual machine migration using adaptive pre-paging and dynamic self-ballooning. In: Proceedings of the 2009 ACM SIGPLAN/SIGOPS International Conference on Virtual Execution Environments, VEE 2009, pp. 51–60. ACM, New York (2009). https://doi.org/10.1145/1508293.1508301

15. Hirofuchi, T., Nakada, H., Itoh, S., Sekiguchi, S.: Reactive consolidation of virtual machines enabled by postcopy live migration. In: Proceedings of the 5th International Workshop on Virtualization Technologies in Distributed Computing, VTDC 2011, pp. 11–18. ACM, New York (2011). https://doi.org/10.1145/1996121.1996125

16. https://github.com/intel-hadoop/HiBench (2018). Accessed June 2020

17. Jin, H., Deng, L., Wu, S., Shi, X., Pan, X.: Live virtual machine migration with adaptive, memory compression. In: 2009 IEEE International Conference on Cluster Computing and Workshops, pp. 1–10, August 2009. https://doi.org/10.1109/CLUSTR.2009.5289170

18. Jo, C., Cho, Y., Egger, B.: A machine learning approach to live migration modeling. In: ACM Symposium on Cloud Computing, SoCC 2017, September 2017

19. Jo, C., Egger, B.: Optimizing live migration for virtual desktop clouds. In: IEEE 5th International Conference on Cloud Computing Technology and Science, CloudCom 2013, vol. 1, pp. 104–111, December 2013. https://doi.org/10.1109/CloudCom.2013.21

20. Jo, C., Gustafsson, E., Son, J., Egger, B.: Efficient live migration of virtual machines using shared storage. In: Proceedings of the 9th ACM SIGPLAN/SIGOPS International Conference on Virtual Execution Environments, VEE 2013, pp. 41–50. ACM, New York (2013). https://doi.org/10.1145/2451512.2451524

21. Kasture, H., Sanchez, D.: Tailbench: a benchmark suite and evaluation methodology for latency-critical applications. In: Proceedings of the 2016 IEEE International Symposium on Workload Characterization, IISWC 2016, pp. 3–12 (2016). https://doi.org/10.1109/IISWC.2016.7581261

22. Koto, A., Kono, K., Yamada, H.: A guideline for selecting live migration policies and implementations in clouds. In: Proceedings of the 2014 IEEE 6th International Conference on Cloud Computing Technology and Science, CLOUDCOM 2014, pp. 226–233. IEEE Computer Society, Washington (2014). https://doi.org/10.1109/CloudCom.2014.36

23. Liu, Z., Qu, W., Liu, W., Li, K.: Xen live migration with slowdown scheduling algorithm. In: Proceedings of the 2010 International Conference on Parallel and Distributed Computing, Applications and Technologies, PDCAT 2010, pp. 215–221. IEEE Computer Society, Washington (2010). https://doi.org/10.1109/PDCAT.2010.88

24. Nathan, S., Bellur, U., Kulkarni, P.: Towards a comprehensive performance model of virtual machine live migration. In: Proceedings of the Sixth ACM Symposium on Cloud Computing, SoCC 2015, pp. 288–301. ACM, New York (2015). https://doi.org/10.1145/2806777.2806838

25. Nathan, S., Bellur, U., Kulkarni, P.: On selecting the right optimizations for virtual machine migration. In: Proceedings of the 12th ACM SIGPLAN/SIGOPS International Conference on Virtual Execution Environments, VEE 2016, pp. 37–49. ACM, New York (2016). https://doi.org/10.1145/2892242.2892247

26. Novaković, D., Vasić, N., Novaković, S., Kostić, D., Bianchini, R.: Deepdive: transparently identifying and managing performance interference in virtualized environments. In: Proceedings of the 2013 USENIX Conference on Annual Technical Conference, USENIX ATC 2013, pp. 219–230. USENIX Association, Berkeley (2013). http://dl.acm.org/citation.cfm?id=2535461.2535489

27. Reiss, C., Tumanov, A., Ganger, G.R., Katz, R.H., Kozuch, M.A.: Heterogeneity and dynamicity of clouds at scale: Google trace analysis. In: Proceedings of the Third ACM Symposium on Cloud Computing, SoCC 2012, pp. 7:1–7:13. ACM, New York (2012). https://doi.org/10.1145/2391229.2391236

28. Ruprecht, A., et al.: VM live migration at scale. In: Proceedings of the 14th ACM SIGPLAN/SIGOPS International Conference on Virtual Execution Environments, VEE 2018, pp. 45–56. ACM, New York (2018). https://doi.org/10.1145/3186411.3186415

29. Shen, Z., Subbiah, S., Gu, X., Wilkes, J.: Cloudscale: elastic resource scaling for multi-tenant cloud systems. In: Proceedings of the 2Nd ACM Symposium on Cloud Computing, SoCC 2011, pp. 5:1–5:14. ACM, New York (2011). https://doi.org/10.1145/2038916.2038921

30. Smola, A.J., Schölkopf, B.: A tutorial on support vector regression. Stat. Comput. 14(3), 199–222 (2004). https://doi.org/10.1023/B:STCO.0000035301.49549.88

31. Svärd, P., Hudzia, B., Tordsson, J., Elmroth, E.: Evaluation of delta compression techniques for efficient live migration of large virtual machines. In: Proceedings of the 7th ACM SIGPLAN/SIGOPS International Conference on Virtual Execution Environments, VEE 2011, pp. 111–120. ACM, New York (2011). https://doi.org/10.1145/1952682.1952698

32. Svärd, P., Hudzia, B., Walsh, S., Tordsson, J., Elmroth, E.: Principles and performance characteristics of algorithms for live VM migration. SIGOPS Oper. Syst. Rev. 49(1), 142–155 (2015). https://doi.org/10.1145/2723872.2723894

33. http://www.mplayerhq.hu/design7/news.html (2017). Accessed June 2020

34. Voorsluys, W., Broberg, J., Venugopal, S., Buyya, R.: Cost of virtual machine live migration in clouds: a performance evaluation. In: Jaatun, M.G., Zhao, G., Rong, C. (eds.) CloudCom 2009. LNCS, vol. 5931, pp. 254–265. Springer, Heidelberg (2009). https://doi.org/10.1007/978-3-642-10665-1_23

35. Wood, T., Shenoy, P., Venkataramani, A., Yousif, M.: Black-box and gray-box strategies for virtual machine migration. In: USENIX Symposium on Networked Systems Design and Implementation (NSDI), April 2007. http://faculty.cs.gwu.edu/~timwood/papers/NSDI07-sandpiper.pdf

36. https://github.com/brianfrankcooper/YCSB/tree/master/memcached (2018). Accessed June 2020

Index-Selection for Minimizing Costs of a NoSQL Cloud Database

Sudarshan S. Chawathe[✉][iD]

University of Maine, Orono, ME 04469, USA
chaw@eip10.org
http://chaw.eip10.org/

Abstract. The index-selection problem in database systems is that of
determining a set of indexes (data-access paths) that minimizes the costs
of database operations. Although this problem has received significant
attention in the context of relational database systems, the established
methods and tools do not translate easily to the context of modern nonrelational database systems (so-called NoSQL systems) that are widely
used in cloud and grid computing, and in particular systems such as
DynamoDB from Amazon Web Services. Although the index-selection
problem in these contexts appears simple at first glance, due to the very
limited indexing features, this simplicity is deceptive because the nonrelational nature of these databases and indexes permits more complex
indexing schemes to be expressed. This paper motivates and describes
the index-selection problem for NoSQL databases, and DynamoDB in
particular. It motivates and outlines a cost model to capture the specific
monetary costs associated with database operations in this context. The
cost model has not only been carefully checked for consistency using the
system documentation but also been verified using actual usage costs in
a live DynamoDB instance.

Keywords: Cloud computing · Cost model · Index selection ·
DynamoDB · NoSQL databases · Physical database design

1 Introduction

Recent years have witnessed a rapid growth in usage of diverse *database and
storage services in cloud-based systems* such as *Amazon Web Services (AWS)*
and *Microsoft Azure*. This growth is fueled by several attractive features of
these systems, chief among which are their low start-up costs and their ability to
scale rapidly (in a few minutes) over several orders of magnitude of throughput
and other system metrics. Related advantages include resilience to a variety
of system failures and the global reach of their network of data-centers. Such
services often use a nonrelational, or so-called *NoSQL*, data model which permits
more flexibility but also complicates database design.

An important feature of these database services is the method used for *billing
for usage*. In contrast to the static or slowly changing billing methods used by

© Springer Nature Switzerland AG 2020
K. Djemame et al. (Eds.): GECON 2020, LNCS 12441, pp. 189–197, 2020.
https://doi.org/10.1007/978-3-030-63058-4_16

conventional on-site relational database systems, cloud-based NoSQL systems typically use billing methods that are sensitive to changes in provisioning and use at time scales of minutes or hours rather than weeks or months. In addition to the finer temporal granularity of billing, these systems also tend to employ finer billing granularity in details of usage, based on a variety of measured and billed metrics. While effective use of such a fine-grained cost structure is potentially advantageous to both client and service provider, and potentially more efficient in a financial sense, realizing such effective use is often very challenging due to the complexity of the cost and billing model.

Secondary indexes, i.e., alternate efficient access paths to data stored in a table, are a crucial feature of database systems, both relational and nonrelational, that permit efficient use of system resources. An important aspect of cloud database services is that system resources are off-site with the service provider and the use of those resources is mapped to monetary costs at a finer granularity. In any database (relational or NoSQL) of even moderate complexity, the *index selection* task, of determining which secondary indexes should be created (and maintained), is a difficult one. The number of possibly useful indexes grows very rapidly with the size of the database schema (table structure), rendering exhaustive examination of all possibilities impracticable. Furthermore, even the conceptually simpler task of determining the degree of merit of a given scheme of secondary indexes is a difficult one, albeit for differing reasons in conventional hosted relational databases and cloud-based NoSQL databases. In the former, a chief source of difficulty is determining how a typically sophisticated but necessarily non-optimal (due to the combinatorics involved) query optimizer will respond to a given scheme of indexes. Recent advances in that context have favored probing the optimizer to answer this question over attempting to model its complex behavior independently. In contrast, NoSQL systems are typically characterized by very simple or completely absent query optimizers, which makes an approach based on independent modeling (v. probing the system) preferable because an accurate model permits potentially fuller optimization compared to what a limited number of probes can hope to achieve.

The main problem addressed by this paper is the development of such a cost model that permits optimal or near-optimal selection of indexes in a cloud-based NoSQL database service. For concreteness, the paper focuses on the *AWS DynamoDB* service, and the finer details are tied to that system. However, the general approach exemplified by this work is adaptable to other services as well. Given the importance and generality of this problem, as well as the prevalence of NoSQL systems, it may seem surprising that the work reported here has not been thoroughly addressed already by earlier work. However, there does not seem to be any reported work on such a cost model despite its need as evidenced by several publications in the practitioner community [3,6,9]. One reason for this disparity may be the difficulty in abstracting the salient features of the cost model from the available system documentation and other resources, which are sometimes difficult to properly interpret (e.g., page 7).

Outline: Section 2 outlines the key features of DynamoDB tables and indexes before stating the index-selection problem in this context. Section 3 presents a detailed cost model that is validated with both the specification and by experiments on a live DynamoDB instance. Related work is addressed by Sect. 4 and a summary appears in Sect. 5.

2 Tables and Index Selection

Tables. In DynamoDB, there are no operations that span multiple tables (other than drastic ones such as deleting the account that owns multiple tables). Therefore it is sufficient to approach the schema-design problem, and in particular the index-selection problem on a per-table basis; such a table is denoted by T below. Each DynamoDB table is required to have a *primary key* with semantics similar to those of primary keys in relational databases: No two items in a table are permitted to have identical primary keys. However, while the primary key of a table in a relational database may be a composite key with an arbitrary number of attributes (key-columns, or key-attributes), the primary key of a DynamoDB table is very limited: It is composed of exactly one or two attributes, the first of which is called the table's *partition key* and the second (optional) is called its *sort key*. Further, the datatypes of these keys are limited to *string, number,* and *binary,* although DynamoDB permits richer types (such as set of integers or list of strings) for other attributes in general. The sequel uses abbreviations *PKey* for the required *primary key* of each table or index (LSI or GSI, described below), *PaKey* for the required *partition key* (also called *hash key*) component of a PKey, and *SoKey* for the optional *sort key* (also called *range key*) component of a PKey.

Secondary Indexes. DynamoDB permits two kinds of secondary indexes: *Global Secondary Indexes (GSIs)* and *Local Secondary Indexes (LSIs).* Analogously to the restricted nature of DynamoDB tables compared with relational database tables, GSIs and LSIs are very restricted in comparison with diverse indexing schemes typically found in relational database systems. Global and local secondary indexes are required to have primary keys subject to the same restrictions as those for base tables, with the exception that there may be multiple items (index entries) for a given value of a primary key. This situation is analogous to that in relational databases, where there may be multiple tuples in a base table corresponding to a single key value in an index. The indexes are required to have a primary key composed of a required partition key and an optional sort key and both keys are limited to single attributes of scalar types. An LSI is subject to the additional restriction that its *PaKey* must be identical to the *PaKey* of its base table (and that its *SoKey* must be distinct from the base table's *SoKey*).

Every index (GSI or LSI) includes, as a minimum, the key attributes of the index along with the key attributes of the base table. Queries using an LSI are permitted to request base-table attributes that are not projected onto the index. DynamoDB automatically fetc.hes the additional attributes from the base table for each index item that matches a query, at additional cost. In contrast, queries on GSIs are simply not permitted to request base-table attributes that are not projected onto the index.

Index Selection. The *index selection problem* is that of determining the set of indexes (combination of LSIs and GSIs) that minimizes the monetary cost of a deployment given an expected workload (composed of item reads, queries, insertions, deletions, and update operations).

3 Costs of Deployment

The cost model used by DynamoDB accounts for read and write operations separately. An orthogonal dimension is whether service is provided in *provisioned capacity mode* or *on-demand mode*. In the provisioned capacity mode, read and write operations are billed based on *Read Capacity Units (RCU)* and *Write Capacity Units (WCU)* respectively. In the on-demand mode, they are billed based on *Read Request Units (RRU)* and *Write Request Units (WRU)*, respectively.

For brevity, the following describes the cost of only *strongly consistent read* operations. For transactional reads, the costs are doubled while for *eventually consistent reads*, the costs are halved. (However, access via GSIs are only at the *eventually consistent* level.)

Reading Items from Tables. Reading items by specifying the primary key (*PaKey* and, if defined for the table, the *SoKey* as well) is accomplished by two operations that are essentially equivalent from the monetary cost perspective: `GetItem` and `BatchGetItem`. In order to simplify the presentation by reducing the number of cases that need separate descriptions, we adopt the convention that if a table does not define a *SoKey* then a requirement to provide it is vacuously met. With this convention, we may consider all read-item operations as providing both *PaKey* and *SoKey* of a table.

A `GetItem` operation reads a single item (or none, if there is no item with the requested primary key) at a cost of 1 RCU times the size of the item rounded up to the nearest nonzero multiple of a blocking factor b_r that is currently set at 4 KB (4000 bytes). (Individual items may have varying sizes up to a maximum of 400 KB per item.) The cost of a `GetItem` that reads an item (or probes for its presence even if it is absent) in table T with *PaKey* value p and *SoKey* value s is simple: $c_g(T, p, s) = \max\{1, \lceil b(T(p, s))/b_r \rceil\}$ using the notation $T(p, s)$ to denote the unique item, if any, in table T with *PaKey* value p and *SoKey* value s. The function $b(X)$ denotes the size in bytes of the set X of items in general. (Here X is either the empty set or a singleton.) Due to the nonrelational nature of DynamoDB tables, size of items in a table may vary significantly from item to item.

The closely related `BatchGetItem` operation permits up to 100 primary key values to be specified at once in order to retrieve up to 100 items with those keys from the table. Cost-wise, a `BatchGetItem` operation with l keys is completely equivalent to l individual `GetItem` operations. The reasons for using it over the equivalent individual items include programming convenience and lower system overheads such as round-trip times. In particular, this equivalence means that the sizes of items in the batch are individually rounded up to multiples of b_r and the sum of these rounded sizes determines the size of the batch for cost purposes. That is, given a set of primary keys $K = \{(p_0, s_0), (p_1, s_1) \ldots, (p_l, s_l)\}$, The cost of a `BatchGetItem` operation with that key-set is: $c_b(K) = \sum_{(p,s) \in K} c_g(T, p, s)$ It follows that $c_b(K) \geq |K|$ (even if there are no items matching any of the keys provided).

Querying and Scanning Tables. A `Query` operation allows reading of zero or more items that have identical *PaKey* values and that satisfy an optionally provided predicate on the *SoKey* (if defined by the table). If items with distinct partition keys are required, a separate query must be issued for each desired partition-key value. In contrast to `BatchGetItem`, here the associated reads are treated as a single operation for cost purposes. In particular, the sizes of the matching items (before any optional *filtering*) are first summed and then rounded up to the next multiple of b_r. As a result, queries potentially provide substantial cost savings over equivalent sequences of `GetItem` or `BatchGetItem` operations that read the same items. The cost of a query on table T with *PaKey* value p and *SoKey* predicate θ may be expressed as:

$$c_q(T, p, \theta) = \max \left\{ 1, \left\lceil \frac{\sum_{t \in T(p,\theta)} b(t)}{b_r} \right\rceil \right\}$$

A `Scan` operation may be thought of as a degenerate case of a `query` that reads all items in a table. For cost computation purposes, a `Scan` incurs the cost for all items in the table whereas a typical, selective `Query` would incur the cost of reading only a small fraction of those. A scan is also notable for being the only operation that permits retrieval of items without specifying a *PaKey*. The cost of a scan is expressed simply as:

$$c_s(T) = \max \left\{ 1, \left\lceil \frac{\sum_{t \in T} b(t)}{b_r} \right\rceil \right\}$$

Other aspects of the above operations, such as *filtering* (server-side post-processing) the items matching a query to limit those that are returned to the invoking application, or returning only the count of items matching a query, do not reduce the costs. For instance, determining the number of items with a given partition key value (a *count* operation in conventional database systems) incurs the same cost as retrieving all the items with that partition key value. Requests to read non-existing items (e.g.., a `GetItem` that specifies a primary key that does not match any items in the table) incur the same cost as if the item were present and read.

Consider a query on base table T using LSI (local secondary index) I with *PaKey* value p, *SoKey* predicate θ, and attribute set A. Let $attr(I)$ denote the set of *projected attributes* of index I. The set of items in table T that have *PaKey* p and a *SoKey* value s satisfying predicate θ is denoted by $T(p, \theta)$. This notation extends the earlier notation of $T(p, s)$ used to denote $T(p, \theta_s)$ where θ_s is the predicate that tests for equality with s. The similar set of items for an index I is denoted by $I(p', \theta')$, where the primed variants of the arguments are used as a reminder that the key attributes of indexes differ from those of their base tables. The *base-table PaKey* value and *base-table SoKey* value of an index item i are denoted by i_p and i_s, respectively. If i is an item in an LSI then $i_p = p'$ because they are values of the same attribute (due to the restriction on LSIs), but $i_s \neq s'$ in general. This notation allows generalizing to GSIs later: If i is an item in a GSI, both i_p and i_s are, in general, different from the values p' and s' of that item's *index PaKey* and *index SoKey*, respectively. The notation $[P]$, where P is a predicate, uses *Iverson brackets*: It evaluates to 1 if the P is true and to 0 otherwise. With these conventions, the cost of a query using LSI I is expressed as follows:

$$
c_q(T, I, p', \theta', A) = \max \left\{ 1, \left\lceil \frac{\sum_{i \in I(p', \theta')} b(I, i)}{b_r} \right\rceil \right\}
$$
$$
+ [A \not\subseteq attr(I)] \cdot \sum_{i \in I(p', \theta')} \max \left\{ 1, \left\lceil \frac{b(T, t(i_p, i_s))}{b_r} \right\rceil \right\}
$$

The summation in the second term, over items matching the query, is notable for being outside (after) the item-wise size computation. For queries returning a large number of small items with at least one attribute not present in the used index, this term is likely the dominant contributor to cost.

Despite the DynamoDB restriction on GSI queries that disallows access to base-table attributes that are not projected onto the index, the above equation may be used to model the cost of index queries that use either an LSI or a GSI with the understanding that in the GSI case, the additional accesses modeled by the second term are made separately by the driving application and not automatically by DynamoDB as part of the same query operation.

Write Costs. Write operations use a blocking parameter b_w that is analogous to the parameter b_r for read operations. Currently $b_w = 1$ KB (1000 bytes), in contrast to $b_r = 4$ KB. The cost of *deleting or inserting* an item with *PaKey* p and *SoKey* s from or into table T that is due to the table itself is simply one unit, or the next higher multiple of b_w for larger items. The max is present to account for the minimum cost that is incurred even on requests to delete non-existing items. The subscript t on c_{dt} indicates that this is only the cost component attributed to the base table.

$$
c_{dt}(T, p, s) = c_{it}(T, p, s) = \max\{1, \lceil b(T(p, s))/b_w \rceil\}
$$

More interesting is the additional cost incurred by the presence of indexes on T. That cost depends on whether its values for the index-key attributes are null and may be expressed as follows for a GSI $I_{P'S'}$, as suggested by the g suffix on c_{dg}, using the Iverson bracket notation. $c_{dg}(T_{PS}, I_{P'S'}, t) = c_{ig}(T_{PS}, I_{P'S'}, t) = [t_{P'} \neq \perp \wedge t'_S \neq \perp] \max\{1, \lceil b(T(p, s))/b_w \rceil\}$.

Updating an item from t to u may incur a cost of 0, 1, or 2 units times the size-based scaling, depending on whether the index-key attributes have non-null values and, additionally, whether they are modified by the update operation. It is convenient to express it using the costs c_{ig} and c_{dg} defined above.

$$c_{ug}(T_{PS}, I_{P'S'}, t, u) = c_{ig}(T_{PS}, I_{P'S'}, u) + [t_{P'} \neq u_{P'} \vee t_{S'} \neq u_{S'}] \cdot c_{dg}(T_{PS}, I_{P'S'}, t)$$

The description of LSI write costs (capacity units) on of the DynamoDB developer guide [1, page 490], when compared with the analogous description for GSI write costs on [1, page 454], may be read as implying that an LSI incurs no cost when an item is updated to change only a non-key projected attribute. However, experimentation reveals that in fact the cost incurred in such a case is identical to that incurred by a similar GSI. Then the write costs of an LSI may be expressed using the above equation used for GSIs, with a couple of clarifications: First, since $P = P'$ for LSIs, and a base-table *PaKey* cannot be omitted, the predicate $P' \neq \perp$ always evaluates to true. Second, the cost in the provisioned capacity mode is allocated to the base table as is the case for all LSI costs.

Storage Costs. Let $attr(I_{P'S'})$ denote the attributes (names) of index I (with index *PaKey* P' and index *SoKey* S'), including all key and nonkey attributes. If the base table for $I_{P'S'}$ is T_{PS} (with *PaKey* P and *SoKey* S) then $\{P, S, P', S'\} \subseteq attr(I_{PS}) \subseteq attr(T_{PS})$. Let b_o denote a constant overhead, in bytes, assessed per index item; its value at the time of writing is 100 [1]. The storage used by the GSI $I_{P'S'}$ on base table T_{PS} may then be expressed as follows:

$$b(T_{PS}, I_{P'S'}) = \sum_{\substack{t \in T_{PS} \\ t_{P'} \neq \perp \\ t_{S'} \neq \perp}} \sum_{A \in attr(I_{P'S'})} b(t_A) + b_o$$

Recall that t_A (the value of the attribute named A in item t) may be absent (modeled as null, $\perp$) except when A is a key attribute (of the base table, not necessarily index). Items that have a null for an index's *PaKey* or, if used by the index, its *SoKey*, do not contribute to index size. At one extreme, if none of the items in T have non-null values for these attributes then the storage cost of the index is 0. At the other extreme, if every item in the base table has non-null values for these attributes, and if the index projects all attributes from the base table, then the additional storage used by the index is $b(T) + b_o \cdot |T|$, where $b(T)$ is the size in bytes of the base table and $|T|$ is its cardinality (number of items).

We may use the above expression of GSI storage costs for LSIs as well, with the understanding that $P = P'$ when it is used for LSIs. However, LSIs (and their base tables) are also subject to a limit on the sizes of *item collections* from which GSIs (as well as their base tables, if they have no LSIs) are exempt. Briefly, an item collection refers to all items in a base table and its LSIs that have the same *PaKey* value. The aggregate size (in bytes) of items in an item collection can be no greater than 10 GB. This limit on item collection sizes adds another design constraint for LSIs, in addition to the limit of at most five LSIs per base table. It is possible, for instance, that an otherwise advantageous choice of an LSI must be abandoned due to the item-collection constraint. DynamoDB design guidelines suggest ways to reduce sizes of item collections. However, since a single LSI may (depending on projected attributes) approximately double the size of an item collection, the constraint may be limiting when certain LSIs are considered even if the base table's item collections are well below the limit.

4   Related Work

The difficulty of reliably predicting monetary costs of DynamoDB deployments has been widely reported in the practitioner literature [6,9,10] including billing surprises of large magnitude.

The authoritative DynamoDB documentation [1] provides detailed, albeit sometimes difficult to interpret information on how operations map to monetary costs. It also provides heuristic guidance on recommended practices for index selection but no systematic algorithms or numerical formulas assist with the process. Index selection is a component of a larger scheme for query optimization in DynamoDB and related systems [5].

The more conventional index selection problem in relational DBMS has received significant attention [4]. However, although there are some similarities, such as the combinatorial explosion in the number of potential indexing schemes with increase in the number of attributes of base tables, the crux of the problem is very different in the conventional relational and cloud NoSQL environments. In the former, a major difficulty is determining the effect of indexes on the query plans used by the query optimizer and their costs. Given the level of sophistication of query optimizers in competitive relational database systems, the preferred approach has been to probe the optimizer for that information instead of trying to model the actions of the optimizer. However, in a NoSQL cloud database setting, the optimizers are either very simple or completely absent, so that modeling is a viable option. On the other hand, the cost model itself is more complicated and irregular.

The problem of materialized view selection [8] may be viewed as an index selection problem generalized to more expressive indexes (specified using SQL queries or similar). In the other direction, physical database design [7] goes beyond indexes and into other systems aspects affecting database performance.

DQL [2] is a notable effort in regularizing the query-language interface of DynamoDB to a syntax that is close to SQL, albeit with significant restrictions.

5   Conclusion

Selecting an appropriate set of secondary indexes for a database given an expected workload of read operations (individual item reads and bulk queries) and write operations (insertions, deletions, updates) has a major impact on the performance of database systems and applications in diverse environments. For cloud-based NoSQL database services, as exemplified by AWS DynamoDB, different selections of secondary indexes can incur monetary costs that differ by orders of magnitude, making the index selection problem in such environments especially significant. Despite the high practical significance and monetary implications of this problem as evidenced by a multitude of reports in the practitioner literature, the problem has received very little attention in the research community. This paper presents the first comprehensive formalized cost model for secondary index selection in DynamoDB. An important feature of this cost model is that it has been carefully verified with not only the system specification documents but also with experiments on a live system (by comparing actual reported costs with those predicted by the model). This verification allows the model to be used with confidence for further research as well as in practice, where the costs map directly to usage charges.

Ongoing work is exploring simplifications of the cost model in order to allow easier application at the potential cost of less accurate results and higher than optimal monetary cots. It is also exploring a simlar approach applied to other NoSQL database services.

Acknowledgments. This work was partly supported by the US National Science Foundation and benefited from the reviewers' comments.

References

1. Amazon Web Services: Amazon DynamoDB: Developer guide. https://docs.aws.amazon.com/dynamodb/ (2019), API Version 10 Aug 2012
2. Arcangeli, S.: DQL–DynamoDB query language: a simple, SQL-ish language for DynamoDB. System documentation (2018) https://dql.readthedocs.io/en/latest/index.html
3. Brazeal, F.: Why Amazon DynamoDB isn't for everyone. A Cloud Guru blog (2017) https://read.acloud.guru/why-amazon-dynamodb-isnt-for-everyone-and-how-to-decide-when-it-s-for-you-aefc52ea9476
4. Chaudhuri, S., Narasayya, V.R.: Self-tuning database systems: a decade of progress. In: Proceedings of the 33rd International Conference on Very Large Data Bases (VLDB), pp. 3–14. ACM (2007)
5. Chawathe, S.S.: Cost-based query-rewriting for DynamoDB (work in progress). In: IEEE 18th International Symposium on Network Computing and Applications (NCA), pp. 1–3. IEEE (2019)
6. Guerrero, J.: How DynamoDB's pricing works, gets expensive quickly and the best alternatives. YugabyteDB Blog (2018) https://blog.yugabyte.com/dynamodb-pricing-calculator-expensive-vs-alternatives/
7. Lightstone, S.S., Teorey, T.J., Nadeau, T.: Physical Database Design : The Database Professional's Guide to Exploiting Indexes, Views, Storage, and More. Elsevier Science & Technology, San Francisco, California (2007)
8. Mami, I., Bellahsene, Z.: A survey of view selection methods. ACM Sigmod Rec. **41**(1), 20–29 (2012). https://doi.org/10.1145/2206869.2206874
9. Ranganathan, K.: 11 things you wish you knew before starting with DynamoDB. yugabyteDB blog (2018) https://blog.yugabyte.com/11-things-you-wish-you-knew-before-starting-with-dynamodb
10. Roussel, A., Branson, R.: The million dollar engineering problem. segment blog (2017) https://segment.com/blog/

Poster Session

A Developer-Centric API Value Chain

Konrad Kirner[✉] and Somayeh Koohborfardhaghighi

Amsterdam Business School, University of Amsterdam, Amsterdam, The Netherlands
konrad.kriner@web.de, s.koohborfardhaghighi@uva.nl

Abstract. In today's digital economy, the creation of digital services attracts widespread interest due to its new role as the main driver of innovation. Application Programmable Interfaces (APIs) and their emerging ecosystem are at the center of this digital service innovation trend. In this research, we propose a developer-centric API value chain and we link it to the topic of online customer reviews (OCRs). The aim of our work then is to highlight the important role of the developers in the API value chain and the success of a provider's API.

Keywords: APIs · API value chain · Mashup · Service composition · Service innovation · Online reviews

1 Introduction

One crucial component of the new digital services today is the Applications Programmable Interface (API), a machine-readable interface which enables applications to connect to each other's distinctive functionalities and to use them without knowing their inner mechanisms [1]. Right now, the API economy is growing in a fast pace and spans over thousands of API-providing companies which can be clustered in many categories. Service developers (re)use company provided APIs or even combine them with other existing ones to deliver new functionalities on top of them or to create new services. This process is called service composition process through which a mashup (a new application) will be created. Service developers by creating new complementary services and thereby increasing the accessibility to new users, add value to the API-providing platforms or companies [2]. On a more holistic level, such companies also can access distinctive resources and services of others by plugging into their API and using their services.

The API value chain first introduced by Jacobson et al. [1]. From a business perspective, this value chain is a sequential line from the business assets of a company to the end-users. The company transforms assets into an API which then is used by a developer for further use. Due to the growth of the software as a service (SaaS) ecosystem, developers have the option to select variety of APIs and their selections therefore significantly impacts the success of a provider's API. Thus, the business success of the provider company is depending on developers' choice making. To highlight the important role of the developer in this value chain, we propose a developer-centric API value chain which is shown in Fig. 1.

© Springer Nature Switzerland AG 2020
K. Djemame et al. (Eds.): GECON 2020, LNCS 12441, pp. 201–205, 2020.
https://doi.org/10.1007/978-3-030-63058-4_17

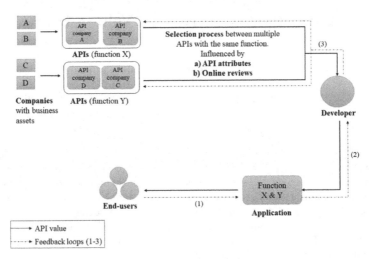

Fig. 1. Developer-centric API value chain.

In contrast to the traditional value chain proposed by Jacobson et al. [1], the proposed developer-centric API value chain shows the important role of the service developers in delivering high-end web services. First, if developers, for example, needs two distinctive functions (i.e., X and Y) for the sake of service composition, they have multiple offerings (i.e., from different companies) for each function. In our example, they have two offers (A and B) for function X and two offers (C and D) for function Y. In this process, we assume that the developers are influenced by (a) API attributes like technical features and the brand and (b) online reviews from the developer community via ratings, reviews, and reports. Second, the proposed value chain consists of feedback loops which can be used to explain how these three actors (i.e., service developer, service providers and end users) are intertwined. The feedback loops (i.e., shown as 1–3 in Fig. 1) are assumed to exist between the end user, the developer and the service providers. As we can see, online reviews are part of the last feedback loop and are visible to the service providers and developers. The importance of this loop is obvious for the service providers since they aim to motivate service developers to favor their APIs over the competitors. Therefore, it is essential for service providers to understand how developers make their choices regarding the process of API adaption [3]. The rest of this paper is organized as follows: In Sect. 2 the relevant literature on APIs and the role of developers in the API adoption process are discussed. In Sect. 3, we formulate our theoretical model which is followed by the conclusion and discussion on the topic.

2   Literature Review

2.1   APIs and Their Role for Service Innovation

APIs are machine-readable interfaces which connect applications and digital services with each other and enable the seamless and easy exchange of data and services. In an API ecosystem, APIs can be used by developers according to the principles of open innovation. It means that API providers open their digital assets to developers which can innovate on top of them. The potential benefits for both groups are enormous. API providers can reach a broader customer base across markets, platforms, and devices, create new markets, extend their brands and foster innovation. Developers can take a shortcut by using available building blocks for developing their new applications without reinventing the wheel all over [1, 4]. The market for APIs and their composition in mashups is already characterized by Yu and Woodard [3]. They pointed to the long tail of the API market which describes the high number of low frequency occurrences which, when cumulated, can outweigh the most frequent events. The authors observed that about half of all APIs (51%) are not used in any mashups at all. These insights are in line with the work of Koohborfardhaghighi and Altmann [5] who found out that established connections between specific APIs are used in a high frequency even though other APIs would have similar functionalities.

The value of APIs and their adoption by developers is rooted in their importance for service creation and service innovation. Den Hertog in [6], argues that service innovation can be structured using four dimensions which are mainly the service concept, the service client interface, service delivery systems and the technological options. These dimensions are interrelated and each of them can be innovated by itself. A new service concept describes how a problem can be solved in a new, often intangible way. The client interface describes how client and service-provider interact with each other. The service delivery system focuses on the internal capabilities and processes of a company which enable the workforce to innovate and to deliver services to the clients in an efficient manner. Even though service innovation can happen without technology, new technological option as a dimension, is the main driver and the enabler of service innovation.

2.2 The Role of the Developer

Developers have an important position within the API ecosystem and their role is clear in the API value chain. Due to their position between the API and the end-users, they can be seen as an important bottleneck within the API value chain [1]. By looking at the developer-centric value chain depicted in Fig. 1, it becomes even more obvious that two things are crucial for the service composition process. Firstly, the professional capabilities of the developers to create a new application, and secondly, their choice making process when picking one amongst several APIs. They have an innovative role in a coevolving ecosystem which depends on both, the APIs, which is offered by providers, and the developer's choice [1, 7]. Developers are also providers themselves. They provide new applications to their own clients or companies [1]. The quality and reliability of an API are assumed to have a crucial role due to the high reputational risk for both the developers and the client company if new mashups or applications fail in delivering the right service. Therefore, the need for quality assurance is an important explanation for why developers decide to pick APIs which are often used by other developers and neglect the long tail of the API market. In this research we believe that similar to the online retail market, user-created feedback can be used to assure a certain quality standard in API market [8]. Thus, in the extension of this research we aim to cover the latest research about the influence of online reviews in the decision making process from a product-centric point of view.

3   Conceptual Framework

Developers can find different information about APIs and mashups on multiple API dictionaries and websites (e.g. programmableweb.com). They have access to the API attributes which are provided by the API provider and the reviews which are represented in the form of the average user rating on each API. These online reviews are not yet used systematically on API directories but can be considered as a tool to overcome information asymmetry and create a quality assurance for existing services. In this study, these two sources of information (i.e., API attributes and online reviews) are assumed to influence the choice probability of the developer in the selection of APIs. The proposed conceptual framework is presented in Fig. 2.

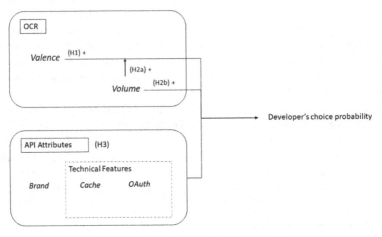

Fig. 2. Proposed conceptual framework.

The proposed conceptual framework consists of two blocks which are assumed to influence the choice probability of the developer when selecting a specific API. The first one is the OCR block, which includes the two OCR dimensions valence and volume. Valence describes the overall satisfaction of users (i.e., service developers) with the API and can be used to make a quality assessment. Volume is particularly interesting because it can not only be used to identify the general opinion of the community about an API, but also to have an estimation of the number of service developers who have had experience of using it. Number of service developers can be an indication of a community support for an API. The second block includes API related attributes which are assumed to influence the developers' choice making. As we discussed in Sect. 2.1 due to the identified power-law distribution of the use of mashups, we can test whether the brand attribute is a major influential factor which impacts the adoption process of APIs. There are also many technical attributes which are associated with APIs. Security schemes such as personal identification for example are often used in the online sector due to the growing security concerns [1]. In this study, OAuth 2.0 is picked as a security attribute for an API. OAuth 2.0 is an open protocol for secure authorization and is a safe way to handle protective data. It helps service providers to prevent data from being used by unauthorized parties. However, this authorization process via OAuth 2.0 can also prevent developers from trying an API due to the time-consuming procedure [1]. Another important technical at-tribute which can be used to make APIs and their response rates fast and reliable is a cache function. If an API works slowly, the application or mashup the developer develops will also work slowly. That is why we include caching as an important factor for developers in the selection of APIs. As depicted in Fig. 2, based on the proposed conceptual framework, now we are able to generate several hypotheses which will be considered and tested as the future extension of this research.

4   Conclusion and Discussion

API positioning and thereby its adoption is increasingly important for the survival of every modern business. The insights derived from this research will contribute to theory as well as to practice. In this study, by introducing a developer-centric view for the API value chain, we position the developers and their decision making at the center of API driven service innovation. Thus, the developers' role as a crucial factor within digital service innovation process is highlighted. This perspective, has not been sufficiently explored in recent research.

References

1. Jacobson, D., Brail, G., Woods, D.: APIs: A Strategy Guide. Sebastopol. O'Reilly Media, Inc, CA 95472 (2012)
2. Iyer, B., Subramaniam, M.: Are you using apis to gain competitive advantage? Harvard Bus. Rev. 1–5 (2015)
3. Yu, S., Woodard, C.J.: Innovation in the programmable web: characterizing the mashup ecosystem. In: Feuerlicht, G., Lamersdorf, W. (eds.) ICSOC 2008. LNCS, vol. 5472, pp. 136–147. Springer, Heidelberg (2009). https://doi.org/10.1007/978-3-642-01247-1_13
4. Vukovic, M., et al.: Viewpoint: riding and thriving on the API hype cycle. association for computing machinery. Commun. ACM 59(3), 35 (2016)
5. Koohborfardhaghighi, S., Altmann, J.: A network formation model for social object networks. In: Zhang, Z., Shen, Z.M., Zhang, J., Zhang, R. (eds.) LISS 2014, pp. 615–625. Springer, Heidelberg (2015). https://doi.org/10.1007/978-3-662-43871-8_89
6. Den Hertog, P.: Knowledge intensive business services as co-producers of innovation. Int. J. Innov. Manage. 4(4), 4–6 (2000)
7. Tiwana, A., Konsynski, B., Bush, A.A.: Platform evolution: coevolution of platform architecture, governance, and environmental dynamics. Inf. Syst. Res. 21(4), 675–687 (2010)
8. Kostyra, D.S., Reiner, J., Natter, M., Klapper, D.: Decomposing the effects of online customer reviews on brand, price, and product attributes. Int. J. Res. Mark. 33(1), 11–26 (2016). https://doi.org/10.1016/j.ijresmar.2014.12.004

Bridging Education Services and Consumer Expectations Through Reusable Learning Objects

Djamshid Sultanov[1] and Jörn Altmann[2(✉)]

[1] Tashkent University of Information Technologies named after Muhammad al-Khwarizmi,
Tashkent, Uzbekistan
sdjamshid@gmail.com
[2] Seoul National University, Seoul, South Korea
jorn.altmann@acm.org

1 Introduction

A competitive job market requires higher education institutions to carefully update curriculums and explore new possibilities of technology-related education. In spite of the reforms in education systems, there is still a gap between the skills that the job market expects and the skill set of new graduates (Hinchliffe and Jolly 2011). This gap fertilizes a rising risk of increased unemployment among early graduates (Nghia 2018; Tan et al. 2017).

When discussing the responsibility of employability of graduates, there is no clear consensus between higher education institutions and the industry. Employers point at the accountability of educational institutions for the employability of their graduates in the workplace (Nghia 2018). Oppositely, academia points out that education systems provide only a minimum skill set, which has to be enhanced after getting employed (Tan et al. 2017).

Considering this discrepancy, the research objective of this study intends to open the discussion on new ways for optimizing education service offerings by fulfilling consumer (i.e., students and industry) expectations and increasing stakeholders' values (i.e., utilities, profits, and social welfare).

As a model for achieving that, this research suggests composite education services that strengthen the reuse of learning objects and, thereby, reducing time and monetary cost.

2 Theoretical Background

Student expectations are the crucial factor for academia to define service variety and quality. In most cases, the socio-economic background, the age, and the gender of the students influence their heterogeneous expectations (Vasconcelos and Almeida 2018). Considering that student satisfaction is also an important factor for the survival of education service providers (ESP) in higher education in the educational service market

© Springer Nature Switzerland AG 2020
K. Djemame et al. (Eds.): GECON 2020, LNCS 12441, pp. 206–210, 2020.
https://doi.org/10.1007/978-3-030-63058-4_18

(Gruber et al. 2010), ESP should adjust the institutional policies and services to the freshman expectations in early states (Bates and Kaye 2014).

As literature emphasizes that the skills of university graduates are not always sufficient to fulfill employer expectations (Hinchliffe and Jolly 2011), there is also the risk of an increased rate of unemployment among university graduates (Nghia 2018; Tan et al. 2017).

The last three decades raised the topic about the modularity and reuse opportunities of educational contents, which is divided into learning objects. A learning object is a small (as small as possible) chunk of an information resource, which can be shared and coupled for addressing learning objectives (Elfeky and Elbyaly 2016). The main concepts behind the learning object are reusability (Redmond et al. 2018), effectiveness in assembling new educational contents, interoperability, and flexibility in designing curriculums (Nurmi and Jaakkola 2006). The literature argues that the motivation behind using learning objects should be the reduction in cost of designing and updating educational contents (Elfeky and Elbyaly 2016) and an increase of access to educational contents.

Learning objects can be based on the decomposition of curriculums, which contain the syllabi of courses that are necessary to obtain a certain major and related skills. A learning object for students aims at providing the knowledge for a specific learning objective of a topic. Each learning object in a syllabus contains different types of knowledge chunks that can be text, figure, software code, audio, video, or presentation material.

Our suggestion to compose education services from learning objects is founded in the need to address student and industry expectations. Student and industry have their particular expectations. The use of reusable learning objects as the core of education services enables quick detections of new or changed expectations and effective responses to them. Reusable learning objects can easily be replaced and updated, which reduces the cost for educational services.

3   Model

Figure 1 portrays the system dynamics model of the value exchanges and interactions of the education stakeholders. Although the system dynamics model already indicates the inherent complexity of a real educational system, the model presented has been simplified such that only the main logic and structural interdependencies have remained. The overall system allows showing the dynamic changes in value creations (i.e., utilities and profits) and parameter values due to interactions between stakeholders.

In particular, the system dynamics model shows that changes in the education service quality (e.g., 'Quality of the Education Service' in Fig. 1) affect the value creation (i.e., utilities and profits) of stakeholders. Moreover, the value exchanges of students and industry let education service provider (ESP) also to react, resulting in the emergence of system dynamics behavior in this complex system. For example, addressing stakeholders' expectations drives the service improvements of ESP, which consequently improves the satisfaction of expectations of students and industry. In addition to this, as the satisfaction level determines the adjustments on future expectations (i.e., a high satisfaction level increases future expectations), ESPs are pushed to improve the education service offerings.

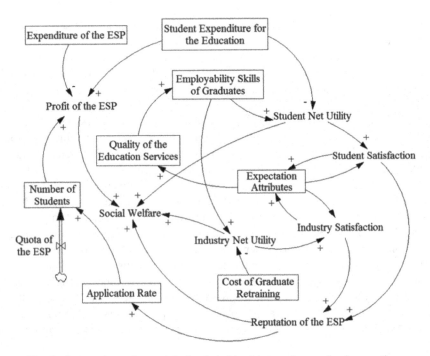

Fig. 1. System dynamics model of stakeholders' interactions and value creations

The impact of reuse of learning objects in educational services is modeled with two parameters "Quality of the Education Service" and "Expenditure of the ESP". By increasing the service quality with incurrence of little expenditure, there is a positive impact on the value creation of stakeholders.

4   Simulation Parameters and Settings

In order to run the simulations on the base of the model in Fig. 1, the following six simulation parameters have been set initially (Fig. 1): quality of the education services, student satisfaction, industry satisfaction, the expenditure of the ESP, student expenditure for the education, and cost of graduates retraining (Table 1). All values of these parameters, which are based on literature references or observations, have been normalized using the min-max normalization method. Consequently, the extracted data varies between 0 and 1 (Jain and Bhandare 2011).

The model of the education stakeholders' interactions and value exchanges is tested with two different scenarios: (1) high-quality education service environment (Scenario 1) and (2) low-quality education service environment (Scenario 2). The scenario 1 represents an environment, in which the ESP addresses the expectations of the students and industry fully. In the second scenario, the expectations of the students and industry are not addressed fully. The two scenarios differ in their parameter values, as depicted in Table 1. For conducting this kind of simulation and analysis, the Vensim software has been found to be capable software (Haile and Altmann 2016).

Table 1. Simulation parameters and their values for the two scenarios considered

Simulation parameters	Scenario 1	Scenario 2	Reference for the parameter value setting
Quality of the Education Services	0.84	0.545	Assumption: $\frac{Student\ Satisfaction + Industry\ Satisfaction}{2}$
Student Satisfaction	High: 0.89 Low: 0.56	High: 0.89 Low: 0.56	(Office for Students 2018)
Industry Satisfaction	High: 0.78 Low: 0.53	High: 0.78 Low: 0.53	(OECD 2015, 2017)
Expenditure of the ESP	High: 0.63 Low: 0.35	High: 0.63 Low: 0.35	(OECD 2018)
Student Expenditure for the Education	High: 0.46 Low: 0.35	High: 0.46 Low: 0.35	(OECD 2018)
Cost of Graduate Retraining	High: 0.31 Low: 0.17	High: 0.31 Low: 0.17	Assumption: $(\frac{Expenditure\ of\ ESP}{2})$
Admission quota of the ESP	1000	1000	Assumption

5 Results and Discussions

Current research discusses the topic of composing high-quality education services from reusable learning objects, in order to satisfy the expectations of consumers (i.e., students and industry). Moreover, employing reusable learning objects for the development of education services improves the speed of service formation, reduces the cost of searching for knowledge, and keeps the educational content up to date.

Our analysis results indicate that meeting expectations of students and industry by the ESP (scenario 1) increases their satisfaction and, in turn, the reputation of the ESP, leading towards an increase in the application rate of students. In an environment, in which ESPs do not care about the expectations of their students (scenario 2), the satisfaction from the service offerings did not show a sensible growing trace. Consequently, if ESPs lag behind industry on delivering knowledge to students, the employability skills of graduates are lowered. If a student expects higher service quality than actually supplied, student satisfaction even shows a slight decline. It stands for the case when a student comes to university with matured viewpoints on building employability skills but does not get the desired knowledge and skill set from the university.

The industry satisfaction shows an even stronger growing trace in the high-quality education scenario (scenario 1) than the student satisfaction. Expectations of the industry are usually based on certain practical aspects that match with the context of the local economy, technology, and society.

Furthermore, as ESP reputation increases, only if the education service supplied is higher than the expectations, ESP reputation does not only dependent on service quality but also on its relation to student expectations. Moreover, as low consumer expectations can also increase consumer satisfaction in both scenarios, there is an incentive for ESPs to improve their service offerings continuously. Not addressing consumer satisfaction results in low employability skills of graduates. It means that ESP cannot contribute to breakthrough changes and reforms in the industry and society.

Acknowledgements. This work was supported by the National Research Foundation of Korea (NRF) grant funded by the Korea government (MSIT) (No. NRF-2019R1F1A1058487) and by the Institute of Engineering Research at Seoul National University with research facilities.

References

Bates, E.A., Kaye, L.K.: "I'd be expecting caviar in lectures": the impact of the new fee regime on undergraduate students' expectations of Higher Education. High. Educ. **67**(5), 655–673 (2014)

Elfeky, A.I.M., Elbyaly, M.Y.H.: The impact of learning object repository (lor) in the development of pattern making skills of home economics students. Brit. J. Educ. **4**(2), 87–99 (2016)

Gruber, T., Fuß, S., Voss, R., Gläser-Zikuda, M.: Examining student satisfaction with higher education services: using a new measurement tool. Int. J. Public Sect. Manage. **23**(2), 105–123 (2010)

Haile, N., Altmann, J.: Value creation in software service platforms. Future Gener. Comput. Syst. **55**, 495–509 (2016)

Hinchliffe, G.W., Jolly, A.: Graduate identity and employability. Brit. Educ. Res. J. **37**(4), 563–584 (2011)

Jain, Y.K., Bhandare, S.K.: Min max normalization based data perturbation method for privacy protection. Int. J. Comput. Commun. Technol. **2**(8), 45–50 (2011)

Nghia, T.L.H.: The skills gap of Vietnamese graduates and final-year university students. J. Educ. Work **31**(7-8), 579–594 (2018)

Nurmi, S., Jaakkola, T.: Effectiveness of learning objects in various instructional settings. Learn. Media Technol. **31**(3), 233–247 (2006)

OECD. Skill needs—Industries OECD Dataset (2015). https://stats.oecd.org/Index.aspx?DataSe tCode=SKILLS_2018_INDUSTRY

OECD. Getting Skills Right: Skills for Jobs Indicators. OECD Publishing (2017). https://www. oecd-ilibrary.org/content/publication/9789264277878-en

OECD. Education at a Glance 2018. OECD Publishing (2018). https://www.oecd-ilibrary.org/con tent/publication/eag-2018-en

Office for Students. National Student Survey—NSS (2018). https://www.officeforstudents.org. uk/advice-and-guidance/student-information-and-data/national-student-survey-nss/get-the- nss-data/

Redmond, C., et al.: Using reusable learning objects (RLOs) in wound care education: under- graduate student nurse's evaluation of their learning gain. Nurse Educ. Today **60**, 3–10 (2018)

Tan, A.Y.T., Chew, E., Kalavally, V.: The expectations gap for engineering field in Malaysia in the 21st century. On the Horizon **25**(2), 131–138 (2017)

Vasconcelos, R., Almeida, L.S.: Academic expectations for engineering freshmen: gender dif- ferences. In: 2018 IEEE International Conference on Teaching, Assessment, and Learning for Engineering (TALE), pp. 209–212 (2018)

Exascale Computing Deployment Challenges

Karim Djemame$^{(\boxtimes)}$ and Hamish Carr

School of Computing, University of Leeds, Leeds, UK
{K.Djemame,H.Carr}@leeds.ac.uk
https://eps.leeds.ac.uk/computing/staff/187/professor-karim-djemame,
https://eps.leeds.ac.uk/computing/staff/499/dr-hamish-carr

Abstract. As Exascale computing proliferates, we see an accelerating shift towards clusters with thousands of nodes and thousands of cores per node, often on the back of commodity graphics processing units. This paper argues that this drives a once in a generation shift of computation, and that fundamentals of computer science therefore need to be re-examined. Exploiting the full power of Exascale computation will require attention to the fundamentals of programme design and specification, programming language design, systems and software engineering, analytic, performance and cost models, fundamental algorithmic design, and to increasing replacement of human bandwidth by computational analysis. As part of this, we will argue that Exascale computing will require a significant degree of co-design and close attention to the economics underlying the challenges ahead.

Keywords: Exascale computing · High performance computing · Holistic approach · Economics

1 Introduction

The Exascale project will accelerate exciting advances and scientific discovery in many diverse fields such as genomics, market economics, astrophysics as well as contribute to the economic competitiveness [6]. Modern High-Performance Computing (HPC) is already at the petascale, using distributed techniques pioneered in the 1990s in response to shortcomings of the previous massive vector machine models. Thirty years later, the pattern is now repeating, as the limitations of distributed computing drive the development of hybrid models where distributed and vector techniques are layered on top of each other. This generational transition in underlying hardware models means that effective transition to Exascale computing and later to yottascale, requires not just development of immediately applicable techniques, but fundamental attention to the underlying models of not computational science, but computer science. Consequently, a separation of concerns is necessary if Exascale is to become widely available in a sustainable manner. This paper argues that algorithmic development to harness the power

© Springer Nature Switzerland AG 2020
K. Djemame et al. (Eds.): GECON 2020, LNCS 12441, pp. 211–216, 2020.
https://doi.org/10.1007/978-3-030-63058-4_19

of Exascale cannot be achieved without considering the fundamental computer science issues that Exascale computing raises. Its primary contribution is the formal identification of the major issues that must be overcome, the hardware and software environments inside which Exascale development will happen, the software abstractions necessary to cope efficiently with ever-larger computations, the programming methodologies based on the abstractions that will enable more efficient application development, the interpretation methods necessary at Exascale, and the underlying economics issues to be addressed to ensure effective adoption.

The paper is structured as follows: Sect. 2 gives an overview of the landscape in the shadows of the petascale cluster abd presents the fundamental computer science challenges that Exascale computing raises. The associated economics issues to productively deploy Exascale are identified in Sect. 3. Section 4 summarises and concludes the paper.

2   Grand Challenges and Research Agenda

The development of the extreme scale supercomputers arena such as Argonne National Laboratory's *Aurora*, Oak Ridge National Laboratory's *Frontier* and Lawrence Livermore National Laboratory *El Capitan* is under way [1]. These three CRAY supercomputers being fielded in the 2021–2023 timeframe will all employ the Cray Shasta architecture, its Slingshot interconnect and a new software platform. Vector and distributed parallelism often demand different approaches with unique optimisations, workflow and shortcuts. Hybrid parallelism, such as will be needed for the next generation, demands the best of both worlds, and poses a challenge that must be overcome in order to realise the potential for not just Exascale computation, but for the yottascale computation that will come after it. Substantial research efforts have been put into Exascale computing over the last few years. The Exascale Computing Project (ECP) in the USA is bringing together research, development, and deployment projects as part of a capable Exascale computing ecosystem to ensure an enduring Exascale computing capability [7]. The EU plans to develop and reinforce the European high-performance computing and data processing capabilities to achieve Exascale capabilities by 2023, and has funded a number of technology projects [2] What becomes urgent is to draw a complete picture of the state of the art and the challenges ahead to exploit the Exascale. Instead of tackling research into the areas of *input, programming, systems* and *output/analysis* separately, the proposed way forward is to take a holistic approach that considers the entire Exascale software stack to: 1) identify the missing functionalities, bottlenecks, unsolved problems, best practice and trends to support Exascale computing across the stack, and 2) to define and integrate new requirements into the design and development process for software. We acknowledge that as Exascale hardware evolves, software and applications need to adapt, and as Exascale application requirements evolve, hardware and software design need to adapt as well. This mutual adaptation process is a problem that needs addressing.

Challenge 1 – Exploiting Exascale Systems. A one million processors supercomputer can run unprecedentedly large scale simulations and offer orders of magnitude greater performance than conventional processors. Moreover, the future direction of Exascale systems is extreme heterogeneity, often of potentially reconfigurable systems. Nodes will be a collection of heterogeneous processors: some general purpose (CPUs), some specialised (such as SIMD units, e.g.. GPUs) and some configurable cores (FPGA fabrics) [9]. Moreover, the shift to hybrid symmetric multiprocessing and distributed parallelism represents one of the biggest challenges that software developers will face. Research is needed to investigate how to automate efficient mapping across the complex and heterogeneous Exascale landscape, and how to adapt workflows to meet infrastructure-level objectives needs addressing, e.g.. through machine learning approaches, as well as the identification of the building blocks for run-time reconfigurable Exascale systems.

Challenge 2 – Application Design and Development. Research is needed to identify the best practice to increase programmer efficiency considering the emerging requirements for Exascale algorithms. Techniques such as constraint analysis and program synthesis to discover code patterns that match heterogeneous hardware needs investigation. Research will identify the required features to improve the performance and interoperability between the current programming models, and how to provide the tool(s) below the Programming Model and interfaces that exploit the best practices in terms of scalability and performance. Domain Specific Languages (DSLs) as higher level abstractions can be used to increase programmer efficiency, hide the hardware complexity and allow hardware independence [8], but must be designed first. Generic computing patterns that allow the implementation of customised algorithms to optimise load balancing, data handling, and support fault tolerance can also ease application development [5]. The Programming Model itself should support ease of programming and migration for legacy code.

Challenge 3 – Middleware, Resource Management and Performance. One of the most critical aspects in the evolution of High Performance Exascale systems is a dedicated middleware to manage the enormous complexity of such systems where deep heterogeneity is needed to handle the wide variety of applications. Intelligent resource management thanks to automated methods using machine learning/data science is the way forward for handling the complexity of Exascale systems and optimise their performance. With current Petascale storage systems support data processing in, or close to, the storage location to improve performance, the identification of the technologies supporting data access for High Performance Exascale Data Analytics becomes key.

Challenge 4 – Data Analysis and Interpretation. The human visual system allows humans to grapple with data in the megabyte to gigabyte range, and recent innovations allow artificial intelligence to operate with similar amounts of data. Beyond this, interpretation involves some form of abstraction, reduction or summarisation of the data [10]. For a terabyte of data, this has meant tools that allow humans to look at 0.1% of the data through slicing, statistical summarisation, custom domain-dependent tests, or visualisation, i.e. a three orders of magnitude reduction in the data presented to the human. At the Exascale, computational analysis of all forms will become increasingly important, but the analytic tools in each field tend to be isolated. Research is needed to map out the tools currently used for data interpretation and analysis, and to define a framework that can be carried forward for tools with wide application at the Exascale.

3 The Economics

The diffusion of Exascale computing will follow the pattern of (old) High Performance Computing but will create visionary ideas and a process of generalised adoption. This gives a very broad set of options that will emerge due to economic constraints, critical mass issues, industrialisation aspects, legacy and usability problems.

Investment. The deployment of Exascale is driven by economic and societal needs and takes into account the changes expected in the technologies and architectures of the expanding underlying hardware and software infrastructure. Data acquisition will continue to fuel demand for more processing as well as enabling workloads that combine HPC, advanced analytics and IoT at scale. However, the investments needed to productively deploy Exascale are substantial. Future business models will be categorised based on criteria that take into account their value propositions, their technological and economic incentives and emerging trends in the market of Exascale.

Software (Re)Engineering. In the discipline of software (re)engineering, making applications Exascale-ready will incur costs, but the resulting software itself will have economic attributes as well. The inherent re-engineering cost factors will include the quality of the software to be re-engineered, the availability of the expertise and tools support for re-engineering as well as the extent of the (possible) data conversion which is required.

New Business Models. Industry and SMEs are currently increasingly relying on the power of supercomputers to work on innovative solutions, reduce costs and decrease time to market for products and services. An example of HPC provision is Cray on Azure to answer the demand for a large-scale, dedicated compute instance in the cloud [4]. They will continue to do so with Exascale, and may provide previously unimaginable scenarios in upstream processing that leverage the Exascale.

Application Deployment. The rise of new disruptive applications such as Cyber Physical Systems, which are evolving into Cyber Physical Systems of Systems and other major technological advances in ICT are profoundly transforming their development and management processes. These are difficult to analyse because they may deployed across a multitude of systems which includes

Exascale facilities, cloud data centres, edge/fog components and networks. Their deployment should take place in an efficient manner, not only technically but economically as well.

Exascale as a Service. Cloud Service Providers such as Microsoft Azure and Amazon Web Services (AWS) are providing elastic and scalable cloud infrastructure to run applications on HPC systems [3]. With Exascale they will face more economic challenges with the provision of costly mixed CPU, GPU and FPGA types and high-performance low-latency interconnects. For these investments to pay off, finding new accounting and pricing models as well as maximising the use of the high-cost infrastructure is a key requirement as the classic cloud service provision model will not be adequate. In an IoT context, Exascale as a service will become a part of the overall application workflow across a number of domains: IoT, edge/fog and cloud, with a complete data flow all the way from the IoT devices up to the Exascale/cloud data centres.

4 Conclusion

The ongoing deployment of Exascale computing is bringing a number of challenges. Research on both Exascale applications and related technologies will expand from the traditional fields which deploy HPC solutions to new ones, in order to not only address the requirements of (often disruptive) applications such as Artificial Intelligence and Data Analytics but the generational transition in underlying hardware models. The paper has argued that a separation of concerns is necessary if Exascale is to become widely available in a sustainable manner. This will require a truly interdisciplinary effort to not only develop applicable techniques, but address the underlying models of both computational science and computer science. Moreover, it has identified key economics issues following such paradigm shift.

References

1. Cray Exascale (2019). https://www.cray.com/company/news-and-media/doe-el-capitan-press-release
2. European High Performance Computing Handbook (2019). https://www.etp4hpc.eu/pujades/files/ETP4HPC_Handbook_2019_web.pdf
3. Amzon High Performance Computing (2020). https://aws.amazon.com/hpc/
4. Cray in Azure (2020). https://www.cray.com/solutions/supercomputing-as-a-service/cray-in-azure
5. Alowayyed, S., Piontek, T., Suter, J., Hoenen, O., Groen, D., Luk, O., Bosak, B., Kopta, P., Kurowski, K., Perks, O., Brabazon, K., Jancauskas, V., Coster, D., Coveney, P., Hoekstra, A.: Patterns for high performance multiscale computing. Future Gener. Comput. Syst. **91**, 335–346 (2019)
6. Gagliardi, F., Moreto, M., Olivieri, M., Valero, M.: The international race towards exascale in Europe. CCF Trans. HPC **1**, 3–13 (2019)
7. Messina, P.: The exascale computing project. Comput. Sci. Eng. **19**(3), 63–67 (2017)

8. Silvano, C., Agosta, G., Bartolini, A.: ANTAREX: a DSL-based approach to adaptively optimizing and enforcing extra-functional properties in high performance computing. In: Proceedings of the 2018 21st Euromicro Conference on Digital System Design (DSD), pp. 600–607 (2018)

9. Terzo, O., Djemame, K., Scionti, A., Pezuela, C.: Heterogeneous Computing Architectures: Challenges and Vision, 1st edn. CRC Press, United States (2019)

10. Tierny, J., Carr, H.: Jacobi fiber surfaces for bivariate reeb space computation. IEEE Trans. Vis. Comput. Graph. **23**(1), 960–969 (2017)

Author Index

Printed in the United States
By Bookmasters